Fifty Fantastic Assembly Stories

Adrian Martin

Brilliant
PUBLICATIONS

We hope you and your pupils enjoy the stories in this book. Brilliant Publications publishes other books for primary school teachers, a few of which are listed below. For more details and for sample pages, please go to our website: www.brilliantpublications.co.uk

Other books you may find of interest:

Brilliant Class-led Assemblies
Brilliant Stories for Assemblies
More Brilliant Stories for Assemblies

Brilliant Activities for Reading Comprehension

Published by Brilliant Publications
Unit 10
Sparrow Hall Farm
Edlesborough
Dunstable
Bedfordshire
LU6 2ES, UK

E-mail:
   info@brilliantpublications.co.uk
Website:
   www.brilliantpublications.co.uk
Tel: 01525 222292

The name Brilliant Publications and the logo are registered trademarks.

Written by Adrian Martin
Illustrated by Brilliant Publications
Front cover illustration by Kay Dixey

© Text: Adrian Martin 2014
© Design: Brilliant Publications 2014

Printed ISBN: 978-1-78317-102-6
E-book ISBN: 978-1-78317-103-3

First printed and published in the UK in 2014

Contents

Introduction

As a headteacher of eleven years (and still counting) I have delivered over one thousand assemblies and read many, many stories to children. Those lucky enough to have shared a really good story with an audience of children will be familiar with the spine tingling power of the written word; the school hall filled with silent anticipation as the story reaches a climax, the sudden simultaneous laughter as many children share a funny moment, the groan when the book is closed at a page-turning stage in the story.

In the early days of my headship I would search bookshops for good stories with a strong moral theme and would often buy a book of many stories, only to use one or two. It was then that I decided to try my hand at writing my own. I am convinced that children will 'get' the message much more effectively if they believe in the characters in the story and for that reason decided to base all of my stories around the pupils and staff of one school. My pupils have loved getting to know the different characters at Mill Lane Junior School and amaze me with their ability to remember the stories long after they have been read.

I believe the stories within this book will provide teachers with an effective starting point in promoting and exploring high standards of behaviour; mutual respect and tolerance for people of all faiths; cultures and lifestyles; values which are, rightly, high on the educational agenda.

©Adrian Martin and Brilliant Publications
Fifty Fantastic Assembly Stories

Dave Wins a Prize

It was a sunny, Spring day in May and Brendan's mum had finally managed to prize his fingers away from the controls of his games console.

'You'll enjoy it,' she said as they set off to the village fête. 'Barbara next door said it was great last year – there were police dogs and everything.'

Brendan liked dogs, but they would have to be doing something fairly special, he thought, if it was going to be worth him giving up an afternoon of gaming. And to his great surprise and pleasure, they were. He stood behind the barrier at the side of the arena and watched, fascinated as Prince, a police dog, ran up and down the see-saw, through the wavy tunnel, over jumps and a high wooden fence and through a hoop that Don, the Dog Trainer, had set on fire. Don only had to give a simple, one word command such as *Go!*, *Stop!*, *Sit!*, *Stay!* and Prince would obey him instantly. Prince was always incredibly alert – his ears pricked and his eyes fixed on Don, waiting for his next instruction. It was as if Don had an invisible remote control pad especially for dogs.

Brendan looked down at Dave, his black Labrador, who was lying at his feet. Brendan hoped that Dave might be inspired by Prince and the other dogs, but Dave had obviously decided that this was an extremely good opportunity for a sleep. Sleeping was something Dave did very well; he

was an expert at it in fact. The woman they bought him from said he was lively and would need plenty of exercise but Dave obviously hadn't heard her say this. Even when he was a puppy he would lie down and close his eyes at the first opportunity. He wasn't particularly fussy about where he lay down – anywhere remotely flat would do. On a walk, Dave would begin to pull on the lead after about five minutes, forcing Brendan to turn around and head back home. To Brendan's annoyance, Dave would then speed up as they approached the house. As Brendan opened the front door Dave would slump to the floor as soon as his paws made contact with the carpet. Brendan then had to get hold of his front paws and drag him further into the house so that he could close the front door. The only times Dave livened up and could be described as anything like lively were when there was a chance of him getting something to eat. At the faintest rustle of a chocolate bar wrapper being opened or the merest rattle of his biscuit box, Dave would spring up from a deep sleep and bound towards the source of the sound. He would then park himself in front of whoever had the food and sit, slavering, with long lines of slimy saliva hanging from his mouth, until he was given something. Then, of course, he would slump to the ground to continue his deep slumber.

'Why can't Dave be more like Prince?' Brendan asked his mum, stroking the snoring mound of fur at his feet.

'Ha ha! Dave? Like Prince?' she said incredulously. 'If you could even get Dave to sit on command it would be a miracle,' she laughed.

Although mum was only joking, Brendan was a little offended by her remark. Dave was his dog; he had pleaded with his mum and dad for almost a year before they had

Fifty Fantastic Assembly Stories

finally given in and got Dave but they were both very clear about who had to look after him:

'He's your dog Brendan. You feed him, you walk him,' they had said.

And Brendan did keep his side of the bargain; he got up early each morning to take Dave out, even when it was raining and even went to the supermarket with his mum and dad to get the dog food. So any negative remarks made about Dave were taken personally by Brendan.

'It's the school summer fair in June,' mum continued. 'Isn't there always a dog show? You could put him in for that. I'm sure he'd win a prize for the world's laziest dog!' And with that she produced such a high pitched laugh that Prince stopped in his tracks and looked straight at her. Dave, on the other hand, didn't move a muscle.

Brendan didn't laugh. He wasn't going to have Dave talked about like that. Dave didn't know it yet, but he was going to be in the dog show at the school summer fair and he was going to win a prize. Brendan had never been more determined to prove his mum wrong and when they arrived home from the fête later that day he began planning Dave's training schedule. Dave meanwhile, who had had a long day, fell into a deep sleep on the kitchen floor.

Brendan decided that a constant supply of food would be essential if he was ever going to get Dave to do anything for him so Sunday began with a visit to the pet shop. He went alone as Dave was asleep on the bottom step of the staircase.

An hour later, armed with a box of Doggy Treats, Brendan shook Dave awake and dragged him out into the garden.

'Right Dave,' he said positively. 'Today is Day One of your training programme.'

Dave looked very uninterested, but perked up when Brendan slipped his hand into his pocket and brought out a Doggy Treat. He bounded towards his owner but was a little surprised when Brendan held up the treat with one hand and pushed down firmly on Dave's back with the other, causing him to sit down. As Brendan forced Dave into the sitting position he said, 'Sit,' in a loud, clear voice, trying to copy Don, Prince's master. He was surprised but delighted that his plan had worked and he finished his command by offering the treat to Dave who snaffled it in one quick movement of his tongue.

'Good boy Dave,' Brendan said, giving Dave a cuddle. 'Let's try that again.'

'Not bad Brendan, not bad at all,' said his mum to herself as she watched from the upstairs window.

She was even more impressed as the weeks passed; Brendan woke Dave from his sleep every day as soon as he arrived home from school and took him into the garden for his training session. As each day passed Dave needed less encouragement to go to the garden. Brendan made sure he took him out every day, repeating the same process and gradually increasing the number of commands. The breakthrough came the night before the school fair. Brendan opened the front door and, rather than having to wake Dave, to his amazement, he was waiting for Brendan, tail wagging, ready to go.

'Good boy Dave!' he said enthusiastically, pushing a treat from his coat pocket into Dave's mouth. He had learned that it was a good idea to have

©Adrian Martin and Brilliant Publications

a treat handy at all times so that he could reward Dave if he ever needed to. The following day at the fair Brendan led Dave round the arena on the school field. Dave wasn't on a lead – he simply followed the lovely smell of Doggy Treats which Brendan had in his hand. Brendan had learned that if he put a treat in his closed hand and held it in front of Dave's nose as he walked, Dave would follow. When he completed a circuit of the arena Brendan gave the command to sit. Dave immediately sat and received the tasty treat. Brendan followed this with a sharp command to stay. This was Dave's favourite command because it meant that he got a treat for not moving. They then had to wait for four other dogs to parade round the arena. Understandably, Dave moved from a sitting position to a sleeping one, but at least he didn't walk away like some of the other dogs.

'Well done Brendan! And Dave isn't it?' It was Mrs Davies, the Headteacher, who was also one of the judges. 'We were very impressed with the way you controlled your dog. Very well done.'

And with that she put a silver medal around Dave's head and stuck a silver rosette with '2nd' written on it, to Dave's back. He didn't notice of course as he had fallen sound asleep in the middle of the arena.

Brendan thanked Mrs Davies and looked up into the audience to see his mum smiling back at him.

'Not bad,' she mouthed.

'Come on Dave,' he said, smiling. But Dave was flat out. And for the first time in months, Brendan didn't mind; he'd achieved enough for one day.

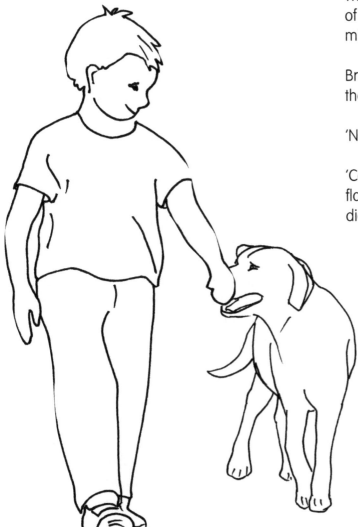

Martin Learns What It Takes

Martin Holmes and Declan Murphy were next door neighbours and could enter each other's back gardens through a gate that Declan's dad had made. He was a keen gardener and had become fed up with the two boys constantly climbing over the fence and landing in his vegetable patch when they wanted to play together. Before school, they would play in Declan's garden, seeing how high they dared to go on the swing before jumping from the seat at its highest point. After school, they would play football in Martin's garden, where there was more grass and considerably fewer vegetables.

The boys' parents were good friends and both families would spend most holidays together camping in Cornwall, Wales and even France. Declan and Martin spent most of their waking hours together, so it was just as well that they were best friends.

At school they were rarely apart and their teachers had long since given up trying to get them to do things separately. So it was no surprise to anyone when, following a demonstration by Mrs Darby, the piano teacher, the boys arrived home with the same request; 'I want to learn how to play the piano.'

Mrs Murphy, Declan's mum, decided not to answer her son until she had spoken to Mrs Holmes next door.

'Has your Martin said he wants to learn how to play the piano?' she asked, pushing open her neighbour's kitchen door.

'Yes. Just. Declan too I take it?' replied Martin's mum. 'Apparently it's cheaper to learn if two learn together. What do you think?'

'I'll be surprised if they stick at it,' replied Declan's mum. 'But it won't do them any harm to try I suppose.'

The mums agreed, weekly lessons were paid for and keyboards were bought, allowing the boys to practise at home. At the beginning of their first lesson, Mrs Darby made it very clear to them that unless they were prepared to practise regularly (at least every day, were her exact words), which meant they would have to play football less, they might as well not even start.

Declan nodded along as Mrs Darby spoke. Martin nodded too, but in his head he was thinking, 'Less football? I don't think so. How hard can learning the piano actually be?'

For the first few weeks both boys practised what Mrs Darby had taught them. Instead of playing football together as soon as they arrived home from school, they went to their own bedrooms to practise on their keyboards. To their parents' surprise they began to get rather good and were soon able to play a few lines of music. Mrs Darby told them that they were picking up the basics quickly and that if they continued to practise daily they might be good enough to play at the Summer Serenade, the school's annual musical evening which was two terms away.

The thought of playing the piano in front of hundreds of people affected the two boys in completely different ways.

©Adrian Martin and Brilliant Publications

Declan loved the idea and could think of little else since the moment Mrs Darby had mentioned it. He made up his mind right there and then that not only would he be playing the piano at the Summer Serenade, but that he would be playing the piano well at the Summer Serenade and everyone in the audience would be mightily impressed by his musical prowess.

Martin hated the idea and had done everything he could not to think about it ever since Mrs Darby had mentioned it. The thought of playing the piano at the Summer Serenade filled him with feelings of dread and fear and he made up his mind right there and then that although he might be going to the Summer Serenade he certainly would not be playing the piano.

Mrs Darby was clever. She had deliberately put the idea of playing at the concert into the minds of the two boys to see how they would react. She didn't want them to waste their time if they weren't serious and she knew that learning to play any musical instrument required practice and perseverance.

From that moment on the two boys went about their piano playing in very different ways. Each day when Declan arrived home from school he would go straight to his bedroom to play his keyboard for half an hour, sometimes longer. He was really beginning to get the hang of it now and was enjoying being able to play tunes rather than just lines of music. There was no doubt about it; he was improving every day.

Each day when Martin arrived home from school he would go straight to his bedroom to play his keyboard for half an hour, sometimes longer. But although he went to his bedroom to play his keyboard, he didn't actually play it; in fact, he did anything he could find to do in his bedroom to avoid playing his keyboard. He watched TV, played on his games console, lay on his bed listening to Declan practising next door, read some of his many football books or did his homework.

Once, when he became bored of doing all the things in his bedroom to avoid playing his keyboard he even tidied his room, such was his desperation to avoid practising. So unlike his best friend, Martin's ability to play the piano did not improve. He had had enough of it and that is when the excuses began. Mrs Darby wanted to know why he wasn't improving at all and, if anything, he was getting worse as the weeks went by. Martin told her that his keyboard at home was broken, that he had lost his music book and (his most far fetched excuse of all) was that he'd hurt the fingers on both hands falling from Declan's swing. Declan certainly couldn't remember this happening and simply looked blankly when Mrs Darby stared at him with a raised eyebrow. Martin carried on giving his excuses week after week, thinking that he was getting away with it. However, unknown to him, Mrs Darby had had her suspicions for quite some time and after giving her yet another ridiculous excuse about having earache, she simply shook her head, smiled knowingly and said, 'You've given up haven't you?'

It was time for him to face up to the truth. He nodded uncomfortably.

'It's fine,' she said. 'It's not for everyone and it's obviously not for you, but there's no point in denying it; make sure you tell your mum and dad when you get home.'

And that was that. Martin's parents were disappointed but not completely surprised – they had wondered for some time why Martin's practice sessions hadn't actually produced a musical sound of any kind. But whilst Martin was dreaming up his excuses, Declan was practising and practising and getting better and better. On the night of the Summer Serenade, Martin was sat in the second row of the audience, and was looking forward to hearing his best friend play.

The school hall had an impressive stage which was raised to give the audience a clear view of the performers. Declan stood at the side of the stage behind the curtain. This was the moment he had practised so much for. Six months ago Mrs Darby had mentioned that if he practised hard and didn't give up, he might be able to play at the summer concert. She didn't really believe it would be possible and was probably more surprised than anyone that Declan was about to perform. So far, the evening had gone really well; children from Years 3 and 4 had made their way to the stage, to play the trumpet, the oboe, the violin, the piano and a whole host of other instruments. All had performed well and had received deserved applause from the audience. Musical evenings could be a little tense, with parents desperate for their child not to make a mistake but Mrs Darby always did a great job of making everybody relax. Finally, it was Declan's turn to perform and as he walked to the very edge of the stage, waiting to be introduced, he could see the many faces of the audience, waiting to be entertained. His mum and dad sat nervously on the front row, clutching the programme which listed the performance order so they knew that Declan was next. They had heard him at home obviously but weren't sure how he would perform in front of a huge audience.

Mrs Darby introduced him and her words made Declan feel confident about himself. She described Declan as the hardest working pupil she had ever taught and told the audience that although he had only been playing for six months it was as if he had been playing for years. And then she called his name and beckoned him towards her. The eyes of the audience focused on him as he appeared and, although he walked tentatively across the stage, his nerves seemed to disappear completely when he sat down at the piano. He placed the sheet of music on the stand above the keys and took a deep breath. The hall, with nearly two hundred people in it, fell completely silent. Six

months ago Declan had never touched a piano key before. Now he was about to perform in front of a large audience. He looked up at Mrs Darby who smiled and mouthed the words, 'You can do it.'

He played superbly, never once looking up at the music. A few seconds into the piece there was an audible gasp from the audience. Declan's mum and dad watched on, beaming with pride. He had learned the piece by heart and was enjoying playing so much that he even had the confidence to look up at the audience and smile at them. He finished with a flourish and received thunderous applause, Martin joining in, clapping as hard as he could. He knew that the applause could have been for him, but he also knew that Declan had tried hard, had shown greater determination and he thoroughly deserved this moment. Declan made his way from the piano to the centre of the stage; this was the greatest achievement of his life so far and it was time to perform his first ever bow.

©Adrian Martin and Brilliant Publications
Fifty Fantastic Assembly Stories

Stephen Discovers He's a Better Runner Than He Thought

Stephen Heyward was computer mad. Not Playstations, Nintendos or XBox, but computers. He was obsessed with them and had been from a very early age. When he was eight months old, his mum had sat him on the kitchen table next to his dad's brand new computer. Stephen was promptly sick all over the keyboard. Whilst his mum and dad ran around the kitchen shouting and panicking, frantically opening and shutting cupboard doors looking for something to wipe away the goo without damaging the keys, or the computer itself, Stephen lay there, gurgling and gently leaning on the letter 'Q'. He was fascinated by the pattern made by the letters, as lines and lines of 'Q's marched across the screen like little soldiers going into battle. Now, at the age of nine, he had not one, but four computers in his bedroom, and two radios, one of which he built himself. His dad had also allowed him half of his shed in the garden so that Stephen could play with his electronics kits and he spent every second he could either in the shed, making things with wires, motors and buzzers, or taking his computers apart, and exploring the complicated maze of wires and microchips inside.

At school, it was he that the teachers asked for, when things went wrong in the computer suite. Rather than just going to the ICT club at school, Stephen ran it. His friends called him 'Chip', short for microchip, and whenever any of their computers or electrical appliances went wrong at home, they would call him for help.

Stephen was happy at school, and even happier at home. Everything was going well. He was doing well in lessons and his future career, as a computer programmer, was all mapped out. But there was one thing that he didn't like, hated even, and that was sport. He just couldn't understand what the attraction was. At break time most of his friends would charge out onto the playground, split into two teams and chase a small plastic ball around for twenty minutes.

So, for his entire school life, he avoided sport of any kind. At times, this was difficult; he spent most PE lessons doing as little as he possibly could. He did what he was told to do and occasionally he found some of the activities easy, but he had absolutely no interest in anything which involved moving about quickly and his teachers knew it: 'If you showed half as much interest in PE as you do in computers,' Mr Lee commented at the end of a gymnastics lesson, 'You'd win a gold medal at the next Olympics!' But Stephen wasn't interested in the Olympics. As far as he knew, there were no events involving computers so he had never bothered with it. Unfortunately for Stephen, Mill Lane Juniors' own version of the Olympics; Sports Day, was only a few weeks away. Of all the sporting events at school, Sports Day was the one Stephen hated the most. The one Sports Day he had taken part in, four years ago when he was in Reception, was still clear in his mind, and made him shudder with embarrassment whenever he thought about it. He had been picked for the skipping race – he didn't know why because he couldn't skip, but his mum had encouraged him and practised a little with him at home. As Miss Patel blew the whistle for the start of the race, the five year old Stephen started skipping. His new trainers were a little too big for him and after a few skips his right one had

worked itself loose. As he brought the rope down for the fourth time it got caught under the Velcro strap. Stephen continued the skipping action, and brought the rope up over his head. What he didn't know was that his shoe was attached to it. When the rope reached its highest point, the training shoe was released. It flew, as if it had been catapulted, through the air. Like most of the other competitors, Stephen had been skipping slightly off course, towards the crowd of parents watching their children. The shoe sailed through the air, bounced off the hood of a baby buggy, and landed with a smack on the Results Table, scattering all the scores onto the floor. Everyone laughed. Everyone, that is, except Stephen. He couldn't carry on with one trainer on. All the other children in the race skipped off towards the finish line, leaving him stranded, with one trainer on and one dirty white sock. He looked at the crowd of people, including his mum. They were all laughing hysterically. Eventually, after what seemed like ages, Miss Patel led him away to his seat, sat him down, and dabbed a soft tissue around his tearful eyes.

And that was the last Sports Day he had taken part in. He had been ill for the ones in Year 1, 2 and 3, and last year he had got himself a job raking the sand pit. But this year Mr Lee had already told him that as it was his second to last Sports Day at the school, he must take part, even if it was only in one event. Stephen's mum and dad had booked the afternoon off work, and as far as he could see, there was no way out. It was one week away, and the excitement in the school was building.

At the trials Stephen had decided to try the three-legged race – at least he wouldn't be on his own in this. And so it was, when the notice board went up in the school entrance hall and all the children crowded around, there was his name, next to the three-legged race category with his partner, Beth Allkins. She was sports mad, Liverpool Football Club mad, and very, very competitive. The exact opposite of Stephen Heyward.

A week later, Stephen and Beth were lining up at the start line, their legs tied tightly together, waiting for Mr Lee's whistle to signal the start of the race. All Stephen could remember was Beth telling him to start with his left foot, her right, and then to march together 'one, two, one, two'. The whistle went, the race began, and before Stephen knew it, they had come fourth. It wasn't actually that bad, he thought, although the look on Beth's face suggested that she didn't quite feel the same way.

'Never mind', she said. 'With a bit of luck I'll win the sprint. See you later Chip.'

And she was gone, to her next race, leaving Stephen to saunter back to his seat, relieved that the whole ridiculous event was finally over.

But unfortunately for Stephen, things were about to take a different turn. Just as he was sitting himself down to watch the rest of the afternoon's events, a hand gripped his shoulder. It was Beth and she was grinning. 'Bad news I'm afraid Chip. Jack's just hurt his ankle in the high jump.'

'And?' replied Stephen, who couldn't understand what this had to do with him.

'And … that means you've got to take his place in the 100 metre sprint – all the other boys are in two events and no one's allowed to do three.'

Stephen's heart sank. He didn't 'do' running. Running was a waste of energy. And he certainly didn't do running in front of the whole school or in front of all the parents or even in front of *his* parents. And he certainly didn't do running when it meant running with the five best runners in the school! The five boys who loved running and spent most of their lives running. What could he do? Could he pretend he had injured himself in the three-legged race? No. It was too late. Noone would believe him. And before he could think any more, the words he dreaded rang out over the school megaphone. Mrs Davies, the headteacher,

Fifty Fantastic Assembly Stories

was calling for the Year 5 boys' 100 metre runners to make their way to the start line.

Reluctantly, very reluctantly in fact, Stephen made his way to the beginning of the running track. He was in the middle lane. On his left was Liam Hodges and on his right, Adam McMahon – the school's two fastest runners. The other three in the race, Paul Simpson, Neil Hampson and Robert Jackson, were all in the school cross country team.

He was going to look stupid. He just knew it. Down one side of the track were the parents, Stephen's mum and dad were positioned right near the finish line, and on the other side were all the children shouting for their favourite. Mr Lee called the boys to attention, and slowly put the whistle to his lips.

'On the whistle boys. Good luck!'

And they were off. And after ten metres Stephen, expecting to see the backs of all the other boys as they ran off into the distance, couldn't see anyone else. Where were they? He could hear them, but he couldn't see them. After twenty metres, the

same. And then thirty and forty. And out of the noise of the crowd, he could hear, clearly, his dad's voice; 'Come on Steve… you can do it. Keep going. You're in the lead!' And from the other side of the track, he heard something he had never heard before; 'Chippy! Chippy! Chippy!' The other children were chanting his name. Actually chanting his name. He was winning. He was actually winning the 100 metre race at Sports Day. But at that moment Liam, in the lane to Stephen's left, tripped and fell and, as he fell, his right arm caught Stephen's left foot. Stephen stumbled and lurched forwards. He could see the grass coming towards him and prepared himself for the pain of hitting the dry ground. But he had been running at speed and his momentum kept him upright and, although he had lost his rhythm momentarily, he managed to stay on his feet. However, in that split second Adam McMahon had not only caught Stephen, but overtaken him.

Stephen had never felt like this before – normally, he'd not be bothered, but for some reason, now, he felt strange, determined.

'So this is what they all see in sport,' he thought to himself. 'Now I get it.'

With 10 metres left, he made one last surge for the line, but Adam was too far ahead. He really was fast. Stephen hit the finish line and walked away in a daze. 'Stephen!'

He continued walking back to his seat at the side of the track.

'STEPHEN!'

He turned back to the finish line. Mrs Newall, the Year 3 teacher, was beckoning him towards her. She was one of the judges and was holding something in her hand. Stephen walked over to her, his legs beginning to stiffen a little.

'Wow!' she proclaimed. 'Since when could you run so fast? You came second! Well done!'

She handed him a rectangular piece of yellow card with the number 2 written on it. 'What do I do with this?' he asked. But Mrs Newall had returned to her judging position for the next race.

'You take it to the results table.' It was Adam McMahon. 'Well done Chip,' he said. 'You had me worried there. Didn't know you could run so fast.'

Stephen followed Adam to the results table, handed his card in and turned to go back to his seat. But before he could take a single step he was lifted up and hugged by his dad.

'I can't believe it. You were amazing.' he said.

'Yeah, not bad for a computer geek!' replied Stephen, smiling.

And after a hug that very nearly squeezed all the air out of him, he made his way back to his classmates, who cheered and clapped as he approached. He kept looking round, expecting Adam to be behind him, but no – Adam was with the rest of Year 5 now, joining in the applause for Stephen, the school's new star runner.

He had an amazing talent with computers, but coming second in the 100m sprint during the school Sports Day, was his greatest achievement yet!

©Adrian Martin and Brilliant Publications
Fifty Fantastic Assembly Stories

Beth Learns to Listen

Beth Allkins, or Casey, as her friends called her, was interested in one thing and one thing only: football. She was ten years old now and in Year 5 at Mill Lane Juniors. For the last ten years, eleven months and three weeks, she had supported Liverpool Football Club. She had spent the first week of her life in hospital with her mum so that didn't really count, but since the day she had arrived home, when she was just eight days old, she had become football mad. And it was all dad's fault. You see, it was dad's job to make sure the baby's room was right for baby Beth. 'I don't mind what you do with it,' mum had said, 'As long as the baby feels safe and happy in there.'

Saying this, she realised later on, was a big mistake. Most dads decorate the baby's room with pictures of animals or Disney characters and paint the walls with calm colours and hang cute, twirly things with animals on over the cot, which play calming music so that the baby can slowly fall asleep, watching the little animals turning whilst the music plays. But Mr Allkins, Beth's dad, was not most dads. He was Beth's dad, and he was a mad Liverpool fan. And when Mr Allkins heard Mrs Allkins say, 'I don't mind what you do with it…' a very broad smile appeared on his face. The thought that the baby might be a girl did not even enter his mind, as he set about making the baby's room 'safe and happy'.

Instead of pictures of animals or Disney characters on the walls, he bought Liverpool Football Club wallpaper. Instead of curtains with pictures of animals or Disney characters on, he bought Liverpool Football Club curtains. Instead of a cute, twirly thing with animals on hanging over the cot, he made his own, with pictures of his favourite Liverpool players. When it turned, instead of playing calming sweet music, it played 'You'll Never Walk Alone' – Liverpool Football Club's theme tune. Everything in the baby's room, absolutely everything, was linked to Liverpool Football Club. The carpet, the light shade, the rocking chair in the corner; he even managed to get

You'll never walk alone!

Liverpool Football Club nappies! But his favourite part of the whole room was the cot. He had spent hours wondering what he could do with the cot, when one Saturday afternoon, at half time during the match, it occurred to him – the best idea he had ever had. The cot was, more or less, the same shape as a football stadium. Yes that was it! And that was it. He spent two months in the garage, every night after work, converting the cot into Anfield – Liverpool's stadium.

The inside of the cot was exactly like being inside the stadium with every stand packed with smiling faces and goal posts at each end. And the outside was exactly like the outside of the stadium. He made flood lights which worked and stuck them to each corner of the cot. The sheets were, of course, bright green, and the outer cover had the pitch marked on it, with the centre spot in the middle and the penalty areas at each end. He finished the cot the day before the baby was due to be born. 'Very soon,' he thought, 'My baby son will be lying on the famous Liverpool pitch.'

And one week later, his baby daughter was lying on the famous Liverpool pitch. It wasn't quite what Mrs Allkins had in mind, but it was too late to change anything now. So, at the age of just eight days, Beth Allkins became a Liverpool fan. She didn't really have much choice. There was one player on the twirly thing above the cot who she used to smile and gurgle at and as the Liverpool theme tune played, she would wait for his face to come round. Jimmy Case – her dad's favourite player of the 1970s.

©Adrian Martin and Brilliant Publications
Fifty Fantastic Assembly Stories

He was a hard tackling midfielder and for some reason Beth liked him. He would be her favourite player too. And that was why her friends called her 'Casey'.

As she grew up, her love for football also grew. She collected everything to do with Liverpool Football Club and anything to do with football. She went to her first match when she was three years old. Liverpool were playing Manchester United. They lost 3–0, and she cried for three hours. Her dad cried for four. By the age of seven, she was as good as any of the boys she knew and better than most of them. She would spend Saturday morning and most of Sunday playing football. Dad would take her to the local community centre where she would stride confidently into the hall full of boys in her full Liverpool kit. As soon as the boys saw her they would run over to her to test her on her knowledge of the game with questions that their dads had given them.

'Who scored a hat trick against Benfica in 1984?'

'Ian Rush.'

'How many times did John Barnes play for England?'

'48. I thought you said you had some hard ones for me this week,' Beth would reply with a grin.

In lessons she tried hard, but her teachers always said that if she put as much effort into her school work as she did into her football, she would be top of the class in everything. Her biggest problem was that she was really bad at listening. If anything other than football was being talked about, she would stop listening after a few seconds and her thoughts would turn to her favourite subject. Occasionally, this got Beth into trouble – nothing serious, not yet anyway, but trouble all the same.

At the end of the first day at the Infant School,

Beth's teacher was telling the children where they would go to meet their parents at home time. 'Follow me out onto the playground and I will lead you to the gate,' Miss Patel said. But by this time Beth was thinking about Kenny Dalglish's winning goal in the European Cup final against Bruges in 1978. When her class went to the cloakroom to get their bags, all the children followed Miss Patel out onto the playground and to the gate. All, that is, except one. Beth was a little slow getting her bag and coat and was left on her own in the cloakroom. When she was finally ready everyone had gone so she walked the wrong way up the corridor, joined the end of another line of children and walked out with them. But they were older children and they went out through another part of the school and to another gate, some distance from the gate where the new children were meeting their parents. Meanwhile, Miss Patel and Beth's mum were stood at the other gate wondering where on earth Beth was. Half an hour later Beth was found, sitting on her bag, on her own, calmly reading her football sticker book.

But her poor listening skills really got her into trouble on an exciting trip out in Year 5. An indoor rock climbing centre had recently opened near to the school and the Year 5 children had been invited to try it out.

'You'll all be perfectly safe,' the instructor had said. 'As long as you all listen carefully.'

Beth's friends gave her a knowing look.

'Don't worry,' Beth said. 'I'm listening.'

And she did. The instructor told them how to connect the ropes to the karabiner – a safety clip on the belt, and how to get into the safety harness, and how to fasten the helmet and as the instructor spoke Beth looked at him. He reminded her of someone and she couldn't quite work out who. And then she realised – Jimmy Case, her favourite footballer – he looked just like him in a

©Adrian Martin and Brilliant Publications

Fifty Fantastic Assembly Stories

Beth Learns to Listen

certain light. And then she was off into her own little football world, inside her head, remembering some of Jimmy's best moments … .

'So whatever you do don't let that happen,' the instructor said, waking Beth from her daydream.

She wondered what it was she mustn't let happen. Everyone else was nodding and looking serious. It was obviously something important, but she'd soon work it out.

And five minutes later she was at the top of the rock, having a great time, ten metres above the ground. She had made it to the top in seconds and now it was the fun bit – coming back down.

'Just jump backwards,' shouted the instructor, 'Your friends will support you.'

Liam and Holly were twenty metres below, supporting her with the ropes. She jumped backwards and they let some rope slip between their fingers, lowering her to the ground. It was great fun. Now it was her turn to support and as she stood there with the rope in her hands she realised that this was the bit she hadn't listened to.

It was Holly's turn to climb with Beth and Liam supporting her. Holly wasn't as confident as Beth and after five minutes she was only halfway up the rock.

'I'll come back down now if that's okay,' she said, shakily.

Fine,' replied the instructor. 'Are you two ready to support her on the way down?' he asked Liam and Beth.

'Yes!' they replied. Beth didn't know what to do but was too embarrassed to admit that she hadn't been listening before.

Holly had watched Beth coming down having so much fun. She jumped back as Beth had done but this took Liam by surprise – he was expecting the instructor to tell her when to jump. The strain of her jumping backwards made him lose his grip on the supporting rope, which slipped quickly through his fingers. Beth wasn't holding the rope tightly enough (as the instructor had told everyone to) and when Holly jumped back the rope snapped out of Beth's loose grip. A split second later there was a sickening thud as Holly hit the ground centimetres away from Beth and Liam. She screamed with pain and lay on the crash mat clutching her left arm. Liam looked at Beth – he knew she should have been holding the rope more tightly. Before she could do anything the instructor was talking to Holly, telling her not to move and that help was on the way.

Holly was taken to hospital while the rest of the class went back to school. They travelled back in silence. Beth felt sick. 'Why didn't I listen? What have I done?' she asked herself.

No one blamed her but she felt sure that they knew it was her fault.

The next day, Holly arrived at school with her arm in plaster. She had broken her wrist. She walked straight over to Beth and Liam. 'I just want you to know, it wasn't your fault,' she said. 'I jumped too soon. It was my fault and I'll be fine.'

Although Beth was really grateful to Holly for being so thoughtful, she still felt terrible inside and decided there and then that from now on, she would listen to every word and leave thinking about football for the weekends.

Fifty Fantastic Assembly Stories

Listening
Harry Gets the Pen!

Harry Jenks didn't take life too seriously. No one ever had to tell him not to worry, because he never did. He approached everything with a smile. The trouble was, he never did anything particularly well. Harry wasn't very competitive; he really didn't care if his team won or lost at football, or if other children knew the answers quicker than he did in maths, or if they could run faster, or jump higher than he could. He was just happy to bumble through life taking each day as it comes. Everyone liked Harry, after all, what was there not to like? He did however, have one weakness – he was very, very untidy. Harry himself didn't see this as a weakness and couldn't see what all the fuss was about and fuss there certainly was.

'True,' Harry thought. 'The bedroom could do with a bit of a tidy, but it's not as bad as dad was making it out to be.'

After several pushes, three or four pulls and a large number of shoves, his dad had finally managed to force open Harry's bedroom door. He fell into the room, tripping over one of Harry's many remote controlled cars and looked down at the floor where his son was sitting. Harry looked up at his dad's face. It was redder than usual and

his hair was standing on end. Harry was about to mention this but there was something about his dad's expression that made him realise it probably wasn't the best time to do so.

'Harry! What on earth?! How can you? Oh … I give up,' he spluttered. And with that he closed the door as best he could and blustered off downstairs.

Harry let out a sigh and continued to read his favourite comic. He was sat on his giant beanbag in the corner of the room. His bedroom carpet, as far as he could remember, was bright red, but not a centimetre of it could be seen for Harry's toys, books, skateboard, mini-snooker table, radio, washing-up bowl and bicycle wheel. He had absolutely no idea where the bicycle wheel had come from and he knew for a fact that all the bikes in the garage had both of their wheels on.

Unsurprisingly, Harry's untidiness wasn't just confined to home. His carefree attitude towards his own personal space was also the cause for bewilderment at school. Everyone knew which cloakroom peg belonged to Harry – it was the only one with nothing attached to it. His coat, school bag and PE bag could always be found on the floor beneath the peg. His desk was exactly the same; completely clear, spotless in fact; quite the opposite to the floor underneath it. Every Parents' Evening would be the same.

'They said you're a nice, happy boy Harry, but you really need to work on your organisational skills,' dad would say on the way home in the car. Harry wasn't listening of course – it was just the way he was, there was nothing he could do about it, he just couldn't work out why everyone kept going on about it. But there was something his mum said after the first Parents' Evening in Year 5 that did actually bother Harry.

©Adrian Martin and Brilliant Publications

Fifty Fantastic Assembly Stories

'Mr Lee says that you're the only one in the whole class still writing in pencil,' she said. 'He also said that despite the teachers constantly telling you what you need to do, you simply don't seem to listen and that because of this, he can't ever imagine you being awarded with the pen.'

One of the lovely traditions at Mill Lane Junior School was that when children proved to their teachers that they could write fluently with a pencil, they would be presented with a pen in assembly, by Mrs Davies. The children became very excited about the prospect of receiving their very own pen and most would practise their handwriting for hours, hoping to impress their teachers enough to be sent to Mrs Davies's office, where their writing would be judged. The youngest child to have ever received the pen was Peter Hartley when he was in just the second week of Year 3. Harry was now in Year 5 and none of his teachers had ever even hinted that his handwriting was good enough to be considered worthy of the pen. Until this point he hadn't realised that he was the only one in the class still to be writing in pencil and hearing his mum say that Mr Lee thought he would never get it upset him a little. It came as a great surprise to Harry therefore when, the following day, Mr Lee told him to take his books along to Mrs Davies at half past two that afternoon. Harry was foolish enough to think his writing was actually good enough and that Mrs Davies would quickly agree. But the reason Mr Lee had decided to send Harry along was to see if the Headteacher could get through to him as none of the teachers seemed to be able to.

'Right then Harry,' Mrs Davies began. 'Let's have a look at your writing and see if we can give you a few helpful tips.'

Harry passed the Headteacher his writing book. He had only had it six weeks and already it looked tatty and uncared for. Mrs Davies looked at it, took a deep breath and opened it at a random page. The last time Harry had seen a face with an expression of sheer shock was when his dad had forced open his bedroom door a few weeks ago.

'Oh Harry,' she gasped. 'This won't do. No, no, no. This won't do at all.'

Harry stood motionless by her desk for what seemed like a very, very long time, whilst Mrs Davies turned over page after page after page. As each page was revealed, she let out long, drawn out sighs, tutting and shaking her head. A lot.

'Right,' she said, shutting the book firmly. 'This is what you need to do.'

On a yellow piece of paper she wrote down a heading, 'What Harry Jenks must do to get the pen.'

She underlined it twice with her pen, pressing down so hard that she almost ripped the paper.

Underneath the heading she made six bullet points and as she wrote next to each one, she read every word slowly and clearly to him. And for the first time in a very long time, Harry listened. To every word. Next to the sixth and final bullet point she wrote, 'Practise EVERY day', writing the word 'EVERY' in block capitals and underlining it. Harry got the message that this word was important.

'I'll see you again in exactly one week,' she said firmly and then fixed his eyes with a steely, blue eyed stare. 'Go!' she said, pointing a finger towards the door.

Harry went and for once, he did not drop the piece of yellow paper on the floor. Instead he gripped it firmly, took it straight to his bag in the cloakroom which was of course empty, and pushed it into the front compartment, closing the zip firmly afterwards. When he arrived home, he forced open his bedroom door and stared at the mess that greeted him. 'Time to change,' he said to himself. An hour later, large parts of his bright red carpet could be

'Ah, Harry, yes,' she said. 'Now, where's that piece of paper I gave you?'

He pulled the paper from his pocket. She sighed as he passed it to her. It was tatty and creased, but for once, not because it had been on the floor but because he had folded and unfolded it every day to remind himself what he needed to do.

'Let's have a look then,' she said, opening his writing book at that morning's piece of work. Just as it had done a week ago, her expression quickly changed from calm to shocked, but unlike a week ago, it broke into a grinning, friendly face.

'I'm almost speechless Harry,' she said, looking back at the work he had done since their chat a week ago. 'The change is remarkable.'

seen and there was enough room for Harry to sit at his desk to practise his handwriting. And practise he did; every night and even every morning before breakfast. A week went by more quickly than Harry had ever known a week go by before but when the day came, the clock seemed to tick in slow motion as he waited for Mr Lee to send him to Mrs Davies's room. He was never normally aware of the time but today he needed 2:30 to come quickly. Mr Lee had noticed a huge difference in Harry since his trip to Mrs Davies last week. Everything about him was tidier – even his hair looked like it had been introduced to a comb. Eventually the classroom clock ticked around to 2:30 and Harry was back in the Headteacher's office.

Harry felt good. He had listened and he had changed, for the better. He wasn't awarded the pen that week. Mrs Davies wasn't a pushover. She needed to see that Harry really had changed. But he did get it two weeks later and as he enjoyed the loud round of applause he received in assembly when Mrs Davies handed him the pen, he realised that listening wasn't such a bad thing to do after all.

©Adrian Martin and Brilliant Publications
Fifty Fantastic Assembly Stories

Jake Gets Tough on Speeding Drivers

It was Road Safety Week at Mill Lane Juniors and Mrs Davies, the Headteacher, had arranged for the local Road Safety Officer to talk to the children about staying safe on the roads. Like most schools, Mill Lane Juniors did the best it could to encourage its children to walk or cycle to school, rather than coming in the car. But, like most schools, the parents of Mill Lane Junior School children were busy and had jobs to go to and had no choice but to use their cars. And, like most schools, this meant chaos outside school at home time. Mill Lane would be filled with cars, parked on both sides of the road. Only the yellow zig-zag lines were free from traffic. Some parents, so desperate to find a space near to the school gates, would arrive at the school at least half an hour before home time, to park.

Jake was lucky; his house was close to the school and now that he was in Year 5, his parents trusted him to get to school on his own. So far this year, he had walked 41 times, cycled 24 times, skateboarded twice and scooted on his new stunt scooter on 37 occasions. Jake loved maths and he had made a graph to show his school journeys. He was particularly interested in the fact that, so far this year, he had not once been taken to school in the car, even when it rained heavily.

He knew this because he had included weather conditions on his graph and had worked out that he had got wet on his way to school 17 times since September; that was 16.3%, he had calculated. 'Jake', his mum told everyone who would listen, 'had a great head for numbers.'

He liked the facts that the Road Safety Officer told the children, his favourite being the particularly startling fact that a car travelling at 30 miles an hour takes a full three seconds longer to stop than one travelling at 20 miles an hour. Jake believed the Road Safety Officer, but if he did have any doubts about this particular fact, he would be

absolutely certain after his journey home from school later that day. He always went home the same way, through the estate. He and his dad had worked out that this was the safest way, as Jake only had to cross one road, Oakdene Avenue, which was a very quiet road. Jake's graph told him that he had crossed this road 104 times on his way home from school this year and, despite stopping to look both ways, not once had there been a car in sight. Until today. Maybe Jake didn't look today because on the 104 previous times no cars had been coming. Maybe he didn't look because he was too busy working out how many Road Safety facts he could remember. But when he scooted across Oakdene Avenue that day, a car was coming. And it was coming quickly. He was half way across the road when he heard the loud screech of the car's brakes. He instinctively leapt from his scooter and fell backwards towards the safety of the kerb. He would have hit his head on the kerb but fortunately the rucksack on his back softened his fall, so apart from being very shocked, he was unhurt. The same could not be said for his scooter, which the car had been unable to stop in time to avoid. There was a loud crunch as the car's tyre hit Jake's scooter, breaking it clean in two. Although everything happened in a split second it felt to Jake like minutes had passed by. As he sat, dazed at the side of the road he became aware of another noise.

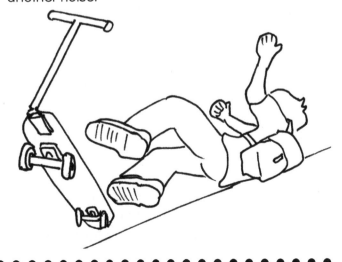

'That could have been your leg you silly boy. You weren't looking where you were going!'

It was the driver, who had wound down her window to shout at Jake and although Jake had never seen her before, he would never forget her face as she scowled at him before speeding off along Oakdene Avenue.

'Unbelievable!' came a softer voice from behind Jake. 'Are you all right Jake?'

It was Declan's mum. She had witnessed the whole thing and couldn't believe the way the driver had spoken to him. She helped Jake up and drove him home, putting the broken scooter in the boot of her car. It was the first time he had been driven home from school this year but he had already decided that he wasn't going to count it on his graph. This was definitely going down as his 38th and sadly his last, scooter journey.

As Declan's mum drove the car, Jake's eyes were fixed on the speedometer. She didn't once exceed 20 miles an hour and he was aware of how slow it felt. He tried to compare the speed they were travelling with the speed of the car that had nearly hit him. Obviously it was an impossible thing to do with any degree of accuracy but he was sure that that car must have been breaking the speed limit.

'She was driving far too quickly,' Declan's mum told Jake's mum as she handed over the broken scooter. 'We should tell Mrs Davies about this.'

And that was exactly what they did. The very next day. Although, much to his mum's disgust, Jake still insisted on walking – he wasn't having his 'Travel To School' chart ruined by a selfish speeding driver. Mrs Davies had a brilliant idea, or at least Phil, the Road Safety Officer had a brilliant idea and told Mrs Davies about it. Another school which had had lots of problems with traffic had set up what they called 'A Pupils' Court'. The police set up a speed trap outside school and when any

motorists were caught speeding they were given a choice of either paying a fine of £60 or going into the school to be questioned by a group of children.

'Ooh that sounds like it might do the trick,' Jake's mum said.

'And Jake could be one of the children to ask a question, if he would like,' Mrs Davies added. Jake nodded. He wasn't too sure that he liked the idea of talking to a driver he didn't know but he knew that Mrs Davies and a police officer would be there so he agreed.

A month later the 'courtroom' was set up in the school library and the police were in position on Mill Lane. Jake was one of six children chosen to be on the panel and they had each been asked to think of something they would like to say to the speeding drivers. Jake didn't have to think for long – he knew exactly what he was going to say to them. It took longer than they expected for the first driver to be led in to the library. Later on, the police told the children that three of the drivers had chosen to pay the fine rather than facing them; this was a sign of how guilty they must have felt, the police had thought. In total, seven drivers chose to meet the children; they were different in many ways – some were men, some were women, some were young, others were older. But one thing they all had in common, was an excuse:

'I was late for an appointment.'

'I didn't realise how fast I was going.'

'The car behind me was making me drive fast.'

They all seemed very sorry and all assured the children that they would never do it again. But it was the last driver to walk through the door who was the most apologetic. Jake knew who it was before she had even walked into the room. He could hear her making excuses to the Police Officer as she walked along the corridor towards the library where the children were waiting. Just as he would never forget her face, neither would he ever forget the voice, after she shouted at him while he sat shakily on the kerb at the side of Oakdene Avenue. It was definitely the woman who had destroyed his scooter and very nearly destroyed him just a few weeks ago.

'Sit here please madam,' the Police Officer told her. 'And these are the children who are going to talk to you.'

She sat down. The children were all sat behind a long desk and Jake was particularly thankful for this; it made him feel safer. Even though she was no longer driving her car, she still frightened him. The woman sat looking at the floor whilst each child asked her a question. She didn't look up once, obviously deeply embarrassed to be there. Mrs Davies was sitting behind the children. 'Jake,' she said. 'Would you like to tell the lady your fact now please?'

Unlike the other children, Jake had not written anything on a piece of paper. He had remembered his fact ever since he had heard the Road Safety Officer say it to the children in his presentation – the same day that this woman had very nearly knocked him over on Oakdene Avenue.

'Did you know,' he began, 'That a car travelling at 30 miles an hour takes a full three seconds longer to stop than one travelling at 20 miles an hour?'

For the first time since she had sat down the woman looked up and was about to say something when she saw the child who had spoken. Jake looked her in the eye and remembered what she had said to him before speeding off again.

'No, I didn't know that, young man,' she said.

She recognised Jake immediately and her expression changed instantly. It was as if she had realised for the first time in her life how dangerous driving over the speed limit actually was.

'I'm sorry,' she said, before looking towards the floor again.

The following day Mrs Davies handed Jake an envelope.

'I don't know what's in it,' she explained. 'The last speeding driver brought it in this morning. Said it was for the boy who gave the fact about braking.' Jake opened the envelope. A note flopped out which read, 'Put this towards a new scooter.' Six £10 notes were attached by a paper-clip to the note – £60. 'The amount she would have to have paid the police if she had chosen the fine,' Jake thought and then he smiled to himself. 'She really was sorry.'

Michael Struggles with a Dilemma

Being a Play Monitor was one of Michael's favourite school responsibilities; he was delighted when he was awarded his Play Monitor badge in assembly as it meant that his teachers had trust in him. Twice a week, on Tuesday and Thursday, Michael would have an early lunch, put on his red Play Monitor cap and make his way to the smaller playground, where the younger children played. His job included getting out the play equipment from the play cupboard, swinging the long skipping rope as the younger ones skipped endlessly, teaching them how to play snakes and ladders on the giant snakes and ladders area painted brightly onto the playground's surface and occasionally refereeing the football matches which took place in the football area. This was his least favourite part of the role because he'd never really enjoyed football and didn't understand the rules.

The younger children loved Michael – as soon as he appeared on the playground they would surround him, pulling his hands and dragging him over to the skipping area. Recently, a dressing-up box had been added to the play cupboard so that the children could play in a variety of strange and wonderful costumes. Today, Michael was stood spinning the rope wearing a long blue dress with a Postman Pat mask over his face and a straw hat on his head. This was the outfit the younger children had chosen for him to wear and, although he looked and felt ridiculous, he didn't mind, as long as they were having a good time. Every now and again one of the mid-day supervisors would ring the bell and a class would line up to be taken in for their lunch. This usually came as a relief to Michael as it meant that some of the children playing with him would have to go in for their lunch, giving him a chance to rest his skipping arm and to remove the ridiculous clothes they had dressed him in. Michael was a very relaxed, laid-back boy who could cope with children pulling him in different directions and making him dress

in strange outfits, but as a class of Year 3 children lined up for lunch, he saw something that made him feel quite uncomfortable. He looked around the playground to see if any of the adults had seen what he had seen but unfortunately he seemed to have been the only witness and he wasn't at all sure what to do about it. Robert Williams was tall for his age, almost as tall as Michael who was two years older. Not only had Michael seen Robert push into the line in front of Joe Lewis, but Michael had then witnessed Robert deliberately raise his leg and bring his foot down hard on top of Joe's foot. Understandably, Joe yelped in pain but Mrs Shelby, the mid-day supervisor, was too busy at the front of the line, making sure the children were lining up sensibly. Michael couldn't understand Joe's reaction. He rubbed his foot but then just stood there in the line, allowing Robert to stand in front of him. When Mrs Shelby walked down the line he said nothing but instead just stared ahead. It was almost as if Robert had some kind of power over Joe and Michael began to doubt what he had seen. Although Michael felt sure that what he had seen Robert do was very wrong, he decided not to say anything at this point, but to keep an eye out for Joe on Thursday when he would be a Play Monitor again.

©Adrian Martin and Brilliant Publications

Two days later, Michael stood on the playground, this time wearing a pink cape and a police officer's helmet. Mrs Shelby rang the bell and once again, the Year 3 children lined up to go into school for their lunch. Michael's eyes were focused on two children in particular. Joe Lewis stood quietly in the line as he had done two days earlier and probably did every day of his school life. Michael watched as Robert Williams slowly made his way from the football area to the line. When he reached the line, instead of joining it at the back as he should have done, he sidled over to where Joe was standing. Michael watched as Joe stood back to allow Robert to squeeze in ahead of him, just as he had done on Tuesday. Robert then raised his right arm and jabbed it backwards, his elbow digging into Joe's stomach. Joe winced, but just as he had done on Tuesday, said nothing to Mrs Shelby who, again, was too distracted by the noise of the other children to see what Robert had done.

Michael decided to follow the line of children into the school. Play Monitors were allowed to go into school when play equipment needed replacing so, after removing his pink cape and police helmet, he grabbed a skipping rope which had a broken handle and followed the line. As he walked behind the children he could see that Robert had swapped places with Joe and was now behind him, prodding him in the back as they walked along. Each time Mrs Shelby stopped the children to remind them to be quiet Robert put his hands by his sides. Michael continued to follow the younger children into the school dining room. He knew he risked being asked what he was doing there but he needed to see for himself what happened next. When he had got his lunch, Robert sat down next to Joe and, when Joe opened his lunch box, Robert grabbed one of the sandwiches and took a large bite out of it, before putting it back. Once again, Joe didn't react and continued to eat his lunch as if nothing had happened.

'He's being bullied,' Michael thought. 'And no one else knows except me.'

With a sickly feeling in his stomach, Michael made his way back out onto the playground, but instead of taking the direct route, he made a detour to Mrs Davies's office. He knew exactly what he had to do.

'Are you sure about this Michael?' the Headteacher asked him, after she had finished writing down everything he told her.

'Completely sure,' he replied.

The next day the Play Monitors were given other jobs to do and it was Mrs Davies who was spinning the skipping rope for the younger children. She often went out at playtimes to chat to the children so no one thought it unusual that she was there. And when Mrs Shelby rang the bell for the Year 3 class to line up, Mrs Davies wound up the rope and focused her attention on Joe Lewis. She had talked to Joe's teacher before school that day about him and Mrs Newall had said that Joe had definitely seemed quieter than usual over the last few weeks. She wasn't particularly complimentary about Robert's attitude when Mrs Davies told her what Michael had seen.

'I can't quite put my finger on it,' Mrs Newall told the Headteacher. 'But whenever anyone is upset about something, Robert Williams is never very far away.'

Mrs Davies watched as Joe walked to the line. He had a strange look on his face, neither happy nor sad, but there was definitely something not quite right about his expression and this concerned Mrs Davies greatly.

She continued to watch as Robert strolled over to the line. As he approached, Joe stepped back to allow Robert into the line, just as Michael had seen him do.

'Michael's got it wrong,' she thought. 'Joe's saving a place for Robert. He's just let him into the line.'

©Adrian Martin and Brilliant Publications
Fifty Fantastic Assembly Stories

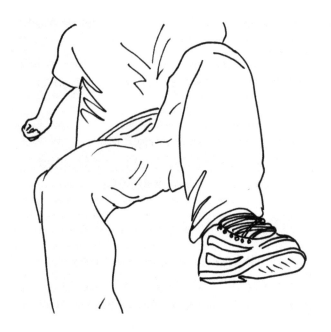

But then Robert lifted his foot and scraped it down Joe's shin. Just as he had when Michael had watched, Joe winced in pain. So too, did Mrs Davies, imagining how much that must have hurt. But despite wanting desperately to stop Robert doing anything else, she pretended that she had seen nothing and instead, followed them into school and then to the dining room. Like Michael had done, Mrs Davies saw Robert swap places with Joe and then prod him repeatedly in the back as they walked along, stopping each time Mrs Shelby looked in his direction. Mrs Davies then watched the boys sit down at a table with their lunch and just as Michael had done, she saw Robert remove a sandwich from Joe's lunch box, take a bite and put it back. To her amazement, Joe did not react, but now that she had seen what Michael had told her with her own eyes, Mrs Davies certainly did. An hour later Robert was

standing outside her office, wondering why he had been sent there.

'Come in Robert,' Mrs Davies said.

Robert walked in but was certainly not expecting to see what he did. His mum and dad were sat at the table at the far end of Mrs Davies's office. Their faces were a deep shade of red and Robert's father looked particularly annoyed.

'Sit down,' Mrs Davies told him, sternly.

It took a few minutes longer than it should have done for Robert to admit what he had been doing, but as Mrs Davies had seen his actions for herself he knew that lying was not an option. Joe was then sent for so that Robert could apologise to him. Understandably, Joe looked nervous and confused when he walked into the Headteacher's office, but the relief on his face was clear for all to see when Robert stumbled his way through an apology and promised never to do anything like it again.

When the parents had left and both Robert and Joe had returned to their classroom (Joe skipping with relief), Mrs Davies went in search of Michael.

'Well done,' she told him. 'You stood up for what is right and because of that, justice was done. I'm proud of you.'

And for the first time that week, Michael could look forward to being a Play Monitor again.

Tom Makes a Terrible Mistake

• •

This assembly is one of two. The first aims to promote discussion about the reasons for Tom doing what he did, what he should do next, and what the Headteacher/his parents/his friends should do so that justice is done.

It was Friday assembly at Mill Lane Junior School and Mrs Davies, the Headteacher, was doing her 'Important Messages' before the children left the hall:

'And remember everyone, when you're walking home from school in your school uniform, you are still representing this school and your behaviour must be as good as it is when you are here.'

Friday's assembly was right at the end of the day, and Mrs Davies often reminded the children about how they should walk home sensibly. The school was very popular, and Mrs Davies was proud of the way the children at Mill Lane Juniors behaved.

Tom was sitting with the rest of 5L, near the back of the hall – the older you got, the further back you sat. He couldn't wait for next year when he was in Year 6, and he could finally sit at the very back, with all the other children in the school in front of him. He was playing with the laces on his school shoes – he leant forward a bit and looked along the line. In assembly, the children sat in 'girl – boy' order. Next to Tom was Erin Bentley, then came Barney, Tom's best friend. Lauren Booth was sitting on the other side of Barney, followed by Sam Parsons, Emily Brooks and finally Joseph Parsons, Sam's twin brother. They were all sitting up straight, listening to what Mrs Davies was saying. Barney was even nodding in agreement, as if he were one of the staff. Tom was not listening to a word Mrs Davies was saying – he tried hard to listen in every assembly and had started well today - he had listened to the whole of the story (which he was sure Mrs Davies had

told before), but when the messages started, he just couldn't help it. His thoughts had wandered into Tom's World, as his mum called it – a strange but wonderful place inside his head that he often visited. Mr Lee, his class teacher, called it 'daydreaming', but he liked to think he was exercising his imagination. He was thinking about next year and how he would be the best Year 6 pupil ever and all the other children in the school would look up to him (even though many of them were already taller than him). He would be the hero of the school … forever.

He felt a sharp pain in his ribs – it was Erin's way of reminding him to sit up straight so that Mrs Davies would choose their class to be the first to leave the hall. Tom immediately sat up as straight as he could, extending his neck to well beyond its normal length so that he would stand out. He decided to smile his sweetest smile as well, hoping that the four baby teeth he still had at the front would catch Mrs Davies's eye. The Headteacher looked at the sea of children in front of her.

'Er … Tom's class I think – well done Tom. You were sitting up so well, and what a lovely smile you were giving me. Lead your class out please Tom.'

Erin scowled at him – it was only because of her that Tom had been chosen. 'Sometimes life could be so unfair,' she thought.

It was on the way home that night that Tom's good luck came to an end. He and Barney normally walked home together – they lived in the same

• •

street. But tonight, Barney was going away for the weekend to visit his Auntie Val in the Lake District – his mum and dad were waiting at the school gates in the car, all packed and ready to go.

'See you Monday Tom!' Barney shouted as he ran in the opposite direction to the car.

'Yeah, sure – have a good time,' Tom replied, reluctantly. He was going to miss playing with his best friend this weekend. He set off down the path on his own – the walk home took him past the Infant School and then into the housing estate where he and Barney lived. Tom walked slowly – it was Friday after all so there was no homework to be done and he had no football practice that night. Normally he and Barney would be chatting on the way home, so Tom didn't really notice the gardens of the houses he passed. Today though, his attention was caught by one particular garden that was full of painted clay figures. Tom's Grandad had a couple in his garden – gnomes, he called them. But Tom had never seen as many as there were in this garden. There was a pond in the middle of the lawn with three gnomes fishing in it. They all wore blue trousers, red jumpers and black wellington boots. One was sitting on a bench, another on a fishing basket, while the third was standing up casting his fishing rod into

the pond. Tom was mesmerised by them – they were tiny, but realistic. They were also all smiling and seemed to be having a great time. As he stood looking at them, Tom's mind once again wandered off into 'Tom's World'. He wondered what it must be like to be a gnome – to be there all day and all night, fishing, never catching anything. Maybe they came to life when it went dark. Maybe they caught tiny fish from the pond and sat around a tiny camp fire eating the fish they had caught and singing songs until sunrise, when they would go back to their positions again.

Tom was startled from his 'daydream' by a voice he did not recognise.

'Bet you couldn't hit one with this.'

'Eh?'

'I said, I bet you couldn't hit one with this.'

It was a boy in a different uniform to Tom's – he was wearing a black blazer and had a round, grey stone in his hand. The boy was bigger than Tom – much bigger, and the badge on his blazer said, 'St Cuthbert's High School'.

'Course I could.'

The words came out of Tom's mouth before he had time to think. They didn't even sound like his words and he couldn't believe he had said them. But he had.

'Prove it,' said the older boy, pushing the stone into Tom's hand and then standing back, arms folded.

Tom was a good footballer – he was one of the Year 5 strikers in the school team. But he had never been a very good thrower. Although he loved cricket, he found it hard to hit the wickets and he had never quite managed to throw the javelin as far as anyone else at the school Sports Day.

©Adrian Martin and Brilliant Publications

Fifty Fantastic Assembly Stories

He rolled the stone over in his hand. It felt dry and smooth and a little bigger than it had looked in the boy's hand. Behind the pond was a small lawn and then the house. He looked up at the windows of the house. No one was watching. In fact, there didn't seem to be anyone in – there was no car in the drive and none of the lights were on.

He took aim at the gnome sitting on the bench, raised his hand and flung the stone through the air.

The next second of Tom's life seemed as long as his whole life so far. He watched, open mouthed, as the stone flew through the air. It missed the gnome he had aimed at by some distance. In fact, it had missed all the gnomes altogether. But what it didn't miss, was the window of the house. There was a loud smack, followed by the sound of shattering glass, followed by silence. Tom stared at the large window – there was a round hole in the middle of it, and four long cracks travelling from the centre of

the hole to each of the corners. His ears began to burn. He could hear his heart pounding. He felt sick.

'Told you, you couldn't hit the gnome,' said the bigger boy. He was backing away at speed and laughing – actually laughing. 'You'd better get out of here,' he said. His walk had turned into a run and seconds later, he was gone.

Tom stood, fixed to the spot staring at the window. Behind him, the doors of one of the houses opened. He ran and ran and ran, and only stopped running when he reached the driveway to his house.

'Where on earth have you been? We've been worried sick.'

It was Tom's mum. He looked at his watch – it was quarter past four – he was normally home by four.

Tom opened his mouth to tell her what had happened. Nothing came out.

'You look like you've seen a ghost,' his mum said. 'Come on in and have some toast.'

Tom followed his mum into the house. He didn't know what to do. He didn't know what to say. He didn't think anyone had seen him so maybe he'd get away with it if he said nothing. The older boy wouldn't tell anyone in case people thought he did it. That was that then – he'd keep quiet, try to forget it ever happened. No one would ever find out …

Tom Learns the Hard Way

● ●

Part One (pages 27–29) describes Tom being 'dared' by an older boy into throwing a stone at a garden gnome – the stone misses and goes through the window of Mrs Knight's house. A neighbour recognised the uniform Tom was wearing and informs Mrs Davies, the school's Headteacher. The news is about to become known to everyone at the school. Will justice be done?

It was Monday morning and the children were gathering on the playground. Tom had spent the weekend worrying about what he had done on the way home from school on Friday.

'You all right Tom? You look awful,' Tom's best friend Barney asked.

'Yeah – I'm fine. Just didn't sleep very well last night that's all.'

Barney and Tom were having their usual Monday morning chat before school when they were interrupted by Emily Brooks, who was very excited about something.

'Hey – have you heard what happened on Friday after school?'

'No Emily. We haven't. What happened on Friday after school?' replied Barney, in a disinterested tone. Emily was a bit of a gossiper and Barney just couldn't see the point.

'Someone threw a stone through Peter Knight's grandma's window, that's what.'

'Who's Peter Knight?' asked Barney.

'He's in Year 3 – blonde, small, glasses, cute.'

'Never heard of him,' replied Barney.

Tom had gone very pale, and began to back away.

'It doesn't matter that you've never heard of him. His grandma's window was broken on Friday after school, and it may have been someone from Mill Lane Juniors,' Emily said loudly.

'Couldn't have been,' said Barney. 'No one from this school would do that.'

Barney noticed that Tom was no longer with them. He looked around to see his best friend sitting on one of the playground benches on his own.

'Strange,' thought Barney. 'What's up with him?'

Moments later, they were filing into the Monday morning assembly with the rest of Mill Lane Junior School. The Headteacher's office was just outside the hall and out of the corner of his eye, Tom could see Mrs Davies talking very quietly to an elderly lady. Mrs Davies had her hand on the lady's shoulder and was shaking her head. She seemed quite upset about something. Tom had a sick feeling deep in his stomach.

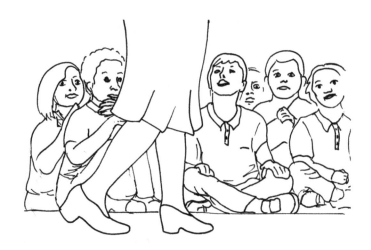

● **Tom Learns the Hard Way** ●

©Adrian Martin and Brilliant Publications

The children sat in silence as they waited for Mrs Davies to begin the assembly. The teachers sat on chairs at the sides of the hall – they usually looked quite serious on Mondays, but they looked particularly serious today.

After what seemed like ages, Mrs Davies finally appeared at the front of the hall.

'Well everyone. I normally start by saying 'Good morning' to you all, but unfortunately I cannot bring myself to do that today. I have just been talking to Mrs Knight, Peter's grandma.' Everyone's heads turned towards 3N, where Peter was sat. His face turned a deep red.

Mrs Davies continued, 'She is extremely upset and I can fully understand why.'

Everyone in the hall sat forward, listening intently to what the Headteacher was about to tell them.

Tom's ears burned. He could feel his face getting redder and redder. There was nothing he could do about it. He felt like everyone was staring at him. He dared to glimpse quickly at Barney. He was leaning forward like everyone else, waiting to hear what Mrs Davies was going to say.

'On Friday evening, at about four o'clock, a stone was thrown through Mrs Knight's window.' Everyone in the hall, children and teachers, gasped.

'Fortunately, Mrs Knight was shopping at the time, so nobody was hurt. The stone went straight through the window and smashed the coffee table in the lounge. If she had been sitting watching the television, who knows what could have happened?'

The hall was silent. Mrs Davies looked very sad and upset.

'But why is she telling us?' thought Barney. 'Maybe we're going to raise money for Mrs Knight to replace her window and coffee table?'

'This is certainly not the way I expect to begin a new week,' continued Mrs Davies, 'But I have to tell you this today because the owner of the house opposite Mrs Knight's saw a boy running away moments after the window had been smashed, and … ' she paused. Tom froze – he knew what Mrs Davies was going to say next and at that moment he would rather have been anywhere else in the world than in Mill Lane Junior School. 'And,' Mrs Davies continued, 'He was wearing a Mill Lane Junior School uniform.'

The children couldn't help themselves – they turned to each other and whispered things:

'Who was it?' 'Who could do that to Peter's gran?' 'How old was he?'

'Right!' Mrs Davies brought the hall to a silence again. 'Someone from this school – a boy – has done something terrible. Something that could have caused serious injury to someone. This person has damaged the reputation of our school. And that person is sitting in this hall today.'

The rest of the assembly was a blur – Tom did not sit up at the end of the assembly. He just wanted to hide from everyone, and when Mrs Davies asked 5L to leave, Tom just about managed to struggle to his feet. As he did so he caught Barney looking at him. Barney knew – they knew each other inside out and couldn't hide their feelings from each other. Tom was behaving strangely and Barney knew something was wrong.

At playtime, Barney pulled Tom to one side. Everyone was talking about the window – who could have done it and what might have happened if Mrs Knight had been in the house. 'You know about this don't you?' Barney asked his friend.

'No – course not. Do you seriously think I'd be that stupid?' Tom replied.

'No I don't – but I do know that you're acting strangely. You know something about it don't you?'

Tom couldn't help himself – tears welled up in his eyes and streamed down his cheeks as he began to tell his best friend what had happened.

When Tom had finished the story, Barney just sat, shaking his head.

'If you don't tell Mrs Davies I will,' he said, clearly.

'What? There's no way I can admit this. No one will ever speak to me again. I can't own up.'

'Look Tom – I'm your best friend and I always will be. Everyone makes mistakes, but you've got to admit this. You'll regret it forever if you don't and that wouldn't be fair on Mrs Knight or you.'

Tom knew Barney was right. If he didn't admit what he had done he would never forgive himself. Every time he walked past Mrs Knight's house he would feel sick. He had absolutely no choice.

At the end of maths, Tom waited for everyone to leave the room, before approaching Mr Lee, his teacher.

'Now Tom – what can I do for you?' he asked. 'Do you want me to go over something again for you?'

Tom took a deep breath. 'The window, Mr Lee,' he said. 'I did it.' And for the second time that day, tears rolled down his cheeks.

Things moved on very quickly from then on. Mr Lee told Tom to wait in the classroom while he told Mrs Davies, and when he got back he told Tom that he was to go to Mrs Davies's office at the end of lunchtime.

Pushing open the door to the Headteacher's room was almost as difficult as telling Mr Lee the truth. When the door swung open, Tom was faced with Mrs Knight, Mrs Davies and his mum and dad. No one shouted – Mrs Knight looked upset and Tom's mum and dad looked very disappointed. Mrs Davies said she was relieved that Tom had been brave enough to tell the truth so that the whole thing could be dealt with fairly. When Tom had explained about the bigger boy, the adults seemed to understand a little more why he had done it although they all agreed that justice had to be done – that Tom would have to be punished, both at home and at school. The end of term disco was next week. Tom would miss that. Tom's dad had bought two tickets for the football match this weekend – Tom would miss that. And then there was the small matter of the window and the coffee table. Mum and dad would pay to begin with, but Tom would pay them back with his pocket money – for the next three months. Justice had to be done.

Tom had learned never to be forced by someone else to do something he knew was wrong – even if they're older or bigger. He had also learned how

good a friend Barney was – if it hadn't been for him, Tom might not have admitted what he had done and justice might never have been done, and he would have felt terrible.

As for Mrs Knight, she forgave Tom, especially when he saved his pocket money for an extra month to buy her a fourth garden gnome for her pond.

©Adrian Martin and Brilliant Publications

Tony's Behaviour Causes Alarm

Mr and Mrs Bailey trudged unhappily from Mrs Davies's office and out into the entrance hall where Tony, their son, was waiting for them.

'What are we going to do with you?' Dad said to Tony. 'Let's go home and talk about it.'

It was the third time Tony's mum and dad had been called into school since the beginning of the year and they were both becoming more than worried about his behaviour. He'd always been so well behaved before but, since starting Year 5, he had been nothing less than a nuisance. All the staff including Mr Lee, his teacher, knew that Tony's auntie had died suddenly in the summer holidays and that Tony had been very close to her. Because of this they understood why Tony was behaving differently and although they let him get away with a few of the less serious things at first, his behaviour had become more worrying recently and something clearly had to be done.

In October, Mr Lee had heard a commotion coming from the boys' toilets at break time. When he had opened the door to see what was going on Tony was hanging from the water pipe near the ceiling. He had climbed onto one of the sinks and made a jump for the pipe which he was dangling from when Mr Lee had entered. The other boys looked horrified when Mr Lee opened the door but Tony, who was facing the other way, was completely unaware that his teacher was there until his rather red face appeared below him. That was the first time Tony's parents were invited into school to discuss his behaviour.

Shortly after the pipe dangling incident one of Barney Smith's football boots went missing from his bag. After a long and tiresome search, Mr Pearson the caretaker told Mr Lee that he had seen Tony outside the classroom on his own at break time. He had wondered what Tony was doing inside when he should have been on the playground like everyone else. He slid open the door of the teachers' cupboard and appeared to put something into the corner of it before sliding the door shut again and going out. Mr Lee had immediately looked in the cupboard and found Barney's football boot. Tony admitted doing it but couldn't give an explanation why – he was one of Barney's best friends and had no reason to hide his things.

'At least you're honest Tony, I'll give you that,' Mr Lee had said, as he and Tony's parents sat round the table after school that evening.

Mrs Davies had asked Tony's mum and dad to come in to see her when Tony had been caught scratching his name into the wooden surface of one of the picnic tables on the playground. Again, Tony admitted what he had done immediately but the adults were becoming more and more worried about him. In the classroom he had become quiet and rarely smiled these days, quite the opposite of the Tony everyone knew before the summer holidays.

Everyone agreed that the unexpected loss of his auntie in the summer was the reason for Tony's sudden change in behaviour. He seemed to be behaving the way he did to get attention but, as Mrs Davies said, she was no expert and so it was decided it would be a good idea to arrange for a specialist teacher to meet Tony. Mrs McDougall specialised in talking to children who had lost someone close to them and from the minute she met him, Tony began to change. They would sit down together for half an hour every Tuesday just after lunch. At first Tony just sat there, not wanting to talk to this person, unsure why she was there and hoping for the session to be over. But it didn't take long for Tony to realise that Mrs McDougall was a kind lady who was just there to help him. She wasn't there to blame him for his behaviour, which he was secretly ashamed of, she wasn't there to put pressure on him by constantly asking him why he was behaving the way he was. She was just there to listen to him. She didn't know Tony's Auntie Jane and this meant he could tell Mrs McDougall all about her and talking about his auntie was something he hadn't done since she had died. As the weeks passed Tony began to look forward to his time with Mrs McDougall and gradually he began to feel better about himself again. There were no more silly behaviours, no more awkward telephone calls inviting his mum and dad into school and in class he was more like his old self, working hard and getting involved again. But then something happened which very nearly ruined everything.

Tony and his friend, Harry Jenks, were waiting outside the classroom with the rest of the class. They usually walked straight into the classroom but Mr Lee was having a meeting in there so they had to wait outside for a couple of minutes. Minutes earlier Tony and Harry had been playing 'tag' with a few of the other boys and when the whistle had gone, Harry was 'on'. As they stood in the line Harry decided it would be a good opportunity to 'tag' Tony, so that he would be 'on' at the beginning of the next playtime.

'That's not fair,' Tony said, laughing. 'You're not allowed to tag me inside school.'

And with that, Tony 'tagged' Harry back.

Now Tony was ready for Harry and as Harry lifted his hand to tag his friend again, Tony moved backwards. Unfortunately he didn't realise that just behind his head was the small red fire alarm box with the thin glass cover which has to be broken when there is a fire. When Tony moved backwards suddenly his head hit the centre of the box and the two boys heard a small crack as the glass was broken. The expressions on the boys' faces changed from enjoyment to horror in an instant as they realised what they had done. Their smiles disappeared and their eyes widened as the piercing sound of the school fire alarm sounded. Children covered their ears and some began to shout above the sound of the alarm. Mr Lee burst out of the classroom and issued clear instructions to the children to stop talking, turn to face the other way and lead out in single file to the playground. As he finished his instruction and began to walk to the front of the line, he looked at the broken glass case on the wall above Tony's head. He then looked down and noticed how red Tony's face had gone.

After Mr Lee had taken the register and was satisfied that everyone in his class was accounted for, he walked along the line of children to where

©Adrian Martin and Brilliant Publications
Fifty Fantastic Assembly Stories

Tony was standing. 'I think we need to talk,' he whispered. 'Come and see me at lunchtime please.'

Tony said nothing. It was his head that had broken the glass case. He had caused all of this bother. The whole school had had to come out onto the playground because he had set the fire alarm off. The children had to line up in alphabetical order when there was a fire alarm and Harry, who was standing in the middle of the line, much further back than Tony, was feeling terrible about the whole thing. Although it was an accident and it was Tony who had set off the alarm, Harry knew that if he hadn't started to play 'tag' the whole thing would never have happened.

At lunchtime Mr Lee told all of the children except Tony to go straight out to play. Harry put up his hand to say something but Mr Lee was in no mood to listen to questions. 'I said everyone out Harry. Which includes you!' Mr Lee was rarely in this kind of mood but the children knew that when he was, it was best to do as he said. Harry walked out of the classroom with the rest of the children.

'Surely Tony will tell Mr Lee what happened,' Harry thought. 'And I'll be called in and then I'll be able to tell him that it was my fault.'

But Tony didn't tell Mr Lee exactly what had happened, because Mr Lee had already made up his mind that Tony was to blame. Since the alarm had gone off, he had thought about the look on Tony's face as he stood next to the broken case. He remembered the time he had caught Tony hanging from the water pipe and the hours he had spent looking for Barney's hidden football boot. Finally, he remembered the disappointed look on the faces of Tony's mum and dad after he had etched his name into the picnic bench. And at the end of a long, exhausting term, Mr Lee made the mistake of asking Tony just one question rather than investigating fully what had happened.

'Did you break the glass Tony?' he asked.

Tony nodded.

Mr Lee then told Tony how annoyed he was that he had let everyone down again, that he had gone back to his old ways after all the help and support from Mrs McDougall and Mrs Davies and his mum and dad. Every time Tony tried to say something Mr Lee put his hand up for him to stop.

'I don't want to hear it Tony,' he said. 'You've really done it this time. I'm going to call your parents again.'

There was a knock at the door. It was Harry and this time he wasn't going to wait for Mr Lee's permission to talk.

'It was my fault Mr Lee,' Harry said. 'It was an accident; I went to tag Tony and he moved his head back and broke the glass. He didn't know it was there. He didn't mean it,' he stopped talking to take a breath.

Mr Lee looked at Tony. 'Is that what happened?' he asked.

Tony nodded.

Mr Lee thought about asking why on earth Harry thought it was a good idea to play tag inside school but stopped himself and looked again at Tony.

'Tony, I owe you an apology,' he said. 'I was really annoyed because I thought you'd let yourself down again, but I was wrong and I am sorry. You'll both have to go to Mrs Davies to explain what happened though, but I'm sure she'll decide it was an accident. Sometimes even teachers make mistakes,' he grinned. And for the first time since the terrible screech of the alarm had begun that morning, Tony smiled too.

©Adrian Martin and Brilliant Publications

Courage

Charlotte Overcomes Her Fear

It was fair to say that the children in Year 5 were excited. They had waited three years for this day and it had finally arrived.

Castlemere Adventure Centre in the Lake District was going to be their home for the next five days. Instead of normal lessons in their classroom, they would be canoeing, rafting, gorge walking, rock climbing, abseiling and problem solving. Castlemere was set in over 100 acres of open fields and woodland; it even had its very own river. Mr Lee had been organising these trips for years now and every year when the children returned home, he would show photographs of the experiences they had had in assembly. It looked amazing. Many of the children in Year 5 had older brothers and sisters who had been on the trip and so everyone was aware of what was in store for them. So it was no wonder that the excitement amongst the children had now reached fever pitch.

'I … just … cannot … wait … any … longer,' Suzie told Charlotte, her best friend, as they waited for Mr Lee to let them board the coach. They had gathered on the playground with their suitcases and bags and were chatting about the things they were most looking forward to.

'I think I'm most looking forward to canoeing Lottie (Suzie always called Charlotte 'Lottie'), or maybe the gorge walking. No, you know what I'm actually looking forward to the most?' she continued, not actually expecting a reply from her friend. 'Rock climbing, yes definitely rock climbing. That sounds amazing. I'm just soooo excited,' Suzie exclaimed.

Suzie was good, no make that very good, at talking. Talking was, without a doubt, her specialist subject and she put a great deal of practice into it. Charlotte often thought to herself that if there was a talking event at the Olympics, Suzie would

definitely get a gold medal for the British team. Suzie continued to explain how excited she was, completely unaware that Charlotte had long stopped listening to a word she was saying. She wasn't deliberately ignoring Suzie, but had simply become lost in her own thoughts. Unlike every other child in Year 5, Charlotte had not been looking forward to the trip with huge amounts of enthusiasm and the reason for this could be summed up in two words; rock climbing. When she was five years old Charlotte had accidentally fallen backwards off a wall at a camp site and landed on the roof of a tent three metres below. Although remarkably she was completely uninjured, she had sat shaking for hours afterwards and had been terrified of heights ever since. Mr Lee had repeatedly told everyone that no one would be forced to do any of the activities, but Charlotte knew that at some point during the week she would have to face up to her fear.

It wasn't long until they were finally on their way. As the coach pulled away from the school gates, tearful parents waved to their smiling children and Mr Lee walked up and down the aisle of the coach, handing out the activity sheets.

'Thank you Mr Lee,' Suzie smiled, as he handed her the yellow sheet which provided them with the activity groups and the order that they would be doing the activities.

'We're in Group 3,' Suzie announced, scanning the sheet for their names. 'Ooh, yippee, guess what we're doing this afternoon Lottie? Guess.'

But before Charlotte could offer a suggestion, Suzie had answered her own question and it was not the answer that Charlotte wanted to hear.

'Rock climbing! We're doing rock climbing Lottie. How exciting is that? Lottie … Lottie, you okay?

©Adrian Martin and Brilliant Publications

Fifty Fantastic Assembly Stories

Suzie asked, 'You seem very quiet today'. 'Not too keen on heights,' Charlotte replied, honestly. 'You know, ever since …'

'Oh, your fall you mean, Don't worry Lottie, you'll have a harness on and a helmet. It's perfectly safe, Mr Lee said so,' Suzie explained, trying to reassure her friend.

'Well at least it's the first activity so I'll get it over with quickly,' Charlotte thought.

Three hours later Suzie was staring directly into Charlotte's eyes as she was fastening her helmet under her chin. Following the instructions of Ben, the climbing instructor, Suzie then checked the tightness of the chin strap and made sure the helmet didn't wobble around too much on Charlotte's head. Charlotte stared at the grey slab of rock in front of her and allowed her eyes to follow it upwards, higher and higher … and higher still, until blue sky peeped out from the very top of the rock, way above their heads. She gulped at the thought of being so high up.

'Right then kids,' Ben said enthusiastically. 'Who's first?'

His question was answered by nine arms shooting up into the air and a chorus of, 'Me Ben, me!' Ben was an experienced climbing instructor and he had already decided who would be his first climber from Mill Lane Junior School that year. The last ten years had taught him that in most groups of ten children, there would be one child who was scared of heights and in this group it was very obvious who that was. One girl, he noticed, had not raised her hand in the air when he had asked who wanted to be first and she definitely had not shouted, 'Me Ben, me!'

In fact, when Ben had asked his question, Charlotte had actually taken a step backwards, quite the opposite action to that of the rest of the group. Ben took his job very seriously and he

knew that it was his responsibility to get every child safely to the top of the rock. He knew that if Charlotte waited to go last, she would have more time to worry and there would be less chance of her doing it.

'Charlotte!' he said. 'Let's climb!'

Charlotte took another step backwards. She hadn't volunteered so why had he picked her, she thought. When she had stepped backwards, the rest of the group had stepped back even further, so that she was now the closest one to the rock face.

'Okay,' Ben announced. 'Suzie, you hold this rope and do exactly what I say. Everyone else, watch and don't say anything, unless it's to encourage Charlotte here. Charlotte, step forward.'

Ben never once asked Charlotte whether she wanted to climb or not. He deliberately gave Charlotte no choice in the matter. There was something about the way he spoke that made Charlotte trust him and as a result, she did exactly what he said, stepping forward towards the slab of rock.

'See that hole there?' he asked, pointing at the rock. 'Put your right foot there.'

Charlotte did exactly that.

'Good. Now, when I say, push up with your right foot and put your left hand in that crack there,' Ben continued, pointing confidently at a crack in the rock.

Before Charlotte could say, 'I'm terrified,' she had pushed up with her right foot, grabbed the crack with her left hand and was higher off the ground than she had been since the incident at the camp site when she was five.

'Well done,' Ben said.

'Go Lottie go!' screamed Suzie.

'Let that rope run through your fingers Suzie,' instructed Ben.

Charlotte felt the rope loosen.

'Now Charlotte, there's another foot hole about 50 centimetres above your left foot. Lift your left foot and jam it in.'

Again, Charlotte followed Ben's instructions but this time, rather than pausing for further guidance, she found a crack with her right hand, gripped it with her fingers and pushed upwards again.

There was a cheer of encouragement from below and something strange happened to Charlotte. She repeated the movements Ben had taught her and within minutes the fingers on her left hand touched something that wasn't cold and smooth, something that wasn't rock. She looked up. What she had touched was green and soft. It was grass. Remarkably she was at the top.

'You're there!' Ben shouted. 'You've done it Charlotte! Now push yourself onto the grass and wait there. I'll be there in thirty seconds.'

Charlotte heaved herself onto the grassy bank at the top of the rock face. She hadn't realised how heavily she was breathing until now and couldn't believe what she had done. Ben appeared with a big grin on his face.

'Wow!' he said. 'Who'd have guessed you were scared of heights? Well done Lottie!'

'How did you know?' she asked.

'Just a lucky guess,' he replied, laughing.

Charlotte looked down at Suzie and the rest of the group, a long way below. They were craning their necks to look up at her and were clapping and cheering. They knew that Charlotte had just conquered her fear and they were impressed with the courage she had shown.

'Can I do it again please Ben?' she asked, laughing.

©Adrian Martin and Brilliant Publications

Hannah Takes to the Stage

● ●

It was October; the month Hannah Ellis had been dreading for quite some time. In October at Mill Lane Juniors the children in Year 5 are told the name of the pantomime they will be performing at Christmas and Miss Morris, the teacher who directs the performance, puts up an audition timetable on the wall outside the classroom. The children don't have to take part, but there was a kind of expectation that everyone should. Everyone at the school got very excited about it and, since the start of the year, teachers would stop Year 5 children in the corridor to ask them if they were going to be in the pantomime this year.

'It's great fun,' they would say. 'It's something you'll never forget. Go for it!'

So far Hannah had successfully managed to avoid this awkward conversation, but she knew that she would have to make a decision sooner rather than later. Her parents knew that she was dreading it and had deliberately avoided raising the subject with Hannah.

Excitement among the children, on the other hand, was building and there was no chance of Hannah avoiding talk of the pantomime on the playground.

'Are you going to audition Hannah? I am. I can't wait. I'm hoping to get one of the main parts but I won't mind if I don't. I just can't wait. I'm nervous about the audition obviously but I've been practising in front of the mirror at home.' Suzie was babbling at full speed, as she did so often, particularly when she was excited.

'I'm babbling aren't I Han? Sorry, sorry. I'm just mega excited that's all,' Suzie continued to babble. Hannah liked Suzie. She was a talker rather than a listener but she meant well and Hannah enjoyed listening to her babblings each day. But

Suzie wasn't the only one getting excited about the pantomime – most of the children in Year 5 couldn't stop talking about it, guessing which one it would be and who would get the main parts.

Hannah was a desperately shy person who found it very difficult to speak out in class, or even when she was working with a group of more than three children. She didn't know the reason why and had just come to terms with the fact that everyone is different and that's just the way it is. She often knew the answers to the questions teachers asked in the classroom and often had good ideas to suggest, but when it came to actually speaking out loud in front of people, she just couldn't do it. And so the thought of actually standing on the school stage in the school hall, in front of more than a hundred people, filled her with dread. No one would have been in the least bit surprised if she had said she wasn't going to take part; everyone would have understood completely. But there was a very good reason why she hadn't said she wouldn't take part. She absolutely loved drama and dreamt of being an actress one day. Whilst the thought of standing on a stage petrified her, she was desperate to act. Mum and dad often took her to the local theatre to watch whatever play was on and she would sit there completely transfixed by the whole thing: the actors, the scenery, the music, the sound effects. She loved everything about it. Instead of TV she watched musicals, of which she was obsessed with and had incredible knowledge, although no one at school knew of her hidden interest. So whilst the thought of taking part in the pantomime filled Hannah with horror, not taking part was simply unthinkable.

'I don't know what to do,' she told her parents over tea one evening.

'Why don't you just give the audition a try and see

● ●

Fifty Fantastic Assembly Stories

what happens?' her mum suggested. 'I can ask Miss Morris if you can audition just for her with no one else in the room.'

Hannah knew that this was what she needed to do and so it was arranged. The normal auditions were in the hall and there were usually a few teachers watching as well as a queue of four or five children waiting nervously for their turn. Hannah couldn't have coped with that. But just her and Miss Morris? Yes, that should be okay. And as it turned out, it was more than okay. She had walked apprehensively into Miss Morris's classroom with the passage she had been given to read. The pantomime was 'Snow White' and all the children had been given some of the wicked witch's lines to read at the audition. Most had read them like robots without any expression or feeling. Suzie had read hers both loudly and quickly. Occasionally someone would show some potential, but no one's audition came close to Hannah's. Miss Morris had watched and listened in utter amazement as Hannah leapt around the room, raising and lowering her voice, changing her expression and best of all producing the loudest, ear-piercing witch-like cackle, so loud and ear-piercing that it actually made Miss Morris jump back with fright.

'Er … wow!' Miss Morris exclaimed when Hannah had finished. 'Thanks Hannah. That … was … incredible! Thank you, you can go now.'

And with that Hannah was gone, breathing heavily as she left the room. She realised that during the audition she hadn't been Hannah Ellis, the painfully shy child but instead had been the wicked witch, determined to trick Snow White and to become the Queen of all the land and to her great surprise she had absolutely loved every second of it. That lunchtime Miss Morris rang Hannah's mum. She explained that although Hannah had shown herself to be a natural actress she was worried about giving her a main part in case she got stage fright when there was a

hall full of people waiting to watch her. After a discussion, the two adults decided to risk it – this could change Hannah forever and it was just too good an opportunity to miss. That afternoon all the children in Year 5 gathered in the hall. Tension filled the air as the parts were slowly given out, Miss Morris beginning with the smaller roles, leaving the main ones until last. With three parts to go; the Prince, Snow White and the Wicked Witch, Hannah became aware that her friends were looking at her. They knew that she had auditioned and they were beginning to realise that Hannah, their very quiet friend, was going to get a leading role in this year's pantomime. To everyone's amazement, Jamie Price was given the part of the Prince and Suzie, the Princess.

'That means you're in love,' Johnny said and everyone laughed.

'Ok, calm down,' said Miss Morris. 'I have one part left to announce and I am delighted to say that the Wicked Witch will be played by Hannah Ellis.'

Hannah wanted the floor to open up and swallow her. Everyone was looking at her and clapping.

'Come and get your part,' Miss Morris said encouragingly.

Hannah made her way to the front of the hall and took the script.

'Thank you,' she whispered.

'You'll be fine,' Miss Morris replied, reassuringly.

That night Hannah had learnt all her lines, even though Miss Morris had given them two weeks.

Several weeks of rehearsals went by and to her amazement, Hannah was at her happiest when she was on the stage, when she could be someone else, but now it was time for the real test. It was the first night of the performance and she was stood at the side of the stage waiting to deliver her first line in front of a packed audience.

'You okay Hannah?' whispered Miss Morris.

Hannah was breathing deeply. 'Think so,' she replied.

She made her way to the edge of the stage where she could see Suzie dressed as the Princess, moving around quite stiffly on the stage, saying her lines to Jamie, the handsome Prince. Hannah could also see some of the faces of the audience which were lit up by the stage lights. They were smiling, following every word. She suddenly felt very nervous as she realised the enormity of what she was about to do. Her mind went completely blank; she racked her brain for the words of her first line but there was nothing in her head. And then she caught sight of something very strange and scary looking to her right. It was a witch and it was wearing a long, black cloak. The witch's hair was jet black and wild, sticking out in all directions and beneath the hair was a face full of wrinkles with a long, pointy, warty nose in the middle. The witch was, of course, Hannah. She was looking at herself in the mirror that Miss Morris had put at the side of the stage to give the children confidence before they went onto the stage. The idea worked for Hannah. Without thinking she strode confidently onto the stage and let out a quiet but evil cackle. The audience immediately booed, recognising the pantomime villain. Hannah raised her hand and hissed back at them. As they booed again Hannah felt a strange surge of confidence running through her body. She had shown great courage to go to the audition and to step forward onto the stage that night and as a result, she would approach life with far more confidence from then on.

Fifty Fantastic Assembly Stories

This page may be copied by the purchasing institution only.

41

Millie Comes Clean

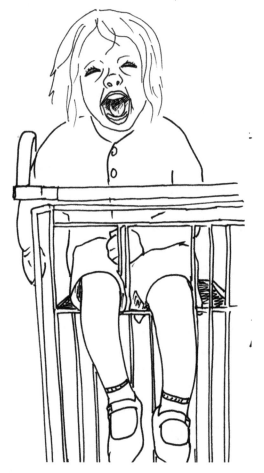

Millie Thomas was, in her words, 'pretty average at most things'; she wasn't bad at writing, she was okay at art, all right at sport and neither good nor bad at maths. She was though, extremely good, some would say incredible, the best in the school, at one particular thing: spelling.

No one could understand why, but she had an amazing ability to spell words perfectly after seeing them just once. She was only 'average' at remembering facts such as the capital of Sweden (Stolkholm) or what 6 times 7 was (42, even though she sometimes said '43'), but if she was shown a word for a few seconds and then was asked to spell it, she had no problem whatsoever. Her 'gift' (as her mum called it) first became apparent when she was just two years old and was sitting in a supermarket trolley being wheeled around by her dad as he did the dreaded weekly shop. Next to a large display of baked beans was a blackboard and on it, in chalk, was a notice which said, 'Special Offer – Buy One Get One Free'. As they approached it Millie stood up in the trolley and began pointing and screaming at the blackboard. An elderly couple nearby actually jumped with fright when they heard Millie's piercing screams and despite several attempts to calm her down there was nothing her dad could do to stop her. After five noisy and stressful minutes in which Millie continued to point and scream at the top of her voice the noise she made changed from a constant single scream to what sounded like her shouting the word, 'Die' over and over again. Dad couldn't understand it. In desperation, his eyes followed her outstretched finger to the blackboard. He read the words on it and suddenly realised what she was trying to say. At this early age Millie sometimes pronounced the letter 'b' as a 'd'. She wasn't saying 'Die' she was saying 'Buy' and she was pointing at the word 'Buy' on the blackboard which was spelled incorrectly. Rather than 'buy' it was spelled 'bye' as in 'goodbye' and remarkably,

at the age of just two years of age Millie obviously knew it was wrong. As she continued to repeat the word 'Die' in a very loud, high pitched voice, he licked his finger and rubbed out the incorrectly spelt word. Millie instantly fell silent, much to the relief of her dad and everybody else in the shop. An assistant arrived to see if there was anything she could do to help.

'Is everything all right sir?' she asked Millie's dad.

'Yes, thanks,' he said, calming down a little. 'I don't suppose you've got a piece of chalk handy?'

With a slightly puzzled look on her face the young assistant slid her hand into the pouch in the front of her overall and handed him a piece of white chalk. In place of 'Bye', he wrote 'Buy' and Millie's face, which had been one of complete misery was

Millie Comes Clean

©Adrian Martin and Brilliant Publications

transformed by a huge grin. After returning the chalk to the confused shop assistant, he continued to push his daughter around the shop, hoping there would be no more poorly spelled notices and occasionally shaking his head in disbelief. In school, Millie's spelling skills were well known. Every Monday the children were given a list of spellings to learn and on the following Friday they were tested. Millie had achieved full marks every week, in every year and it was now the very last week of Year 5. A few weeks earlier Mrs Davies, the Headteacher, had shown Millie a book which was all about the history of the school and had read her an extract from one of the previous Headteacher's entries. It had said that one pupil, Alistair Frompton, had managed full marks in his spelling tests for three consecutive years, from 1963 to 1966!

'If you get full marks in this week's test you will equal that record,' Mrs Davies explained. 'What an achievement that would be!'

Millie wasn't the competitive type – she had never really thought of herself as 'the best' and had certainly never had any wish to go down in the school's history. She didn't have to make any extra effort to be a good speller and so didn't consider it an achievement that she had got full marks in all her tests so far. But ever since Mrs Davies had mentioned this fact to her she had begun to get excited about the idea.

She opened her spelling book to look at this week's spelling list. At the top was the title, 'The 'i' before 'e' except after 'c' rule'. Mr Lee explained that whenever a word has the letters 'i' and 'e' next to each other, the letter 'i' always comes before the 'e' unless there is a letter 'c' in the word before them. To Mr Lee's amazement, most of the class looked completely confused by his explanation, including Millie but she wasn't worrying because she knew that as soon as she had seen the words, she would be able to spell them correctly. At least that was what normally happened. But

when Mr Lee began to read the words out at the time of the test that Friday, the last day of the year, something in Millie's head felt different. Maybe the words of Mrs Davies had put pressure on her, maybe she was losing her touch, but whatever the reason, Millie just didn't feel as confident as she usually was. There were ten words and as she looked at the nine that she had written down, waiting for the last one, she checked the rule that Mr Lee had explained. 'Word number one – 'friend' – there was no 'c' so it must be 'i' before 'e',' she thought. "Receive' – there is a 'c' so the 'e' comes before the 'i'. Yes, I get it now.'

'Word number 10' announced Mr Lee, 'Achievement.'

Millie wrote the word out in her test book, just as she had seen it written many times before in books she had read, on the achievement certificates she had been given in assembly. But then she stared at it with the 'i' before 'e' rule running through her head.

"I' before 'e' except after 'c',' she thought. 'But there is a 'c' in 'achievement' although it's right at the beginning of the word. Does that make a difference?' Millie began to panic.

She crossed it out and wrote it again, changing the order of the 'i' and the 'e'. 'That doesn't look right,' she said to herself, crossing it out and re-writing it a second time. After three attempts she settled on the 'e' before the 'i' and closed her book. For the first time in three years she had been unsure and for the first time in three years she had made a spelling mistake.

Immediately after the test the children swapped books, Mr Lee displayed the answers on the whiteboard and the children began the marking process. Millie's eyes went straight to the bottom of the list of words on the board. And there it was. Her first spelling mistake in three years.

'Remember everyone,' Mr Lee said, 'The 'i' before 'e' rule only applies when the 'c' comes immediately before. But I'm sure you all remembered that,' he chuckled.

He then called out each child's name and the marks were announced. Suzie Walsh was marking Millie's as she had done all year and when Mr Lee called Millie's name, Millie braced herself and waited for Suzie to say, '9.'

Mrs Davies would be so disappointed.

'10, as usual,' Suzie said.

The class applauded. They knew that this meant Millie had equalled the school record for spelling. But Millie was sure she'd spelled 'achievement' wrongly. Certain, in fact. She looked at Suzie who was smiling back at her. Had she marked it right deliberately so that Millie could get the record? She didn't seem to be smiling in a suspicious way.

'Right everyone, after that excitement, give your books back to your partners please,' Mr Lee instructed.

Suzie and Millie swapped books. Millie opened it at the test page. '10 out of 10 – Well done, you've got the record.' Suzie had written below the list of words. Each one had been ticked. But 'achievement' was wrong. It looked like Suzie had just assumed Millie would get them all right and ticked every word without really checking.

What should she do? Mrs Davies would be along shortly to congratulate her. Mr Lee had recorded '10' in his mark book. No one would ever know. Except Millie. It was now or never. If she left it any longer the whole situation would have gone too

far. She raised her hand slowly above her head as the classroom door opened and Mrs Davies walked in.

'Yes Millie?' asked Mr Lee.

'I spelled 'achievement' wrong,' she said. 'I put the 'e' before the 'i'. That's wrong. Suzie mustn't have noticed.'

Mrs Davies, Mr Lee and the rest of the class stared at Millie.

'Well, I don't know about you Mr Lee,' began Mrs Davies, 'But I think that admitting a mistake like that is an even greater achievement than spelling the word correctly! That must have taken a great deal of courage to say.'

A surge of relief swept through Millie's body. And the following year, she got ten out of ten in her spelling test every week!

©Adrian Martin and Brilliant Publications

Fifty Fantastic Assembly Stories

Max Admits It's His Fault

There were four words that Max Bridges was particularly fond of: 'It's … not… my… fault'. He often got himself into trouble, but it was never his fault and he always had an explanation which began with these four words. Despite being kind and understanding, the teachers at Mill Lane Junior School could not help the way they felt about Max.

'I just don't know what I'm going to do with him,' spluttered an exasperated Mr Lee, striding into the staffroom in search of a cup of coffee. 'Nothing is ever his fault,' he added, spooning heaps of coffee into his 'Best Teacher' mug.

'Tell us about it,' chorused several of the other staff who had taught Max in the past. They were relieved not to have him in their class any longer.

When he arrived at the school half way through Year 3 some of the other children seemed amused by Max, but now they had tired of him and Max was becoming quite unpopular, with both the staff and the children. He was tall for his age and extremely competitive, which was fine, but every game he played, he played to win and if that meant playing unfairly, that was fine by Max. He was always the first one onto the playground at playtime, bursting through the door and charging over to the equipment trolley to grab the football. It was his ridiculous rule that whoever got the ball chose the teams, so, clutching the ball in his hands he would make sure that his team had all the best players. They would then thrash the other team and each time Max scored he would charge around the pitch

cheering and copying the latest goal celebration he had seen on the TV. Whenever the ball went out of play, whoever had kicked it, Max would claim it. Whenever anyone tackled him he would roll over shouting, 'Foul!' so that he could get the ball back. He would often get the ball from his opponents by pushing them over and shouting, 'Accident! Not my fault!'

Some of the better players had simply stopped playing because they were fed up with Max's attitude.

'Why's Jake not playing?' Max asked one lunchtime.

'Because your team always wins and you don't play by the rules,' Martin told him, honestly.

'It's not my fault I'm the best player,' Max replied.

It wasn't just on the playground where Max behaved unreasonably. The Year 5 children are encouraged to play games with the younger ones and Mr Lee had given Max a set of dominoes to play with Emmie, a quiet girl in Year 3. But rather than teaching her the rules and allowing Emmie to win now and again, Max took great delight in beating the young girl 10–0 and whooping each time he won. In the end Mr Lee moved Emmie to another group and left Max to play on his own.

'The idea is to play with her, not to see how much you can win by,' Mr Lee said angrily.

Max waited for his teacher to

move out of hearing distance before muttering, 'It's not my fault she didn't know the rules.'

In assemblies Max continually dug his knee into the back of Simon Hoggard in the row in front. Simon complained to his teacher at the end of assembly but when she challenged Max about it, his predictable response was, 'It's not my fault – he keeps leaning into my knee.'

At Max's first Parents' Evening in Year 3 Mrs Newall told Max's parents how concerned she was with his behaviour and that, in her opinion, if he didn't change he would become unpopular with the other children. The response from Max's dad astonished Mrs Newall:

'It's not his fault,' he said. 'He's just a typical boy.'

They closed the classroom door and walked off down the corridor. 'So that's where Max gets it from,' Mrs Newall said – to herself, of course.

Max continued to behave the way he always had done. He didn't change. He didn't listen to the advice of his teachers. He continued to blame everyone else when no one wanted to play football with him anymore. He seemed completely unable to change.

But there was one experience Max was soon to have, not a very pleasant one, some would say a particularly unpleasant one, from which he would finally learn.

The Year 5 trip to Castlemere Adventure Centre was fast approaching. It was a five day trip to the Lake District and Mr Lee needed to sort out the bedroom groups. He took all of the boys into the school hall where he had marked out a large scale plan of the bedrooms using squares of yellow cones to represent each room. In each square was a piece of paper with the name of each bedroom written on it. The bedrooms were named after trees as the centre had its very own

wood.

Oaktree had six beds in it, Jake noticed, whereas Maple had only four. 'This is going to be tricky,' he thought.

Mr Lee began by sitting the boys on the hall floor and talking to them.

'In a moment I'm going to ask you to choose your bedroom groups for the trip,' he said. I don't want anyone to be left out so remember to think of others and not just yourself.'

Mr Lee was concerned about Max – he had noticed how children were choosing not to play with him anymore and, as Mrs Newall had predicted a couple of years ago, Max had become unpopular. Mr Lee had spoken to Max's parents about his behaviour on several occasions since the start of Year 5, but just like Max, they continued to blame everyone else.

But Max wanted to go on the trip and so Mr Lee would have to try his very best to make sure he had a good time and right now that meant making sure he had a bedroom to go to at night.

'Right,' Mr Lee announced. 'In a moment I want you to stand up and choose your groups. When you have chosen, go and sit inside one of the coned squares. And remember,' he added, 'Don't leave anyone out.'

There was a crescendo of noise as the boys called to one another, arms were grabbed and huddles were formed. Gradually groups of boys moved from the space in the centre of the hall to the coned areas around the sides. Mr Lee watched Max and, what he feared would happen, happened. As Max approached each group of boys they turned their backs, causing him to move back to the centre again. After five minutes all the children were sat in their rooms. All that is, except one. Max stood, on his own, in the middle of the hall, looking lost and very alone. *Mr Lee* walked over to him. He had to do something. He simply couldn't allow this to happen.

'Are you all right?' he asked Max.

Max nodded, but it was clear that he wasn't.

'Which group would you like to be with?' Mr Lee asked.

Max pointed to Jake's group. Five boys, including Jake, sat in the coned square that Max was pointing to. The piece of paper Jake was holding had the word 'Sycamore' and the number '6' written on it. Mr Lee took Max over. He and Max sat down on the floor with the boys.

'Would you mind having Max in your room boys?' Mr Lee asked.

They said nothing but he could tell that they did mind. Mr Lee had been a teacher long enough to know when children were not happy about something. Max looked embarrassed. It was time for honesty, Mr Lee decided.

'What is it about Max that you don't like?' he asked the group.

'He never plays fair,' said Martin.

'He always takes over,' added Jake.

'He pushes me over all the time,' continued Harry.

It was as if Mr Lee had turned on a tap – he and Max sat and listened as the boys gave endless examples of the things Max did that put them off being with him. After what seemed like a very long time, the boys finally fell silent.

'Anything else?' Mr Lee asked, determined to give them the chance to get everything out in the open. They looked at each other. Jake said two words; 'It's never … ' and the others joined in to complete the sentence, 'his fault!' they said, strongly.

Mr Lee looked at Max. This must have been a very difficult experience for him. His classmates had rejected him and had finally told him why. Max had been staring at the floor, unable to look the boys in the eye.

'It's my fault,' he mumbled.

'What was that Max?' asked Mr Lee.

Max looked up and repeated, this time more clearly, 'It's my fault. I was just trying to make you all like me,' he added.

'How about giving him another chance boys?' Mr Lee implored.

'One last chance,' Jake said. The others nodded.

And they all hoped that maybe, just maybe, Max would finally learn from his very painful experience.

Learning from experience

Ralph Finally Learns From His Painful Mistakes

Ralph could be a bit of a nuisance. He was a nice enough boy and always had a smile on his face, but he got himself into trouble far too often. He just didn't seem to learn from his mistakes. He was ten years old now and as his teachers kept reminding him, it was about time he started to think before he acted.

When he was seven his class went on a school trip to the zoo. As they entered the monkey house Mrs Newall gathered everyone around and told them that no matter how friendly the monkeys looked, no one should put their fingers anywhere near the bars of the cage. Ralph had seen lots of films with monkeys in and he knew they didn't bite. Mrs Newall obviously didn't know as much as him. He put his finger through the bars and in a flash, one of the monkeys jumped up and bit him, taking a chunk out of his finger. He cried for two hours and had to go to hospital to have an injection in case the monkey had infected him. The injection made him cry even more than the bite. On the way home from the hospital in the car Ralph's mum said, 'Well I hope you've learned never to go too close to wild animals. They might look cute but they can be very dangerous.'

She looked at Ralph through the rear view mirror of the car. He nodded, as he sucked the lollipop that the nurse had given him for being brave.

'I mean it,' she continued. 'Don't touch something when you don't know what it can do.'

But despite this rather painful experience, Ralph needed a further reminder not to touch things before he actually learned not to. His second painful experience was at the school fair. He'd been looking forward to it for ages because for the first time ever, the school had a Reptile House. As soon as he arrived he headed for it. There were snakes, owls, scary spiders, lizards, and the animal Ralph was most interested in: rats.

He paid his money at the door and immediately focused on the area of the room where the rat cages were. He walked past Lauren Booth who was having her photograph taken with a big, fat, hairy tarantula which was crawling over her hand. He walked past Harrison Whitley, who was beginning to turn a rather worrying shade of purple, as a very long, thick python began to wrap itself around his neck. He walked past Beth Allkins, who was stood, rooted to the spot, petrified by the piercing eyes of an eagle owl which was perched on her arm. And he walked past Liam Hodges, who was standing nervously, as a bright green lizard crept very slowly up his right arm, its beady eyes bulging out of its head and its long black tongue darting in and out. He walked past everyone who was holding any animal that wasn't a rat. But he stopped stock still when he reached the rat cage. Ralph loved rats. He didn't just like them, he loved them. He loved them so much that if he was given the choice of holding a rat for ten seconds, or eating a huge cream doughnut (his favourite treat), he would choose the rat every time.

Ralph peered into the cage. A brown rat that had been snoozing in a pile of sawdust immediately leaped up, jumped onto its giant rat wheel and sprinted round proudly for about 30 seconds. The wheel made a pleasant whirring sound as it spun, expertly powered by the rat's impressive legs. To Ralph's amazement it jumped from the spinning wheel and ran to the front of the cage where Ralph was looking in. In one movement it stood up on its back legs and grabbed the bars with its front paws. It looked right into Ralph's eyes and opened its mouth as if it were about to say something to him.

'You like rats then do you?' boomed a deep voice. Ralph nearly jumped out of his skin. This voice could only belong to a giant.

©Adrian Martin and Brilliant Publications

Fifty Fantastic Assembly Stories

Ralph Finally Learns From His Painful Mistakes *Learning from experience*

Ralph turned in the direction that the voice had come from. He was standing facing a pair of hairy knees. Slowly he followed the knees upwards. The knees led to a brown pair of shorts held up by a thick black belt. The belt had a silver buckle which was shaped into the head of a snake with its jaws wide apart. Ralph's eyes continued upwards to a green jumper which he noticed was more than a little dirty. Bits of sawdust, straw and what Ralph thought must be snake spit suggested to Ralph that its owner did not use the washing machine very often. Near the top of the jumper, to the right, was a badge with a group of animals on it which Ralph could not quite make out, (a) because it was so dirty and (b) because it was so high up. Above the badge was some writing – 'Ron's Reptiles'. And then came the beard. Ralph had never seen a beard like it. To describe it as bushy would be an insult to bushes everywhere. Think of the biggest bush you can, multiply its bushiness by ten, and you would be somewhere near imagining just how bushy this beard was. It didn't just cover a large amount of its owner's jumper, but grew outwards, both left and right, as if trying to escape from the face it was growing out of. Ralph noticed a couple of strands of straw poking out from the beard but decided not to point them out.

Suddenly the beard started moving towards Ralph. He stepped back. The beard, followed by a round, red face with sparkling brown eyes arrived in line with Ralph's head. Above his eyes was a perfectly round, completely bald, shiny head.

'I said, you like the rats then do you? I'm Ron. Ron's Reptiles.'

Ralph, who until this point had been too scared to speak, realised that Ron's voice was a friendly one.

'Oh I love 'em,' said Ralph. 'My favourite animal in the whole world, but mum won't let me have one.'

'Well,' said Ron, 'They are a bit tricky to look after. They need plenty of exercise you see and mums

these days, they're just too busy running around.'

Ralph thought about his mum. She was always running around. She was supposed to be here now but was late – probably still in a meeting at work.

'This is Samson,' Ron said, pointing at the cage.

Samson was still standing up on his two back legs looking at Ralph, his nose constantly twitching. His light brown fur was beautifully shiny. Ron obviously spent more time cleaning Samson than himself.

'Would you like to hold him?' asked Ron.

'Yes please!' shouted Ralph excitedly.

'I'll get him out then. He's very protective of his cage. He only allows me to put me hand in 'coz I'm the one who feeds him see.'

Ron eased open the clasp on the small side door of the cage and lay his hand on the floor of the cage. Samson eagerly scuttled over to Ron's giant hand and jumped into his palm. Ron expertly lifted Samson out, his long tail dangling between Ron's giant fingers.

'Now be careful with him,' warned Ron. 'He won't bite now he's out of his cage but he can be a bit lively.'

He gently placed Samson into Ralph's outstretched hands. Samson immediately rolled onto his back with his paws in the air.

'He wants you to scratch his tummy,' said Ron. 'He doesn't do that for many people. He obviously likes you.'

Ralph tickled Samson's tummy and the rat squealed with delight, before jumping back on his feet and rubbing his face against Ralph's fingers. After ten minutes of this, Ron said, 'I think we'd

Fifty Fantastic Assembly Stories

better put him back in his cage now Ralph – I can't let him get too used to you in case he thinks you're his new master.'

Ron scooped Samson up with one hand, opened the side door of the cage with the other, and gently pushed him back into the cage.

'Anyway, nice to meet you,' said Ron. 'Someone needs me over there.'

And he was gone, leaving Ralph on his own, standing next to the cage, with Samson standing on his hind legs again, looking longingly into Ralph's eyes.

'What was it Ron said?' wondered Ralph. 'He only allows me to put me hand in because I'm the one who feeds him?'

Ralph looked at Samson. Samson was so cute. They had made friends. Samson knew Ralph now. They'd spent ten minutes together and Samson had loved Ralph tickling him. He looked so sad on his own in the cage. Ralph had watched how Ron got him out. He knew how to open the side door. Without thinking any more Ralph undid the clasp on the side door and placed his hand flat on the floor of the cage, just as Ron had done. But Samson didn't jump onto Ralph's palm. He ran across his cage and sunk his teeth into Ralph's finger. Ralph let out a piercing scream which silenced the whole room. Ralph tried to withdraw his hand but Samson was in no hurry to let go. He was making sure this hand knew it wasn't welcome in his cage. Ron moved as quickly as a very large man could, removed the lid from the cage, and put his hand around Samson's body. Immediately, Samson let go and Ralph pulled his hand out of the cage. Blood was pouring from his finger, causing Ralph to feel very sick. His mum, who had just arrived, ran towards him.

'What on earth has happened?' she asked.

'I only wanted to hold him again,' cried Ralph.

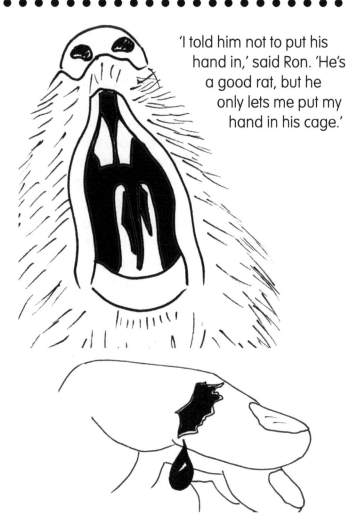

'I told him not to put his hand in,' said Ron. 'He's a good rat, but he only lets me put my hand in his cage.'

'Don't worry,' replied Ralph's mum. This isn't the first time, is it Ralph?'

Through his tears, Ralph looked at his mum and shook his head.

After another injection and four stitches at the hospital, Ralph and his mum were on their way home again.

From the back seat, sucking on the lollipop the nurse had given him for being brave (again), Ralph noticed his mum was about to speak.

'I know,' he said. 'Never touch anything when you don't know what it can do. Sorry mum. I won't do it again. And I really mean it this time.'

©Adrian Martin and Brilliant Publications

Fifty Fantastic Assembly Stories

Tom Proves He Has Learned From His Mistakes

● ●

This story follows on from the two stories in which Tom is 'dared' to throw a stone at a garden gnome by an older boy from a local secondary school – the stone misses and goes through the window of Mrs Knight's house. Tom is persuaded by his best friend Barney, to admit what he did and justice is done – he pays for the window and for a fourth garden gnome for Mrs Knight's garden (pages 27–32).

This story tests Tom's ability to learn from his experience and to stand up for both himself and his friend when confronted by the same older boy.

The children were all gathered in the school hall for the usual assembly – but today was different. Tom wasn't sitting with the rest of his class – he was in the corridor outside the hall. He hadn't been naughty, quite the opposite, in fact: he was about to play an important part in the assembly. Standing next to Tom was a small table and on it, was the garden gnome he had saved up for a month to buy – not for himself, but for Mrs Knight, Peter's nan, for her garden, to show her how sorry he was for breaking her window. He'd already paid for the window – that had taken all of his pocket money for three months, but he'd decided that she deserved something more so that he could really show her how sorry he was. Four months without any pocket money – he'd not been able to buy any football cards, sweets, books or computer games. It had been hard, but he understood that it was what he deserved – justice had been done and he had definitely learned a great deal from the whole thing. He was looking forward to next week's pocket money, which he would be able to spend on whatever he wanted.

Mrs Knight was sitting at the front of the hall in one of the comfortable chairs for special visitors. She had no idea that Tom had saved up for a new gnome for her. Neither did she know that Tom was a short distance away from her, squinting through the gap in the double doors waiting for Mrs Davies to call him in. Tom listened as the Headteacher told everyone what had happened on that horrible Friday night, four months ago. Through the gap in the doors he could just about see his class,

listening to Mrs Davies. They knew about the gnome of course, but Mr Lee, their class teacher, had told them not to tell anyone else in case Peter Knight, Mrs Knight's grandson in Year 3, found out and told his nan. It had been difficult, but they had managed to keep it a secret. Every now and again, some of Tom's classmates glanced over to the doors that he was standing behind – he knew they couldn't see him, but couldn't help jumping backwards when they looked in his direction. And then he had to move back, because the doors were being opened – Laura Cook in 6B was the Door Monitor and had been asked by Mrs Davies to open the door. Tom picked up the gnome from the table, supporting it underneath with one hand as the man at the garden centre had told him. He looked at Mrs Davies who was beckoning him into the hall.

'Come on in Tom – I'm sure you'd like to introduce your new friend to Mrs Knight,' she said, with a smile.

The children in the hall all chuckled at Mrs Davies' joke. Tom looked at all the children – they were all looking at him – a sea of eyes staring at him and the gnome. But then his eyes caught those

● ●

This page may be copied by the purchasing institution only.
Fifty Fantastic Assembly Stories

● ●

of Mrs Knight, who was standing now. He forgot about the children in the hall and rushed over to her.

'This is Eric,' he said, holding the gnome up to her. 'That's my dad's name and mum thinks he looks just like him.' Everyone laughed. Mrs Knight hugged Tom tightly – he was surprised how much strength she had for a small elderly lady, but he knew from this that she knew he was really sorry, and that he would never do anything like that again.

'And from this experience,' Mrs Davies explained, 'It is important that we realise that we must always learn from our mistakes. I think what Tom has done today has proved that he has certainly learned a valuable lesson.'

After the assembly, Mrs Davies, Mrs Knight and Tom walked to Mrs Knight's house and introduced Eric to Bob, Sid and Kevin – the other gnomes in the garden. Mrs Knight placed Eric right in the centre of the garden. He just stood there, hands on hips, looking out across the pond.

'Eric,' said Mrs Knight. 'He's the best gnome I've ever had. Now then – some cake I think.'

And that was that. For the next few months, every Wednesday after school Tom and Barney popped round to Mrs Knight's house to help tidy the garden and to fish the crisp packets from the pond – some of the children from St Cuthbert's just didn't seem to care about litter – 'Why do they do that?' Tom wondered.

And then one Wednesday night after school as Tom and Barney turned the corner into Mrs Knight's road, they stopped dead in their tracks. Two children – older children – a boy and a girl, were standing behind Mrs Knight's wall, pointing at the gnomes. They were from St Cuthbert's High School, and the hairs on the back of Tom's neck stood on end when he heard the boy speak – he instantly recognised the voice.

'Bet you couldn't hit one with this,' he said.

It was the same boy who had dared Tom to throw the stone. Barney grabbed Tom and pulled him into the bushes where they couldn't be seen.

'What're you doing?' Tom whispered.

'They might see us,' said Barney.

'I don't care – I'm not going to let them damage the gno….'

But he didn't finish his sentence because Barney put his hand over Tom's mouth and signalled him to be quiet.

The older girl was talking.

'No way Jonno – do you think I'm that stupid – you think you're so big and clever – you do it.'

'Easy,' replied the boy.

Tom tried to shout something – anything, to distract the older boy, but Barney kept his hand over his friend's mouth. There was a smacking sound followed by quite a large splash.

'No!' Tom managed to remove Barney's hand from his mouth and shout out.

Within seconds, the older boy and girl had run towards the noise and were looking down at Tom and Barney.

'Well, well, well,' said the older boy. 'If it isn't the little window breaker. Fancy meeting you here.'

He leant down and grabbed Tom's school jumper dragging him from the bushes.

'Come and look at what you've just done,' said the boy.

● ●

©Adrian Martin and Brilliant Publications

He walked Tom over to Mrs Knight's garden. The older girl and Barney followed. Tom looked at the pond – there was a gap where Eric used to stand – he leant forward and looked into the pond and could just about make out the outline of the gnome he had bought for Mrs Knight.

'What do you mean – what I've just done?' shouted Tom. 'You did it. We saw you, didn't we Barney?'

Barney didn't get time to answer.

'Oh no,' said the girl. 'We saw YOU do it, didn't we Jonno?'

'Yeah – a right little vandal he is – he was the one who broke the window you know.'

Then he bent down so that his face was right next to Tom's and said, 'You tell anyone about this, and we'll …

'And you'll what?'

It was Mrs Davies. And she was with a man who was dressed very smartly indeed.

'And you'll what, Mark Johnson?' he said. Barney realised who he was – Year 5 had been to St Cuthbert's last year for an athletics afternoon and this man had presented the medals at the end – he was Mr Thompson, the Headteacher of St Cuthbert's High School.

Barney looked at Jonno's face – all the colour had drained from it. He looked extremely pale and not very well at all. Barney was beginning to enjoy this. He looked at the girl – she didn't look very well either.

Tom wasn't having quite as much fun as his friend – he was still in shock and was worried about Eric who was still at the bottom of Mrs Knight's pond.

Mr Thompson looked at his two pupils, and, in an icy voice that could have frozen Mrs Knight's pond over, said, 'My office – first thing tomorrow. And don't even think about making any stories up. There are witnesses who saw everything you did. Now go home.'

The two older children set off for home in different directions. Mr Thompson shook Mrs Davies' hand, thanked her, apologised to Tom and Barney, and then marched off.

'Well, we'd better go and see how Eric is,' said Mrs Davies. 'And Secret Agent Knight,' she added, pointing to one of the upstairs windows of the house. There was Mrs Knight. She had seen the whole thing and had telephoned Mrs Davies as soon as she had seen the older children. Mrs Davies had then phoned Mr Thompson and arranged to go straight to the house.

'Impressive,' said Tom.

'I didn't do it for you,' said Mrs Davies. 'I did it for Eric.' And then she laughed, thank goodness – it was one of her jokes. And for once, it was actually quite funny.

Apart from a couple of scratches, and a nasty water stain, Eric was fine – and no doubt would tell the other gnomes about his underwater adventure when it went dark. At least that's what Tom thought. As for the two children from St Cuthbert's – well Tom didn't find out what happened to them, but he had an idea that it wasn't very pleasant. Mr Thompson looked like one of those Headteachers who didn't stand for any nonsense.

Mrs Davies took great pleasure in telling the children in assembly about what Tom and Barney had done – and it was true what she said – Tom really had learned from his experience and he was really rather proud of himself.

This page may be copied by the purchasing institution only.

Edna Gets Her Purse Back

• •

Edna Townsend made the best jam roly poly and custard any of the children at Mill Lane Juniors had tasted. She was the school cook, until last week when she had retired on her 60th birthday, after 42 years working at the school. Thursdays were jam roly poly days and the children would happily queue up for half an hour to taste Edna's glorious pudding. On the day of her retirement she had been presented with a giant, cardboard jam roly poly pudding which all the children had signed.

It was Thursday and while a week ago she was washing up the many dessert bowls in the school kitchen, today she was looking forward to using her bus pass for the first time. On Saturday it was her granddaughter Alice's birthday and she was heading into town to buy her a present. She took the brand new bus pass from her purse and ran her fingers across the letters of her name printed on it. 'Where has all the time gone?' she wondered to herself. Before leaving the house she looked fondly at the huge cardboard pudding sitting on the dining room table and smiled as she closed the front door.

Unfortunately the thoughtful and amusing gift from the children at school was to play an important part in Edna's day turning out far worse than she could imagine. As she closed the front door the image of it remained in her mind and, instead of zipping up her handbag as she would normally have done, she thought about it being presented to her by Mrs Davies in assembly and remembered all the children clapping. As she made her way down the street towards the bus stop, instead of checking her handbag was zipped up tightly as she would normally do, to check that her purse was safely inside, she thought about the many compliments the children gave her as they handed back their dessert bowls, scraped clean. So instead of her handbag being firmly fastened, the zip was undone and her purse wasn't secure

inside; the corner of it was poking out of the handbag and with every step Edna took, it edged its way out further. When the bus hissed to a stop Edna stepped on and showed her pass to the driver.

'You don't look old enough to have one of those,' he chuckled. 'Let's have a closer look. Well I never,' he continued. 'Pensioners are getting younger these days!'

Edna blushed. She knew he was only joking, but it still felt nice to be told she looked younger than she was.

Instead of putting the bus pass in her purse, Edna kept it in her hand so that she could look at it on the journey. She knew it was a little vain of her, but she wanted to look at the photograph on the card to see if there was any truth in what the driver had said. Of course this meant that she did not put the card back into her handbag and therefore, she did not discover that its zip was open and that her purse had crept even further out and was now very much more out than it was in. After settling into a seat near the front of the bus Edna recounted the driver's words and had a good look at her photograph on the bus pass. 'Actually I don't look that old,' she thought to herself. 'Maybe jam roly poly's good for you after all,' and without thinking she chuckled out loud. As she did so, the bus lurched forward, snapping Edna out of her lovely daydream. It had stopped at some traffic lights and although Edna didn't think he was supposed to, the driver opened the doors to allow a young couple onto the bus.

'I'm not supposed to do that,' he told them. 'But you've caught me in a good mood. It's your lucky day!'

Surprisingly, neither the young man nor the young

• •

©Adrian Martin and Brilliant Publications

lady said anything to the driver, not even a simple 'thank you' which Edna thought rather rude, especially as he had allowed them on when he shouldn't have done. Edna watched the couple, probably in their late teens she thought, as they moved down the aisle of the bus, giggling to each other and sat in the seats directly behind her.

She had been so deep in thought when the bus had stopped suddenly and so surprised by the jolt it gave her that she hadn't heard the thud of her purse as it dropped from her bag and under her seat. Neither was she aware that as the bus had accelerated away from the traffic lights her purse had slid backwards a little further and was now closer to the feet of the couple behind her than to hers. The bus eventually arrived at her stop and she got off saying a cheery 'goodbye' to the friendly driver. It was as she got off the bus that the teenage couple caught sight of Edna's purse under the seat in front of them. Most people who found a purse or anything of value, on the floor of a bus, would attempt to find out who it belonged to. Most people would leap up and ask the bus driver to stop the bus so that they could check if it belonged to the old lady who had only just got off. The very least most people would do was to hand the purse in to the driver. But this couple didn't do any of those things. They simply picked up the purse, opened it and took out the sixty eight pounds from it; the money that Edna was intending to use to buy her granddaughter's birthday present. After taking the money they got off the bus and threw the empty purse into a hedge.

Edna only realised that her purse was missing when she reached into her handbag to pay for Alice's gift at the checkout. She was obviously very upset, but at least she could get back home on the bus as she still had the bus pass in her coat pocket. She spent the whole journey home wondering where on earth her purse could be. Neither the police nor the bus company were able to help; no purses had been handed in they were sorry to say. But fortunately, Edna was about to

find out that, although there were some uncaring, greedy people in the world, there were also many who were kind and thoughtful.

On their way home from school, Millie Thompson and Jess Harper spotted a purse under the hedge next to the path. It was already open and had no money in it but there was a library card with the name, 'Mrs E Townsend' written on it and a photograph of Edna, their school cook who retired last week. The library card included Edna's address which was just around the corner from school, approximately two minutes walk from where they were. 'She must have dropped it,' Millie said. 'Let's take it to her.'

Edna was very grateful to the two girls for bringing her purse back but the girls could tell that the whole thing had upset her.

'There was £68 in that this morning,' she told them. 'I've no idea what happened to it.'

She knew that somehow the money had been stolen and Edna hated the idea of someone rooting through her purse, taking her money and then just throwing the purse away.

'Why would anyone do that?' she asked the girls as she poured them some juice and offered them a biscuit.

But of course they had no words to explain why anyone would do such a thing. They did however make the decision as they walked home together, that they were somehow going to get Edna her money back. It was a car boot sale at school on Sunday and Millie and Jess seized their opportunity. After a considerable amount of huffing and puffing they had filled five large bin bags with teddy bears, books and old toys that they had completely forgotten they ever owned. Millie's dad wasn't too happy about getting up early on Sunday morning, but by half past eight the car boot was raised and the girls were rather

pleased with the way their stall looked. By twelve o'clock one scruffy yellow teddy bear lay forlornly on the trestle table.

'Poor old Bertie,' Jess exclaimed. 'You're coming back with me.'

She grabbed the scruffy bear that her Auntie Sue had bought her for her fourth birthday and stuffed him into her bag.

'£60!' Millie announced proudly after counting their takings. Jess opened her purse and gave Millie £8. 'That's for Bertie,' she said. 'He's worth every penny. See you at Edna's in an hour.'

When the girls handed over the money Edna couldn't believe how thoughtful they had been and found it impossible not to shed a few tears when they told her the amount was exactly £68.

'It's a small price to pay for the best jam roly poly in the world,' Jess said.

The following day at school Millie and Jess were called to Mrs Davies's office. Two identical packages were sat on the Headteacher's desk.

'I've had a visitor this morning,' Mrs Davies explained. 'A very grateful visitor indeed. She asked if you could open these at lunchtime.'

At twelve o'clock, sat at a table together in the dining hall, Millie and Jess were the envy of their friends and every other child in the school, because even though Edna had left over a week ago, they sat eating their own individual portions of jam roly poly and custard!

©Adrian Martin and Brilliant Publications

Fifty Fantastic Assembly Stories

Liam's Magic Trick

Liam's grandad, Len, lived on his own in a small terraced house next to Liam's school. At home time, Len would walk down the path from his front door and stand at the gate waiting for Liam to arrive. When they reached Len's house, Liam and his friends would gather around the gate waiting for him to perform one of his many tricks. As a young man Len was a part-time magician and could be found at the local community centre every Saturday night sawing people in half and making things disappear. He was a bit of a celebrity in his local town and once appeared on the local television news when, memorably, he made all the rain clouds disappear on the weather map, even though it was pouring down outside.

'What have you got for us today Grandad?' Liam would ask each day.

'Today boys, I'm going to make your homework disappear!' Len would reply.

He said this every day and every day the boys cheered, joining in with the joke. Len would then perform one of his card tricks for them and despite his age, none of the children could work out how he did it. Sometimes, as a special treat when it was one of the boys' birthdays, Len would produce his magician's hat and wand and amaze them by actually making their homework books disappear. They would then let out a groan when he made the homework reappear again, but they loved Len's tricks and wouldn't have missed them for the world.

So it was to their great disappointment and concern when the boys arrived at Grandad Len's gate one day, and there was no Grandad Len there. At first they thought it was one of his magic tricks and waited patiently for him to appear from behind one of his large pot plants, but when there was still no sign of him after ten minutes the boys realised that something was wrong and reluctantly made their way home.

'Where's Grandad?' Liam shouted, barging in through the front door in a panic.

'He's had a bit of a fall,' explained Liam's mum. 'But he's all right. Just a bit shaken and he may have fractured his ankle, so he'll be in hospital for a few days. He certainly won't be performing any magic tricks for a while I'm afraid.'

'How did it happen?' Liam asked.

'He stepped out of his front door and slipped on a plastic bottle,' mum replied. 'He's always telling me about the litter that gets thrown into his garden.'

'Is he?' Liam asked.

'He reckons a lot of it comes from the school,' mum continued. 'Most of it's crisp and snack wrappers.'

Liam couldn't believe what his mum was telling him. Lots of his friends did bring crisps for their lunch and most of the children had a snack at break time, but he still found it difficult to believe that they wouldn't put the wrappers in the bin. It upset Liam to think that litter from his school could have caused Grandad Len's accident and he made the decision there and then to do something about it.

The next day at school Liam and his friends arranged to see Mr Lee, their teacher, at playtime. They were all very fond of Grandad Len and were ashamed to think that their litter may have caused him to fall on his own path.

Until now, Liam hadn't been aware of the litter in

the streets around school, but since Grandad's accident, his eyes were constantly drawn to the rustling crisp packets and empty drinks cans on the pavements and in the hedges. 'Why would anyone do that?' he thought to himself. 'There are plenty of litter bins around.'

On the way home from school one day Liam had watched incredulously as a girl in Year 3 had dropped her drink carton on the pavement and even though he was sure her mum had seen her do it, they just walked on, leaving it on the ground. Liam was normally quite a placid, calm person, but for the first time in his life, litter had made him angry.

His idea, which he explained to Mr Lee and his five friends at playtime, was to organise a litter-picking event in the local area. Mr Lee liked the idea, but explained that it would need to be planned really carefully if it was going to work. So plan, and plan carefully, was exactly what they did.

Mrs Davies, the Headteacher, wrote a letter to all the parents and to the local shopkeepers explaining what the school was planning to do. Mr Lee told the children in assembly and the boys designed posters which they stuck firmly to the school fence and lampposts.

At half past nine on the morning of the event, Liam stood nervously outside Grandad Len's house. He had chosen Saturday for two reasons; firstly he thought more people would be able to help and secondly, but mainly, because at one o'clock that afternoon, Grandad Len was coming home from hospital.

'But will people come?' Liam asked his mum as the clock ticked towards eleven o'clock, the arranged meeting time.

He didn't have to worry for long because at ten o'clock, with one hour to go, people began to arrive. Mr Lee, Mrs Davies and most of the staff

from the school arrived with litter pickers and bin bags. They were followed by all the local shopkeepers who had actually agreed to close their shops for an hour. Then came countless children from school with their parents, both local Community Police Officers and best of all, two of the nurses who had been looking after Grandad Len in hospital.

'Anything to get away from his magic tricks,' they chuckled. 'He actually made the doctor's stethoscope disappear yesterday!'

By ten past eleven, twelve bin bags were brimming with rubbish. After an hour more not one item of litter could be seen within a mile of the school; pavements, walls, hedges and gutters had been cleared and 50 bin bags sat bulging outside Grandad Len's house. The Community Police Officers had made an arrangement with the council for the bin wagon to make a special trip at mid-day.

The exhausted crowd of helpers cheered as the wagon drove away, taking the unwanted litter with it.

'Well that's better,' said a relieved Mrs Davies. 'Now we've just got to make sure it stays that way. I've organised a timetable so that each class carries out a litter pick at least once a week.

That was music to Liam's ears. He knew that although they had done a great job, the litter problem was far from solved and he was delighted that litter from his school would no longer end up on Grandad Len's path. An empty crisp bag that had been blown from the back of the bin wagon danced along the pavement towards Liam. As he stamped on it and bent down to pick it up a flash of brilliant white in the distance caught his attention. It was the ambulance carrying Grandad Len and it was a little early. Pushing the crisp packet into his pocket Liam stood with his back to Grandad's gate and waited for the

Fifty Fantastic Assembly Stories

ambulance to pull up in front of him. The doors at the rear of the ambulance opened and the driver lowered a ramp to the floor. Grandad Len looked a little confused when one of the nurses who had been looking after him appeared to help push his wheelchair down the ramp.

'I thought it was your day off dear,' he said.

'I wouldn't miss this moment for the world,' she replied.

And as she pushed his wheelchair onto the pavement, the crowd of litter pickers who had, until now, been hidden by the ambulance, appeared in front of him.

'Well I never,' he laughed. 'I wasn't expecting a welcoming party!'

The crowd joined in the laughter. Len's attention then switched to Liam and his friends. They were still holding their litter picker sticks and Len began to realise what had been happening.

'What have you been up to?' he asked Liam.

Liam smiled knowingly at his Grandad and as the ambulance pulled away, Len's eyes scanned the road, the pavements, the hedges and finally, his own garden path. He couldn't remember the last time he had seen the road looking so tidy; there wasn't one piece of litter in sight.

'Now that's what I call a real magic trick,' he shouted with a huge smile on his face. 'You've made the litter disappear!'

Community
Tom Does Some Gardening

● ●

This story should be read after the story, 'Tom Proves He Has Learned From His Mistake' in which Tom buys Mrs Knight a garden gnome called Eric to apologise for accidentally breaking her window (pages 51–53).

You may remember Peter Knight. His gran, Mrs Knight, has a pond in her garden with garden gnomes sitting around it. You may also remember that a little while back Tom Gould accidentally smashed Mrs Knight's front window, after being dared by an older boy from the local secondary school, to throw a stone at one of the gnomes. You may also remember what happened after that; Tom finally admitted what he had done and had to pay for the broken window out of his own pocket money – three months worth. He also missed the end of term disco and the Premiership football match for which his dad had bought tickets.

After saving up the money for the window Tom decided to save for a further month to buy Mrs Knight a gnome for her pond which he named Eric, after his dad.

You may also remember that the older boy, 'Jonno', returned to Mrs Knight's pond after school and threw a stone at Eric, knocking him into the pond but Mrs Davies arrived on the scene with the headteacher of the secondary school and the boy was caught 'red handed'. Eric, thankfully, survived the assault, and regained his rightful place alongside the other gnomes by the pond.

We can now re-join Tom and his best friend Barney, to see how they're getting on since their experience.

After the incident with 'Jonno', Tom got back to enjoying school life again and although he didn't do so deliberately, he lost touch with Mrs Knight. It was the summer term in Year 5 and he was

beginning to look forward to being in Year 6 next year. He was in the local cricket team and spent most of his time there in the summer. Most nights, he would rush home from school, wolf down some tea and run to the cricket club for a match or a practice session. He had real hopes of being the England wicket keeper one day and he knew how much practice he had to put in to be the very best.

Tom and Barney were on the way home from school one evening, chatting away to each other when Tom stopped dead in his tracks.

'What's up?' Barney asked.

'Look at that,' came the reply.

'What?' asked Barney again.

Barney followed the direction of Tom's finger, which was pointing towards Mrs Knight's garden.

'Hmm….a bit of a mess, isn't it,' said Barney.

'A bit of a mess? It's a lot of a mess,' Tom replied angrily. 'How's it got in such a state? I can hardly see Eric.'

Normally, Mrs Knight's lawn was the best lawn around. She spent most days feeding it, mowing it, even cutting the edges with a pair of scissors so that they were perfectly neat. Normally, Mrs Knight's pond was perfect – crystal clear water, with bright green lilly pads floating on it, the water fountain bubbling away, and an endless number of butterflies, dragonflies and other insects

● ●

©Adrian Martin and Brilliant Publications

Fifty Fantastic Assembly Stories

buzzing around. At this time of the year, the pond was usually teeming with tadpoles and frogs. And of course there were the gnomes; Eric, standing, hands on hips, looking out across the pond as if he was the boss; Bob, enjoying a snooze on a bench; Sid, sat on a fishing basket and Kevin, casting his fishing rod into the pond. These were Mrs Knight's pride and joy, especially Eric, who Tom had bought for her. Normally, Mrs Knight would clean each gnome each day to make sure they looked their best for the many people who walked past the garden.

But today, Mrs Knight's garden told a completely different story. The lawn was overgrown, and yellow dandelions were beginning to sprout out from it, making it look untidy. The fountain had been turned off and the pond water was no longer crystal clear – there was so much litter floating in it that it was impossible to even see the water. Crisp bags, chocolate bar wrappers and drinks cans covered the surface. Poor Eric was completely covered by a plastic supermarket bag which was flapping furiously in the wind, as if he was trying to throw it off.

'And her curtains are shut,' Tom continued, looking at the window he once smashed with a stone.

'So?' replied Barney.

'It's four o'clock in the afternoon Barn. Why would her curtains be shut? Something's wrong here and I'm going to find out what.'

The next day on the playground before school Tom waited for Peter, Mrs Knight's grandson, to arrive so that he could ask him about his gran.

'She's in hospital,' Peter explained. 'She had to have an operation on her hip – all that gardening, the doctor said. Dad says the garden will have to be concreted over when she gets out – there's no way she'll be able to cope with it.'

'But why is it in such a mess?' asked Tom.

'Mum and dad have been too busy with work and visiting Gran in hospital to do anything about it,' Peter replied.

At that point the whistle went, signalling time for the children to go into school. Tom had not enjoyed his conversation with Peter. He was relieved that Mrs Knight was going to be all right, but the thought of her garden being concreted over made him deeply unhappy.

'Surely something can be done,' he thought, as he joined the line of children moving into school. At morning break, while everyone else rushed outside to enjoy the sunshine, Tom walked in the opposite direction to find Mrs Davies, the Headteacher.

'That sounds like a great idea Tom – I'll have a word with Mr Pearson to see if he can help and you see if you can get a group of your friends together.'

Mr Pearson was the school caretaker – he was proud of the fact that he was able to repair anything that the children brought to him – bikes, scooters, tennis rackets, you name it, he would fix it. Tom had no doubt that anything that was damaged in Mrs Knight's garden would be as good as new once Mr Pearson had got his hands on it.

Before he had realised what he was doing, Tom was the leader of a community consisting of 12 children, Mr Pearson and four parents who lived near to Mrs Knight and wanted to help out. In fact, when Mrs Davies told the children in assembly about the idea, most of them had wanted to help, so she had had to draw names from a hat in assembly to make it fair. Tom couldn't believe how many people wanted to help save Mrs Knight's pond – the thought of walking past her house and seeing a dull, flat piece of concrete instead of Eric and his friends made Tom determined to succeed.

'Why should Mrs Knight have to suffer just because

she's getting old?' he thought. 'That garden gives her lots of pleasure. She'd be devastated if it was covered over.

To his horror, Tom had discovered that Mrs Knight was coming out of hospital on Friday and today was Thursday, giving Tom's group just one evening to sort out the garden. The community group all agreed to meet at Mrs Knight's house at four o'clock. Mr Pearson brought along the school lawn mower and the other adults turned up with gloves, garden shears, trowels and other gardening equipment with names that Tom simply couldn't remember.

By five o'clock that evening, the garden was transformed. The lawn was cut to perfection – Mr Pearson had done a superb job, mowing stripes of equal width, so straight that they looked as if they had been drawn with a huge ruler! All the litter around the garden and floating in the pond had been removed, filling two large bin bags. Two of the children had even gone round the edges of the lawn with scissors, to make it as neat as when Mrs Knight does it. Tom had been given the job of … you guessed it – cleaning the gnomes! All that remained to be done was to turn the fountain on again. After a bit of time spent cleaning the water pipe and making sure the electrics were working, Mr Pearson flicked the switch and the water began to bubble away. Tom may have imagined it, but out of the corner of his eye, he was almost sure he saw Eric wink at him.

The following day Tom could hardly

concentrate – he was so excited at the thought of Mrs Knight returning home to see her garden in such great shape.

She was arriving home at two o'clock and Mrs Davies had given the helpers permission to miss their afternoon lessons so that they could welcome her home.

Tom and the others arrived at the house at quarter to two. To their dismay, two chocolate bar wrappers and a crisp bag were floating in the pond.

'Unbelievable! Does no one care about the environment any more?!' Tom shouted to no one in particular.

He rushed through the gate, picked up the litter and stuffed it into his pocket. As he did so, a car turned into the road and approached the house. Mr Knight, Peter's dad, jumped out and ran round to the passenger side. Before he could get to it, the door swung open and Mrs Knight, with a bit of a struggle, heaved herself out of the car. 'I don't need any help thank you Brian,' she said. 'I'm not that old that I can't get out of a car to see what a mess my garden's i….'

As she saw the garden she stopped speaking immediately. Her eyes widened as they scanned the beautifully striped lawn, the immaculate edges, the crystal clear water of the pond and her four gnomes smiling back at her.

It was probably the best feeling Tom had ever had. He felt really proud that he done something good, something real, not only for Mrs Knight, but for the community they both lived in.

'And we'll come every week to help out,' he said to Mrs Knight, as they set off back to school. 'There'll be no need for concrete. I promise.'

'Never,' replied Mrs Knight and she winked at him, just like Eric had done yesterday.

©Adrian Martin and Brilliant Publications

Bernard Stops the Bullies

Bernard was a bit odd. He didn't mind admitting it. He knew he was odd, and oddly, he enjoyed being odd, and he enjoyed people thinking he was odd. His teachers were extremely fond of him but would always be polite in their descriptions:

'Bernard?' Mr Lee said, when asked to describe the Year 5 pupil. 'He's a bit … erm… ooh, er… I'm not sure I can think of the word… erm… . Different. Yes, that's it. Bernard. Different. Definitely different. But very friendly. Always friendly. Lovely lad Bernard. But certainly different.' (Mr Lee was Bernard's teacher. He would never call Bernard odd. But 'interesting' is the code word teachers use for 'odd'.)

Bernard's friends also thought he was odd. They never actually called him odd. That would have been rude. But they definitely thought he was odd. And they liked him for it.

So what was it that made Bernard 'different'?

Well, he did odd things. He was a bit of a fan of Doctor Who. No, that's wrong. He wasn't a bit of a fan of Doctor Who. He was a lot of a fan of Doctor Who. That in itself of course does not make him odd. Many children and adults are fans of Doctor Who. But do they sleep in a tardis? Bernard does. Bernard persuaded his grandad to build a tardis around his bed, so that when he went to bed at night, he had to open the tardis door, just like Doctor Who. Bernard would walk through the tardis door, in his Doctor Who pyjamas, and climb into bed, which of course, was covered in a Doctor Who quilt.

But his Doctor Who habits weren't the only things to make Bernard odd. Oh no. There were others. He had odd eating habits. For his lunch he would eat the oddest sandwiches (from his Doctor Who lunchbox). Peanut butter and tuna, was his favourite combination. He always had this on Mondays and Fridays. Tuesday was raspberry jelly with roasted peanuts. Wednesday was cold baked beans with lettuce, and Thursday was chicken and, wait for it…. Marmite. Yes, that's right. Chicken and Marmite. His friends had learned to accept it. He'd been eating these strange sandwiches ever since he started school and he was never going to change.

'I like the flavours,' he would say. 'Far more interesting than everyone else's.'

And it wasn't just his Doctor Who habits and his strange sandwich choices. Oh no. Bernard was odd in other ways too. He had odd pets. He kept woodlice. Yes, woodlice. In a large glass tank, in his bedroom, next to the tardis. He would regularly put fresh pieces of rotting wood in the tank to keep his little pets happy. Bernard couldn't understand what his friends found so interesting about their cats and dogs. Woodlice were far more interesting. They ate wood, for a start. How much more interesting can a pet get?!

And it wasn't just Bernard's Doctor Who habits, his strange sandwich choices and his pets that ate wood, that made Bernard odd. Oh no. Bernard was odd in other ways too, but for now, you'll just have to accept my word for it.

Bernard was in Year 5 now – 5L to be precise. He was beginning to work out what life was all about. He was beginning to realise that some people are very friendly, and kind, and fun to be with (these people were Bernard's friends), and then there were the other kind of people. These were not Bernard's friends. Bernard was beginning to realise that being interested in unusual things was not without its problems. Although his friends seemed to think he was interesting and fun to be with, there were others who used Bernard's unusual habits to be unkind to him.

And one thing Bernard hated more than anything else in the world was conflict – disagreements, arguments. He could never understand why people did it. What was the point? Someone would always get upset. Usually, everybody got upset! He just couldn't understand it.

Bernard's mum and dad had always told him to be proud of who he is, and not to worry about what other people thought. 'If you want to eat chicken and Marmite sandwiches, you eat 'em,' Bernard's dad said to him.

'Yes, and why shouldn't a boy have woodlice as pets?' asked his mum. 'We're proud of you Bernard.'

Bernard's teachers had always supported him and encouraged him to share his unusual interests with the rest of the class. During the science topic on mini-beasts in Year 3 Bernard had been a great help. He'd even brought his pets in to take part in an experiment.

Maybe those who said unkind things to him were jealous.

Bernard could remember the unkind comments some members of 5L had made that day.

'Huh!' shouted Andy, as the children trooped from the classroom, 'Who wants to know all that rubbish about woodlice? What good do they do? What a waste of time.'

'What a stupid thing to have as a pet. Bet he's got names for them all too,' sniggered Tracey as she walked past him with her friends, who joined in with her giggles.

Bernard was hurt by those comments and later that evening he thought long and hard about what he could have said in reply. He could have been nasty back. He could have said to Andy, 'It's not rubbish about woodlice. You have no interests apart from football. That's all you're bothered about – kicking a silly little ball around, trying to get it through two silly little posts, and most of the time, they're not even posts – they're silly little jumpers, or silly little cones.'

But he didn't.

He could have said to Tracey, 'They're not stupid things to have as pets. They're really interesting and easy to look after. And I don't have names for them. They're woodlice. I'm not stupid.' Bernard knew that Tracey had a pet dog that she never took for a walk, despite promising her mum and dad that she would. He could have made a comment about that. But he didn't.

No. Bernard simply ignored the nasty comments made by Tracey and Andy, and instead went to play with his friends.

Andy and Tracey's comments were unkind. But they weren't the only ones. You can imagine what happened in the school dining room when Bernard produced his odd and wonderful sandwiches:

'What's it going to be today Woodlice Man?' Andy's gang would say, straining their necks to see what was in Bernard's lunch box. 'Is it sherbet and cheese? Or maybe Mars Bar and sprouts?'

©Adrian Martin and Brilliant Publications

Each comment would be followed by laughter and giggles, but Bernard just opened his lunch box and ate his odd, but tasty sandwiches.

Bernard's friends couldn't understand how he could just ignore them. He never seemed upset by what other people said to him. Of course, inside, Bernard was seething with anger. He secretly wanted to push his chicken and Marmite sandwiches into Andy's face so hard that the Marmite stung the inside of his nostrils. But that would have been a waste of bread, and chicken, and Marmite. He wanted to go round to Tracey's house when she wasn't there and put some of his woodlice into her bed so that when she woke up the next morning, they were crawling all over her face, and up her nose. But that would not have been fair on his woodlice.

So instead of saying something nasty back when Andy said one of his nasty comments, Bernard simply imagined him with a face full of chicken

and Marmite sandwich, his nose stinging. And when Tracey said something nasty, he simply imagined her with a face full of woodlice, some crawling up her nose, and her screaming. So he didn't need to say anything, because he knew that if he did, he would lose. There were more of them, and let's face it, he was a bit odd.

And you know what happened after a while?

Andy and Tracey stopped being nasty to Bernard. Once they realised that he wasn't going to get upset by their comments, and he wasn't going to say anything back, they gave up.

Bernard remembered the day the comments stopped. He sat down at the table in the dining room. Nothing. He opened his sandwich box. Today was raspberry jelly and peanuts on wholemeal bread. Mmm. No comments. No giggles.

He also remembered what happened in the playground that same day. Andy said something nasty to John in Year 4. John said something nasty back, they had a big argument and both ended up missing afternoon play. On the other side of the playground, Tracey said something behind Lucy Chapman in Year 3 and Lucy hit her with a skipping rope. They both missed afternoon play and Mrs Davies sent a letter home to her mum.

Meanwhile, Bernard played with his friends, and had a really good chat about who was the best ever Doctor Who.

This page may be copied by the purchasing institution only.
Fifty Fantastic Assembly Stories

65

Conflict
Debbie Realises Her Mistake

Helen and Debbie were inseparable. They had been friends since pre-school when they had been sat next to each other on the playmat. Debbie had looked at Helen, grabbed her nose between her thumb and forefinger and given it a firm tweak. Unlike all the other children Debbie had done this to, who let out an earth shattering scream followed by an unnecessary amount of sobbing, Helen just looked back at Debbie and giggled. From pre-school they went to the same primary school and, as long as their teacher allowed it, they would sit next to each other in class. They went to the same dance club, wore the same clothes and even liked the same food. Debbie's house was in the road next to Helen's, just a couple of minutes' walk away, so as soon as they arrived home from school, Helen went round to Debbie's house or Debbie went round to Helen's. Soon after the girls became friends, their parents got to know each other too and it wasn't long until both families shared camping holidays together. The girls were now nearly ten years old and had rarely been out of each other's sight since their meeting on the playmat. Neither had they ever argued, or ever even got close to disagreeing about anything. But following an idea by their teacher Mr Lee, all that was about to change.

'I've had a great idea for your homework this week,' Mr Lee told the class. 'Rather than our usual writing and maths homework I'm going to set you a practical task.'

Helen winked at Debbie – practical tasks were their favourite because they could do them together.

'But,' continued Mr Lee, 'And this is especially important for you two,' he said, looking at Debbie and Helen, 'You must do this task ON YOUR OWN!'

Helen frowned. Debbie frowned. 'Not fair,' they whispered.

'Oh but it is perfectly fair,' responded Mr Lee. (Helen wondered whether teachers had magic powers which allowed them to hear even the slightest whisper.)

'As you know, in science we are learning about 'sound'. Your task is to make your own musical instrument from anything you can find lying around at home. Parents can help,' Mr Lee said, 'But it must be your idea and you must make the instrument. You've got two weeks to do it.'

The class were excited about the task and Mr Lee allowed them a couple of minutes to discuss their ideas before stopping them again with a final piece of information;

'When all the instruments have been handed in, we'll have a vote to see which one is the best.'

For once, as the girls arrived home that day, they did not go to the other's house. Instead, they set to work on their instruments. The next day in school, most of the children in class 5L discussed their instrument idea with each other. But for the first time, Debbie and Helen did not. Debbie had intended to tell Helen about her idea to make a guitar but for some reason as they walked to school together that morning she had decided to talk about what she had had for tea last night, instead. Helen had intended to tell Debbie about her idea for a drum with different functions, but when Debbie had started talking about what she had had for tea last night, she thought that maybe Debbie wanted to keep her idea a secret for some reason, so decided not to say anything either. Time passed quickly and the deadline day to hand in the instruments soon arrived. Children in 5L marched into the playground with their musical creations hidden in bags and boxes of all different shapes and sizes. As they made their way into the classroom Mr Lee instructed them to put their

©Adrian Martin and Brilliant Publications

Fifty Fantastic Assembly Stories

instruments onto the workbench at the side of the room, where a large space had been created. Helen took her 'Multi-Drum' from her bag and placed it carefully on the bench. Helen had begun with a large biscuit tin which she had decorated with musical wrapping paper. In the tin she had put approximately 30 dried lentils. Where the lid would normally be, she had stretched some clear plastic sheeting, securing it with seven coloured elastic bands which formed strings. Helen had included chopsticks to hit the clear plastic drum skin causing the lentils to jump up and down in the tin, creating a pleasing shaking sound. When the elastic bands were plucked, the lentils jumped about even more. Helen had made her multi-drum with no help from anyone else and was rightly pleased with it. She was also pleased with the reactions of her friends, who were very complimentary about her creation. But then Debbie revealed her instrument; the guitar. There were gasps from the other children as she removed the guitar from the black bin bag she had brought it in. Helen couldn't believe her eyes as Debbie placed the guitar next to her drum. Unlike any of the other instruments, Debbie's guitar actually looked like the instrument it was intended to be. The wood had been cut into a guitar shape and joined together perfectly with wood glue and tiny tacks before being painted bright yellow. Real guitar strings stretched over the perfectly circular hole in the centre and up the arm of the guitar, where they had somehow been attached to the tuning keys allowing the strings to be tightened or loosened. Helen knew Debbie very well. She was good at art but there was no way she could have made the guitar on her own. She couldn't help herself:

'Your dad's made that,' she said. 'This was supposed to be your homework, not his.' And with that, Helen stomped off to her seat.

Debbie was shocked. Yes, her dad had helped her with the guitar. True, he had spent several hours with it in his workshop at the bottom of the garden,

but it was her idea and she had painted it. She couldn't understand Helen's reaction. For the rest of the lesson Helen didn't look in Debbie's direction and refused to say a word to her. At play time Helen disappeared somewhere, Debbie wasn't sure where and at lunchtime she remained silent until Debbie couldn't stand the awkwardness any longer and asked her what was wrong.

'I just can't believe what you've done,' Helen said, holding back the tears. 'Your guitar is so good – you've made me look ridiculous.'

Debbie was shocked by Helen's reaction. This was the first time they had ever had a disagreement and Debbie wasn't going to let a silly guitar ruin their friendship.

'Right,' Mr Lee explained. 'We've all had a good look and play of each of the instruments. Now it's time to vote.'

The children were each given a yellow piece of paper and after being told to think carefully about their decision, they were instructed to place their piece of paper onto their favourite instrument. After a few minutes all the children had cast their vote and most instruments had one or two yellow tickets on them. Three instruments had by far the most – Debbie's guitar, Tony's trumpet made mainly from a watering can and Helen's drum. Mr Lee counted the votes for each one. 'Six each,' he announced and was about to declare a draw when Debbie raised her hand. She had seen another yellow slip of paper on the floor beneath her desk and grabbed it before anyone else saw her.

'Yes Debbie?' Mr Lee asked.

'I'm sorry Mr Lee but I've not voted yet. I just couldn't decide,' Debbie lied, keeping her fingers crossed.

'Er … well, all right then Debbie. It looks like you'll

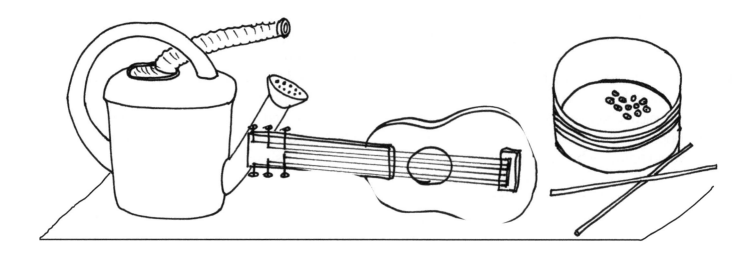

have the deciding vote then. You can't vote for yourself remember,' Mr Lee added.

Debbie walked over to the instruments. The eyes of the class were focused on her and the yellow slip of paper in her hand. Everyone knew about the conflict that the musical instruments had created between the two friends. Debbie strode purposefully towards the three instruments and placed her voting slip firmly onto the skin of Helen's drum – some of the lentils jumped a little.

'She did it completely by herself.' Debbie declared.

Everyone clapped and Helen's face turned a deep shade of red.

The next day at school Mr Lee went out onto the playground before school began and beckoned Debbie over to him.

'I added up all the votes for the musical instruments,' he said.

Debbie gulped.

'And there were 33.'

Debbie knew what Mr Lee was going to say next. 'There are only 32 children in the class.' Debbie gulped again.

'You lied about not voting didn't you?' Mr Lee added.

She nodded.

'I know you did it out of kindness Debbie, but it was dishonest and I'll have to do something about that.'

Debbie nodded again.

'So I've decided to keep it a secret,' he said, smiling. 'Now get back to your best friend and don't do anything like that again.'

Debbie thanked Mr Lee and ran back over to Helen.

'What was all that about?' Helen asked.

'Oh nothing,' replied Debbie, her second white lie in as many days.

©Adrian Martin and Brilliant Publications

Jess Finally Enjoys Her Lunch

• •

Every morning before school was the same in Jess's house. Mum had to be off to work by half past seven whereas dad worked nights and only got in at quarter past seven. Mum would get Jess out of bed and make her lunch and dad would make sure she got to school safely before going to bed for the rest of the day. Jess made her own breakfast of cornflakes and a glass of orange juice.

'I've made you ham sandwiches for your lunch,' mum would say to Jess.

'But I don't like ham mum. I've told you before.'

'You'll get what you're given young lady,' came the reply. 'And you'll be grateful for it,' mum added.

Jess's mum did not appreciate her daughter's bad manners. 'When I was a little girl I had to have a school dinner every day because we weren't allowed to take sandwiches then,' she told Jess. 'And they were horrible – that was long before Jamie Oliver came along and made them as nice as they are these days. You don't know how lucky you are,' she continued.

Jess couldn't bear this conflict between her and her mum. She knew how busy her parents were and causing an argument by complaining about her lunch would have been ridiculously selfish she thought.

'Thanks mum,' she said.

'I should think so too,' mum replied.

Later that day, Jess and her two best friends Hannah and Millie, made their way into the dining hall and sat down. They were all hungry after working hard in their lessons that morning but unlike her two friends, Jess would remain hungry

for the rest of the day. Within seconds, Hannah and Millie had unzipped their lunch boxes and were munching away on their sandwiches. Jess, on the other hand, had no intention of eating her ham sandwiches and to avoid the awkward questions from her friends, she lifted the lid of her lunch box. Sat next to the ham sandwiches on white bread, were an apple, a chocolate biscuit and a mini bag of crisps. Jess hated ham; there was something about its texture that made her feel physically sick. Apples were her least favourite fruit and she wasn't a great fan of crisps. Her mum called her a fussy eater and she was probably right, but if she knew that her daughter was hardly eating any of the lunch she prepared for her, she would be horrified. Hannah and Millie were too busy munching, guzzling and chatting to notice that their friend had not eaten a thing. Jess pushed the sandwiches into the lining of her lunch box as she had done many times before and when other children arrived at the table, causing a distraction, she slid the apple into her pocket. By now Hannah and Millie had finished their sandwiches and had begun eating their snacks. Jess tore away the wrapper from the chocolate biscuit and nibbled at the chocolate. She ate half of it and slipped it back into her lunch box.

'Wow Jess, have you finished already?' Millie asked. 'I hardly noticed you eating.'

'You've not stopped talking that's why,' Jess replied, fastening down the lunch box lid. As she sat waiting for her friends to finish their lunch her stomach rumbled loudly, but fortunately the noise in the school dining hall was far too loud for anyone to hear.

Jess found it particularly difficult to concentrate in the afternoons. Unsurprisingly her stomach ached with hunger – half a chocolate biscuit, a bowl of cornflakes and a glass of orange juice for breakfast

• •

Fifty Fantastic Assembly Stories

where do you put it all? There's nothing of you.'

Dad was right. Jess was looking extremely thin and pale these days. She just smiled at him and continued eating but his questions were about to be answered, leading to the conflict between Jess and her mum finally being resolved.

The doorbell rang. It was Mrs Hewitt who lived in a house at the end of the cul-de-sac.

'Can I have a word?' she asked Jess's dad.

'Sure, yes, come in,' he replied, taking her into the kitchen.

Mrs Hewitt took one look at Jess and said, 'Somewhere else perhaps?'

'Er, yes. Okay,' replied dad, puzzled. 'The lounge. This way.'

Jess's mum arrived home from work and opened the front door. She could hear adult voices from the lounge and was on her way to investigate when the phone rang.

'Hello is that Mrs Harper?' Mr Lee asked.

He shared his concerns with Jess's mum and asked if she could have a chat to Jess to see if there was anything troubling her.

'Thanks Mr Lee, I'll talk to her – see what I can find out and ring you back tomorrow.' She put the phone down just as her husband came out of the lounge with a woman from the end of the cul-de-sac. She had met her once before but couldn't recall her name.

'Thanks Mrs Hewitt. It won't happen again,' dad said. 'Thanks for letting me know. It won't happen again.'

He looked at his wife.

was nowhere near enough to give her the energy she needed to get through the day.

Mr Lee had noticed that Jess seemed to lack energy in the afternoons. She hardly spoke and she produced much less work than she did in the mornings.

Jess walked all the way home from school with her friends apart from the last hundred metres or so. Her house was at the end of a cul-de-sac and she was the only one from her class to live there. Halfway down her road there was a council bin on the pavement and each day Jess would slow down as she approached it to empty out her untouched sandwiches, her apple and crisps. As soon as she got through the door she threw down her school bag and marched straight to the fridge.

'Is that you Jess?' called dad from upstairs; after working all night he slept until Jess arrived home. As he entered the kitchen he was greeted by the familiar sight of his daughter sat at the kitchen table spooning cornflakes into her mouth whilst taking giant bites from a large piece of toast.

'How do you get so hungry?' he asked. 'And

©Adrian Martin and Brilliant Publications

Fifty Fantastic Assembly Stories

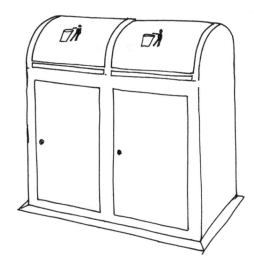

'What won't happen again?' she asked him. 'What was all that about? Mr Lee's just been on the phone, worried about Jess – she's constantly tired at school apparently.'

'That makes sense,' dad said. 'Let me explain.'

He walked into the kitchen and took his daughter by the hand.

'Come with me,' he said firmly. 'Both of you.'

Jess and her mum followed him out of the front door and along the pavement towards the end of the cul-de-sac.

'Where on earth are we going?' Mum asked. 'I've got no time for a walk.'

But dad continued to walk and every step took them closer to the bin which contained Jess's lunch; the lunch that Jess's mum had made her and paid for. Jess began to realise where dad was taking them. Mrs Hewitt must have seen her emptying her lunch box into the bin. Mum continued to ask where they were going until dad finally stopped beside the bin.

'Great,' she said, sarcastically. 'You've brought me to a bin.'

He lifted the lid. Even he was surprised when he

looked inside and he knew why he was there. The bin hadn't been emptied for at least a fortnight and as Jess's mum peered inside, her eyes widened with the sight of piles of neatly wrapped ham sandwiches, snack packs of crisps and at least a dozen apples.

'What….?' she stammered.

'Jess's lunches,' dad explained.

'I can see that,' mum replied.

'Probably a fortnight's worth,' he continued.

'I can see that too,' mum replied again.

Dad put the lid down and the three of them walked back to the house, in silence.

'Why didn't you say anything?' Mum asked Jess as they sat around the kitchen table together.

'I did!' replied Jess. 'You're always in such a rush.'

Jess's mum couldn't disagree with this. She was always in a rush. But she hadn't realised that when Jess said she didn't like ham sandwiches that she didn't actually like ham sandwiches. She thought she was just being fussy.

'From now on,' she said. 'We make your lunch the night before school. And we make it together.'

'No ham,' said Jess.

'No ham,' replied mum.

'And no apple,' Jess grinned.

'Definitely no apple,' mum smirked.

The next day, for the first time in a very long time, as Jess, Hannah and Millie queued up for their lunch, Jess couldn't wait to open her lunch box.

Friendship

Barney Shows True Friendship

● ●

Best friends were always close. But few were closer than Tom and Barney.

They were best friends and had been forever. Literally. They had been born in the same hospital and their mums were in the beds next to each other after they were born. As their mums and dads became friends, so did they. Both families went on holiday together every year and spent most weekends in each other's houses. The mums and dads would be in the lounge, laughing, while Tom and Barney would be upstairs, playing on Tom's computer, or reading Barney's Guiness Book of Records, or kicking a ball about in the garden.

Tom's birthday was the 3rd October and Barney's was the 4th. They lived in the same street and went to the same nursery, the same infant school, and now, the same junior school – Mill Lane Juniors. They were now 9 years old and had just gone into Year 5 – they were in the same class but were in different groups for maths and literacy (Tom found these subjects easier than Barney). As soon as they got out onto the playground, they would be together, swapping football cards, playing football, playing basketball, shooting each other with their fingers, and of course, teasing the girls.

Tom and Barney didn't understand girls. The girls on their playground just seemed to stand around or sit on the benches talking – 'What were they talking about?' they wondered. One time, when Barney was waiting for Tom to come out onto the playground, he thought he'd have a go at joining in with a conversation the girls were having. It couldn't be that difficult. Erin, Lauren and Emily were sitting on one of the benches eating their lunch and talking at the same time. He could never do that and was impressed that they seemed to be able to do it so easily. He walked over to them casually. The nearer he got, the louder

and faster they seemed to talk, whilst munching their sandwiches at the same time. He couldn't understand why, but he began to get nervous – there was no way he could talk that fast, even when he wasn't eating. He couldn't work out how they seemed to know which one was going to speak next – there was no pointing, or commands like, 'It's your turn Erin.' They just seemed to know when one had finished and it was another's turn to speak. The boys he knew never did this – they just played, or chased each other. He was close now, very close, so close he was almost touching them. There was a sudden silence, as they stopped their conversation and looked at him. They had stopped speaking and munching and were wondering what he was doing, staring at them. He opened his mouth to speak, but nothing came out. Lauren was just about to ask him what he was doing when his best friend came to the rescue; 'BARNEY – IT'S YEAR 5'S TURN FOR FOOTY! WHAT'RE YOU DOING TALKING TO GIRLS??' 'Oh yeah – coming Tom. Bye girls!' The girls looked at each other, shrugged, and carried on, talking and eating, quickly. Why didn't the girls like playing with cars? Why didn't they ever have any football cards to swap? And why didn't they ever shoot each other with their magic fingers? Tom and Barney simply didn't understand them. Girls, they decided, were strange.

There were many times over the years when Tom and Barney had relied on each other's friendship and one in particular, that they would never forget – in October last year, Mr Barnes, who ran the football team, told the children in assembly that he had entered the school in a Year 4 tournament on Saturday and that he would pick the team at the next practice. Tom and Barney both loved scoring goals and wanted to be in the team as strikers. Unfortunately, that year, there seemed to be loads of great strikers in Year 4. At the practice, Tom had a great game, and scored twice. He even

● ●

©Adrian Martin and Brilliant Publications

Fifty Fantastic Assembly Stories

passed the ball to Barney when he could have scored his hat-trick, but he passed it to his best friend instead. Unfortunately, Barney hit the bar. Barney had one of those games; whatever he did went wrong. Afterwards, Mr Barnes had a quiet word with Barney, and Tom could see his friend was disappointed. The team list went up the next day and sure enough, Barney's name wasn't on it although Tom's was. Tom felt terrible – he really wanted both of them to play in the tournament on Saturday. He even considered telling Mr Barnes that he couldn't make it on Saturday but his dad told him that that would be letting the rest of the team down.

It was Friday, the day before the tournament, and for the first time since they started school, the two boys did not play together at break or lunchtime that day. Barney stayed in to do a job at break, and went to Athletics Club at lunchtime without telling Tom. At home-time, Barney had gone before Tom had even found his coat in the cloakroom. Tom felt terrible. He wished he'd not scored those goals at the practice now.

The next day, the morning of the tournament, Tom got out of his dad's car at the local secondary school in his new school kit and met up with the rest of the team.

Barney, meanwhile, lay in bed with the covers over his head.

'Barney! You're breakfast's ready!' shouted dad from the kitchen.

He felt so bad about not being part of the team that he wanted to stay in bed all day.

Dad had cooked him his favourite breakfast – scrambled eggs and bacon with a larger than usual splodge of ketchup on the side. The smell drifted up the stairs, under Barney's bedroom door and made its way to Barney's nostrils. He couldn't resist. Dad's plan had worked and a few minutes

later, Barney was sitting at the breakfast table in his football pyjamas, opposite his mum and dad. 'They'll be kicking off around about now,' Dad said. He decided to talk about the tournament – after all, he was certain Barney was thinking about nothing else.

'Mmm,' replied Barney, unable to manage an actual word.

'I wonder if Tom will score?' asked Mum.

'Probably,' Barney said. 'He's our top striker.'

And slowly but surely, Barney found himself feeling better. He stabbed a slice of bacon with his fork, heaped some scrambled egg on top and pushed it into his mouth. As he munched, he began to talk more about the tournament and how he hoped they would win.

'Why don't we go along and support them?' Dad suggested.

'Could we?' Barney asked. The thought of being there made him feel happier than he had for days.

'Course we can,' Dad replied. 'Eat up and get some clothes on.'

Three wins out of three got the team into the final. Tom played superbly and scored no fewer than five goals. They sat in a circle on the grass at the edge of the pitch listening to Mr Barnes as he went through the plan for the final. Just as he finished talking a car turned into the car park. 'It's Barney,' Tom said, jumping up and running over to the car. Barney could see the delighted look on Tom's face and instantly knew he had done the right thing. As he got out of the car his friends surrounded him, telling him every detail of their three victories. And even though he wasn't in the team, he felt a part of it. He'd come to support the team, despite being left out. Mr Barnes put his hand on Barney's shoulder. 'Thanks for coming Barney. You're just in time to see the final. And I'm sure the team will play even better now you're here.'

And that was true. But unfortunately their opponents, Newtown FC were in no mood to lose. They had won all of their matches too and within 30 seconds of the final starting Mill Lane Juniors were losing. Barney immediately blamed himself for coming. 'Maybe I've put them off,' he thought. And he was just about to ask his dad to take him home when Tom headed the ball passed their goalkeeper into the bottom of the net.

The game then became very tense, with few chances for either team and after a considerable amount of nail biting and pacing up and down by the parents and particularly Mr Barnes, it ended 1–1.

'Penalties,' announced the referee.

Barney stood with the team as, one by one, each player took a penalty. Tom took his kick first and, just as Barney had done in the practice match, hit the bar, much to the delight of Newtown FC. Fortunately however, as good a team as Newtown were, they obviously didn't practise penalty taking very often and not one of them hit the target, making it easy for the rest of Tom's teammates and Mill Lane Juniors were soon crowned champions. As the parents lined up with their cameras, Mr Barnes made sure Barney was on the team photograph, standing next to Tom, his best friend.

'Thanks for coming Barney – you'll always be my best friend.' Tom whispered, as everyone else shouted, 'Champions!' for the cameras.

©Adrian Martin and Brilliant Publications

Doris Saves the Day!

● ●

Samantha, or Sam as her best friends called her, could not have been happier at Welling Street Primary School. She had lots of friends who she had known for most of her life and had just received a glowing report from her teachers at Parents' Evening. So when her parents told her that she was going to have to leave because mum had got a new job over 100 miles away, she felt physically sick and stayed in her room for four hours. She understood why they had to leave – 100 miles was too far for mum to travel each day – but she felt like her world had been torn apart and it wasn't long before her life changed completely. Samantha was unaware that while she was away for the weekend with the Brownies, mum and dad had been house hunting and had seen one they liked near to mum's work. They had bought the house and had to move in a few weeks.

Just two weeks later, after a very tearful farewell to her friends, Samantha was sitting at her new desk at Mill Lane Junior School wearing her new uniform. She was sitting next to other Year 5 children who she didn't know, listening to her new teacher. At playtime, Charlotte and Suzie, who were looking after Samantha, took her down corridors she had never walked along. She walked past children she didn't know and out into a playground that she had never played on. At lunchtime, although the food looked similar to the food at her old school, it was served to her by cooks she didn't know and she ate it in a dining room which was bigger and different to the one she was used to. She was introduced to lots of children but, despite trying hard, she found it impossible to remember their names. Charlotte and Suzie had made Samantha feel really welcome but they lived at the other end of the village and so at home time they waved her a cheery goodbye and walked in the opposite direction.

Samantha began walking home alongside lots of other children she did not know. Even though there were many children around her she felt completely alone and wished more than anything that she could be back at her old school, skipping happily home with the many friends she had made there. But just as she was beginning to feel sorry for herself, two girls who she hadn't met that day caught up with her and one of them asked her a question:

'Are you the new girl in Year 5?'

'Yes,' said Samantha. 'I'm Samantha; my best friends call me Sam.'

'Well Sam,' said Yasmin. 'I'm Yasmin and this is Tina and we're your new best friends.'

Obviously, Samantha didn't know Yasmin and Tina. She didn't know that they were in Year 6 and she didn't know what everyone else in the school knew – that Yasmin Porter and Tina Belling were trouble and should be avoided if at all possible.

'Let's go to the shop for some sweets,' Tina suggested.

'But I've no money,' replied Samantha.

'Oh you won't need money Sam,' Yasmin said, confidently.

Samantha wasn't sure what Yasmin meant by this – there was something about the two of them that made Samantha feel uncomfortable but she couldn't quite work out what and at least they were friendly (at least they seemed friendly).

Samantha was already familiar with the sweet shop – she remembered it from when she and mum had walked from school to home together, so that Sam would know how to get home on her own. They'd gone in because mum had a sudden need for some chocolate and Doris, the friendly

● ●

©Adrian Martin and Brilliant Publications
Fifty Fantastic Assembly Stories

owner of the shop, had given them a warm welcome.

Minutes later the three girls had arrived at the shop and as Samantha pushed open the door a bell tinkled, making Doris aware that she had customers. Doris was standing behind the counter and smiled broadly when she saw Samantha. However, Samantha couldn't help noticing that when Doris saw Yasmin and Tina her smile disappeared completely and was replaced by a look of suspicion.

'Hello Doris,' Samantha said, smiling.

'Hello young lady. You're new to the area aren't you?' Doris replied. 'I remember you coming in with your mum the other day. I'm a bit surprised to see you with those two though.'

Yasmin and Tina had disappeared down an aisle lined with tins of dog food, boxes of cereal, cartons of juice and lots and lots of sweets. Before Samantha could reply to Doris there was a sharp 'Psstt…' which, it turned out, came from Yasmin. Samantha followed the sound down the aisle to the back of shop out of Doris's sight.

'Anything you fancy?' asked Tina.

'Well I have got a bit of a weakness for Liquorice Allsorts,' Samantha said.

'Take them,' Tina said.

'But I've got no money, I told you before,' Samantha replied.

'Just take them,' continued Tina. 'She can't see you.'

Samantha realised what Tina meant. She looked at Yasmin.

'It's fine,' Yasmin said. 'We've done it lots of times. She's no idea,' she continued, gesturing towards Doris.

Samantha wasn't sure why she grabbed the bag and stuffed it into the side pocket on her schoolbag, but that is exactly what she did. Maybe she felt pressured by the other two girls. Maybe she was confused because the girls were telling her to do it and she was new to the area. Maybe she just wanted to do it. Whatever the reason was, Samantha was beginning to feel decidedly unwell and wanted nothing more than some gulps of fresh air. She ran down the aisle and out of the shop, banging the door behind her, the bell catching in it and making a dull, tinny noise instead of its usual, welcoming chime.

'Not sure what's got into her,' giggled Yasmin as they ran out after Samantha. 'Bye Doris!' And they were gone, leaving Doris alone in her shop.

'Wow Sam, you didn't look the type to steal. You're definitely one of us now,' Yasmin shouted as her and Tina left the shop. But Yasmin was talking to thin air, because Samantha was no longer there. She was running as fast as she could in the direction of her

©Adrian Martin and Brilliant Publications

home and as she ran, she could feel the weight of the Liquorice Allsorts bag in her coat pocket and she suddenly felt very lonely indeed.

But as she turned the corner to enter the road she lived in, she had to swerve out of the way to avoid two people running in the opposite direction. The two people turned out to be two girls and the two girls turned out to be Charlotte and Suzie, who turned out to be real friends to Samantha. When Charlotte had arrived home that day and told her parents about Samantha, they had told her that she should go round to Samantha's house to invite her round for tea, so both her and Suzie had done just that, only to be told by Samantha's mum that she still wasn't home from school. Feeling guilty and slightly worried, the two girls headed off to find Samantha and that is exactly what they had done.

Samantha told the two girls what had happened.

'We should have warned you about those two,' said Suzie. 'They're trouble with a capital 'T'. Where are the sweets now?'

'Here,' Samantha said, prodding the bulge in her coat pocket.

'Come on,' Charlotte instructed, grabbing Samantha by the arm and marching her back along the pavement.

The bell tinkled again as Samantha, Charlotte and Suzie walked through the sweet shop door.

'Hello girls,' Doris exclaimed, smiling. 'Now young lady,' she said to Samantha. 'These two girls are the ones you need to be friends with, not those other two. Trouble they are. Nasty pieces of work.'

'I've got something to tell you Doris,' replied Samantha. 'I took these before.'

She pulled out the sweets from her coat pocket and pushed the packet across the counter.

'I'm really sorry. It was me. I did it. Not them,' she admitted.

She was about to say 'sorry' again when Doris spoke; 'Oh I know dear.'

'What?' asked Samantha.

'Oh yes, I saw you take them. On the camera. There. See?' Doris said, pointing to the CCTV camera in the corner of the shop.

'But why didn't you say anything?' asked Samantha.

'Thought I'd wait to see if you'd come back,' Doris explained. 'You didn't seem their type to me and when you ran out of the shop I had a feeling you'd be back.'

'And you were right Doris,' Suzie said.

And for the first time since she had moved, Samantha did not feel lonely; she realised that she was very lucky indeed, because in Suzie and Charlotte, she had two really good friends.

Doris pushed the sweet packet back across the counter towards Samantha. 'Take them,' she said.

These were exactly the same words that Tina had used an hour ago to tempt Samantha into stealing the sweets, but unlike before, there was a kindness in the way Doris had said them.

'I can't take them Doris. They're your sweets and I've no money,' Samantha replied, confused.

'I want you to have them,' Doris continued. 'But on one condition.'

The girls looked at each other and waited. 'That you share them with your real friends!' Doris said, laughing.

Fifty Fantastic Assembly Stories

Friendship
Erin Values Her Friends

●●

It was lunchtime at Mill Lane Junior School, and when the weather was dry and warm enough, the children were allowed to eat their packed lunches outside and, after a morning of problem solving and adventure writing, the children in Year 5 were doing just that. Erin, Lauren and Holly were sat on one of the wooden benches at the side of the playground eating their sandwiches – and chatting – at the same time. (Girls seem to be able to do this without thinking and these three particular girls were especially good at it.) They had been friends ever since their very first day at the Infant School six years ago. As they sat there in the sunshine chatting away, Erin thought back to when they first met and how the three of them had become such good friends. She was surprised at how much she could remember, almost as if it was yesterday.

A gaggle of mums and dads were standing on the pavement outside school, waving through the school railings. Bushes grew on the other side of the railings which made it difficult for the parents to see through, but where there were gaps they crammed together peering through the bars, waving to their tiny children. Erin remembered thinking how funny the parents all looked, squashed up together, their hands reaching through the railings like chimpanzees at the zoo, reaching out for the bananas the zoo-keeper threw towards them at feeding time. For the next few years many of the parents would stand outside the school gates like this, watching their children playing together on the playground, until the teachers appeared to take them into school. They would also be there again at home time. Some of them would arrive half an hour before school ended, to get the best viewing space between the bushes. The first day at school was an emotional day for many of the parents and Erin's mum stood there with tears streaming down her cheeks, as she watched her

daughter run confidently away from her and into the playground. Erin did not understand why her mum was so upset; she thought her mum would be happy to get rid of her so that she could get back to doing what adults do, whatever that might be. Erin couldn't wait to go to school – she'd had enough of C-Beebies and Postman Pat and had never really understood why all the other children loved Bob The Builder so much – every episode seemed to end the same way – something would get broken and then somehow or another, Bob would manage to fix it.

Erin could even remember arriving at the school gates on that first day. Her mum was gripping her daughter's hand so tightly that Erin had to prize her fingers from her grip; it was as if their hands were super-glued together. Then came the farewell hug; Erin remembered thinking that all the air was going to be squeezed from her body. But the farewell hug wasn't anywhere near as bad as the farewell kiss – the very thought of it, even now, four years later, made Erin shiver – her mum had bent down to Erin's level and was about to peck her daughter on the cheek when she was accidentally pushed in the back by another parent. Instead of a small peck, she ended up licking Erin's face, from the very base of her chin right to the top of her nose. At that point, Erin and her sticky, gooey face, ran to the playground, towards the other children. She remembered watching some of them as they waved back at their parents whilst others were dabbing their teary eyes with their jumpers after their farewell hugs.

Moments later Erin remembered a group of tall, smiling people appearing on the playground. One of them blew a whistle and as the piercing sound cut through the air on the playground it had a magical effect. Everyone stood still and stopped talking (even the parents stopped waving). 'Ah,'

●●

©Adrian Martin and Brilliant Publications

Fifty Fantastic Assembly Stories

Erin remembered thinking. 'These must be the teachers.'

Each class was then herded up like sheep, the children forming a line behind their teacher (Erin's was called Miss Patel) before following them into the school. Just as she was about to enter the school building, Erin turned to look one last time at the group of parents. Most of them, dads included, were now crying, some were actually wailing and leaning on each other for support. 'Oh, they're worse than us,' Erin muttered under her breath. And at that moment, just as she was beginning to think all the other children were a little babyish for her liking, one of them said something which made Erin want to be her friend.

'I know. They're very odd, aren't they? You'd think they'd be happy, getting rid of us for the whole day.'

The voice came from the girl walking behind Erin who turned out to be Lauren. Erin smiled. She was surprised to find someone else who felt the same way as she did and it wasn't long before the two friends became three. In the cloakroom, Erin and Lauren soon realised that, apart from one other girl, they were the only ones who were not crying. All the other children had obviously caught the crying disease from their parents and were sobbing and wailing just like them. Before long, the girls also realised that they seemed to be the only ones who were able to put their bags on their pegs and take their coats off, without help from one of the smiling teachers. Erin, Lauren, and the other girl, stood outside the classroom door waiting to be told what to do next, whilst the rest of the class just stood helplessly in the cloakroom, waiting for someone to unzip their zip, take off their coat, and lead them to the classroom door. The other girl, it turned out, was Holly – she made Erin and Lauren laugh by pulling her eye lids down and looking up at the ceiling to make it look like the coloured parts of her eyes had disappeared. And that was that – from that moment on, Erin knew that they would be friends. That's one of the

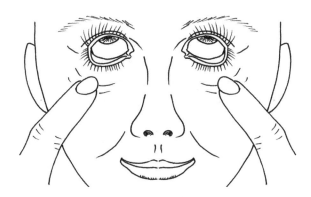

things about friends; they just 'click' somehow; they share the same sense of humour, the same interests and just want to be together all the time. But just as Erin's first ever day at school was beginning to turn out well, Miss Patel announced that everyone would have to sit in alphabetical order to begin with. Most of the other children didn't know what this meant and just stood there looking confused, but Erin was unlike most of the other children. She spent a good deal of time at home reading and unlike the other children, she already knew her alphabet. In fact, she knew it backwards as well as forwards, so she knew full well what Miss Patel meant when she said the children would have to sit in alphabetical order. It meant that she wouldn't be able to sit next to her new friends. Unless, by some very strange coincidence, their surnames began with the same letter. Erin couldn't believe her own ears when Miss Patel said, 'Right children, on this table, we'll have Erin Bentley, Lauren Booth and Holly Brooks.'

Amazingly, the three girls were put on the same table anyway and from that moment on Erin knew that they would be friends for a very long time. And that was what happened. But it wasn't always easy, especially as there were three of them and sometimes they had to work hard at being good friends. At school, there were many times when the children would be asked to find a partner so that they could work in pairs. Erin dreaded activities like this as they always meant that one of them would be left out.

She remembered the time in Year 4 when Mr Barnes was taking the class for PE and after a warm-up game of 'Stuck in the Mud' he asked the children to get themselves into pairs for the first activity. 'Here we go again,' Erin thought as all the children ran towards each other, grabbing their friends, making sure they were all with someone. The girls looked at each other, not sure what to do – they were a three, not a two. They could hear Mr Barnes saying, 'Come on, hurry up. If you can't pick yourselves I'll choose the pairs myself.'

Before long, all the children had got themselves sorted – all, that is, except Erin, Lauren, Holly and one other boy who noone ever seemed to want to work with. It was Joseph Parsons, one of two identical twins who was often left on his own for some reason. Erin, Lauren and Holly clung onto each other, determined not to be split up, hoping Mr Barnes would let them work as a group of three. But Erin could see Joseph standing on his own and felt bad as he was beginning to look upset. She looked at Lauren and Holly, untangled herself from them and skipped over to Joseph with a big smile on her face. 'Hi Joseph, will you be my partner?' she asked him.

At first Joseph was shocked, but shrugged and, with a relieved look on his face said, 'Yeah, okay.'

Erin hadn't wanted to leave her two friends but she knew she had to do something. Friendship, she realised, was about trusting each other and although she didn't like the thought of her two friends playing without her, sometimes friends have no choice.

Six years after meeting each other outside Miss Patel's classroom in Reception, there they were, sitting on the bench, eating their lunch. Holly and Lauren had stopped eating and chattering because they had noticed that Erin had gone into one of her daydreams.

'Erin!' said Lauren.

But there was no reaction. Erin's eyes were open but slightly glazed as she dreamily thought about their times together.

Holly moved her hand across Erin's eyes and clicked her fingers in front of her face. Lauren tugged her sleeve and finally, Erin was back with them.

'What on earth were you thinking about?' asked Holly. 'It was as if you'd gone into a trance.'

'Oh nothing really,' Erin replied. 'I was just thinking how lucky we are to be friends.'

But Holly and Lauren didn't hear her, as they had gone back to chewing and chatting again, like good friends do.

©Adrian Martin and Brilliant Publications

The Show Must Go On

• •

Friendships aren't always easy and sometimes people have to do things for their friends that they would really rather not do. When Erin Bentley, Lauren Booth and Holly Brooks met on their first day at school, they didn't realise that they would become best friends for the rest of their lives. They made each other laugh and enjoyed doing the same things and soon after meeting each other, became inseparable.

There were two things that they were all interested in, one slightly more unusual than the other; they each had an impressive collection of pencil cases, of all shapes and sizes from different countries around the world. Erin's favourite was a fluffy pink llama pencil case which her grandma had brought her back from Peru. This was the 63rd in her collection which she kept crammed together on the shelves in her bedroom. Lauren's favourite was a pencil case disguised as a calculator; not only was it disguised as a calculator, it had calculator buttons which actually worked. Lauren's mum and dad had bought this for her tenth birthday – they remembered being really excited about giving their daughter her first brand new bike. It had taken months to save the money for it, but on the morning of her birthday Lauren walked straight past the shiny pink mountain bike to the smallest gift at the top of her present pile; as she tore away the birthday paper, revealing the calculator pencil case she let out a shriek of joy and cradled it like a baby for the rest of the day. Like Erin, Lauren now had 63 pencil cases which she kept in perfectly straight rows in a huge box under her bed. Like Erin and Lauren, Holly had 63 pencil cases but unlike her two best friends, Holly preferred a more traditional style. Her favourite was a plain wooden, rectangular case which had two levels and was opened not by a zip but by sliding out the wooden lid. She loved the feel of the lid as it slid along its carefully carved runners. But her favourite part of this pencil case

was when the lid was removed completely and the top level swung outwards revealing the lower level beneath. Holly had seen this in a craft shop in Wales on the first day of their five-day holiday. It was priced at £12.50 and she had £15 to spend while she was there. As soon as she saw it she knew she had to have it and quickly worked out that if she spent no more than fifty pence each day on sweets, she would have enough money at the end of the week to buy it. It was hard work; after all, fifty pence does not buy much these days and her younger brother Thomas didn't help by spending all of his money on sweets, guzzling them in large amounts in front of Holly each day. But she was determined to save the money and on the final day of their holiday she walked purposefully into the shop and became the proud owner of the classy, wooden, sliding top pencil case. After showing it to her two friends, Holly placed it carefully in her wardrobe with the rest of her collection.

Each of the girls had encyclopaedic knowledge of every one of the pencil cases in their collection; where they were bought, how much they cost and how many pencils they could hold. It was easy to see why the girls were such good friends.

Fortunately, the other hobby they shared was less unusual. When they weren't looking for pencil cases, they were dancing. In the school playground, before school began, at playtime and lunchtime, even on their way home, they danced. Lauren and Erin lived opposite each other and Holly's house was just two houses away so when they got home from school, having danced most of the way, they would gather in one of the houses and dance until tea-time. At the weekends and in the holidays they would dance together all day long, thinking up routines and practising them over and over again until they all knew each move by heart. On Wednesday and Friday evenings they

• •

Fifty Fantastic Assembly Stories

attended 'The Dance Mill', the local dance school where they had been going since they were just five years old. To begin with they had stumbled around, colliding into each other, not being able to remember any of the moves their dance teacher Becky had taught them. But slowly, with practice, they got better and better and now, everyone who saw them perform was impressed by their moves. They even had a great name thought up by Erin's dad – their surnames all began with 'B' and there were three of them.

'You all used to love watching 'C-Beebies,' he said. 'And your last names all end in 'B', so you can be "The 3-Beebies!".'

And for once, the girls agreed with him. So *The 3-Beebies* they were. Every so often the dance school would put on a performance for the parents to come and watch and although the girls enjoyed these occasions, none of them were as excited as when Mrs Davies, the Headteacher, announced in assembly that she had decided to hold a Talent Show for the whole school to watch and that anyone in Years 5 and 6 could

enter. On hearing the news Lauren, Erin and Holly immediately began rehearsing their routine. Becky provided them with a dance mix combining seven different dance tunes and before long they knew their routine so well that they could have danced every move, perfectly in time, without the music.

Two weeks before the date of the Talent Show, Mrs Davies asked everyone who wanted to perform to meet in the school hall for their auditions. Each act would have one minute to impress her enough to allow them to perform.

'One minute?' asked Bernard incredulously. He was a very big fan of Doctor Who and had written a sketch in which he, playing the Doctor, would be attacked by two Daleks (played by Stephen and Adam with pedal bins over their heads). 'How can I possibly impress Mrs Davies in one minute?' he continued.

'I think she's been watching too many talent shows on the telly,' muttered Stephen, desperately trying to pull the bin over his ears.

In the end, however, it was only a couple of the acts that did not meet the approval of the Headteacher.

Bernard would get his chance to fight the Daleks in front of the rest of the school and the three girls would perform their dance. Best of all, Mrs Davies had been so impressed by the girls that she had asked them to be the final act. 'We want it to end on a high,' she said. 'And you three are definitely the ones to do it.'

The girls had never felt so good about themselves, apart from when they had received their most prized pencil case that is.

With a week to go before the show there was a buzz of excitement around the school. At playtimes children could be seen practising their acts together in corners of the playground; there were joke tellers, magicians, gymnasts, musicians, singers, dancers and of course, Bernard and his two bin-wearing friends, who spent most of their playtimes bumping into each other as Bernard became more and more frustrated by their lack of acting skills.

The Sunday before the talent show was Holly's birthday and after a trip to the cinema followed by as much pizza as they could eat, they went back to Holly's house to play in the garden and practise their routine one last time. It was just after their final practice that disaster struck. Like most children, Holly had a trampoline in her garden and the three girls decided it was time to take advantage of it. As they bounced around trying to jump higher than one another, Lauren lost her balance and landed awkwardly on the edge of the trampoline. As her foot hit the hard edge, her ankle gave way and she fell in a crumpled heap on the trampoline, clutching her ankle and crying in pain. Fortunately her ankle wasn't broken, but it was badly sprained and there was no way she would be able to dance for at least a couple of weeks.

'Well that's the end of the dance then,' Holly said, despondently. 'There's no way we're doing it without you.'

Erin agreed. 'We're *The 3-Beebies*, always have been and always will be,' she said. 'We'll tell Mrs Davies tomorrow.'

Mrs Davies couldn't believe her eyes when she saw Lauren tottering into school on crutches. 'I'm sure there's something we can do girls,' she told them. 'Just give me a while to think. You know what they say – 'The show must go on!'

Later on that day she called them into her office and put her idea to them. Their act began with them sitting on a chair each and then jumping

off them as the music began. 'Lauren can sit on the chair in the middle, covered in a sheet and at the end of the dance you two can lift the sheet to reveal her. That way you can all still be in the talent show.'

The idea of sitting under a sheet whilst her friends performed the dance didn't exactly fill Lauren with great joy but at least if it meant *The 3-Beebies* closing the show then that's exactly what she would do.

Bernard's Doctor Who act went better than expected and the curtain closed as he made his way off the stage with Stephen and Adam still trying to remove the bins from their heads. It was now time for *The 3-Beebies* to perform the final act and Erin and Holly helped Lauren into the chair in the middle of the stage before covering her over with the sheet. They took up their positions, the curtain opened and the music began. The audience immediately began to clap in time to the beat and from under the sheet Lauren imagined every move her friends were making, enjoying the moment more than she thought she would. On the final beat of the music, Erin and Holly, standing either side of the chair, flung the sheet behind them to reveal Lauren sitting there with a beaming smile on her face. The audience clapped enthusiastically and Mrs Davies told everyone how proud she was of all the performers.

'I think Lauren deserves a special mention,' she added. 'True friends stick by each other no matter what and today, Lauren made sure that Erin and Holly could still show off their amazing dancing skills.'

The children applauded again and the three girls looked at each other, knowing that their friendship had just become even stronger.

True Friends Play Fair

Arthur and Samir were best friends. 'Inseparable they are,' their mums told each other regularly. And they were. They played tennis and football together, both played in the school band, Arthur on drums, Samir on guitar, and they both shared the same, whacky sense of humour. Both were able to laugh at themselves which was just as well, as they often provided moments of fun for their classmates, usually unintentionally. Samir often reminded Arthur of his funniest and possibly most embarrassing moment; he had been sitting behind his drum kit on the far side of the stage whilst the band were performing in front of the school. As he beat the drums energetically, the chair he was sitting on inched its way closer and closer to the edge of the stage where a drop of approximately half a metre awaited him. The teachers looked on nervously and some of the children on the front row began to giggle as the chair, and Arthur, approached the drop. There was nothing anyone could do. Mrs Darby, the conductor, was too busy concentrating on the music to notice and it would be too impolite of the teachers to stop the music half way through. Arthur himself was blissfully unaware of the danger he was in and continued to beat his drums as hard as he could, enjoying himself immensely. Until the final note. Mrs Darby raised both her arms and held them above her head, the signal for the rest of the band to hold their final note. When she lowered them in a dramatic flourish, the band all stopped instantly. Arthur, on the other hand, did a back flip off the stage and landed safely in the chair with his legs and those of the chair, pointing upwards towards the ceiling; a big grin on his face. Once the applause and the laughter had finally subsided, Mrs Davies said it was the best ending to a musical piece that she had ever seen, although she wasn't so sure she would like to see anything like it again.

Just as Samir reminded Arthur of this embarrassing incident whenever he got the chance, Arthur reminded Samir of the moment he had made everyone laugh. They were canoeing on a river whilst on the school's adventure week in the Lake District. Samir and Arthur were in the same canoe and, with Arthur at the front, they managed to somehow drift wildly off course into a number of over-hanging trees on the left side of the riverbank. The branches of the trees hung down onto the surface of the river and as Arthur ducked, Samir decided, wrongly as it turned out, to grab hold of the branch above his head, with both hands. The canoe was moving at a reasonable speed and continued through the trees, but only

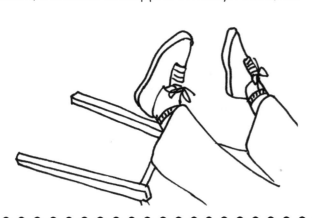

©Adrian Martin and Brilliant Publications

Arthur emerged in the canoe at the other side. Samir was left dangling on the branch, above the water, until, after a great deal of pointing and giggling from his classmates and Arthur in particular, Samir let go of the branch and quietly plopped into the cold river, bobbing up and down in his life jacket with a broad smile on his face.

They loved school and made the most of all the activities it offered them. But one opportunity that came their way at the beginning of Year 5 was about to test their friendship to the very limit. Each year the children had the chance to become a member of the School Council. One child from each class was elected by their classmates and until now, neither Samir nor Arthur had gone for the position. But this year was different and even though neither of them thought they had a chance of being elected, Mrs Davies had encouraged all the children to make the most of their opportunities in assembly and so they had both decided to give it a go. Seven members of 5L were aiming to be elected, speeches were written and the presentation ceremony was underway.

'I promise to do my best for you if I am elected as your School Councillor,' Arthur said. 'And finally, I'll try my hardest not to fall backwards off the stage!'

The class laughed and gave him a well earned round of applause. Samir was next and after a nervous start, he delivered his last line with confidence:

'If I am elected,' he said, 'I will promise I will do my best for you and I will not .....(he paused) ... hang around!'

Again the children laughed and applauded as they were reminded of Samir hanging from the tree over the river last year.

'Well that's the end of the speeches,' Mr Lee told the class. 'You have one vote each, so think carefully about who you choose.'

He looked at the candidates. 'You can vote too,' he said, 'But you mustn't vote for yourself.'

The children wrote the name of their choice on a piece of paper and posted it into the Ballot Box, as Mr Lee called it (it was actually a shoe box with a hole in the top).

At break time Mr Lee counted the 32 votes; Hannah, Samantha and Jake had two votes each, but way out in the lead were Samir and Arthur with an impressive thirteen votes each. A draw then.

The children came back into the classroom after break, eager to hear the results. Mr Lee couldn't remember there being a draw before and after telling the class what had happened and everyone had given all of the candidates a deserved round of applause, he decided to allow all the children to vote again, but this time the election would be between Samir or Arthur. Once again he told the children to think carefully about their decision and reminded Samir and Arthur that they could also vote, but not for themselves. The atmosphere in the classroom had grown even more tense than it had been earlier, as the children scribbled their choice of either 'Arthur' or 'Samir' on their papers. Even Arthur and Samir became nervous. This was a difficult situation for them both – they normally did everything together, not against each other. The strangeness of the situation and the tension in the room had a particularly strange effect on Arthur. He was not normally the competitive type but he had a sudden desire to win, to be better than his best friend. This sudden desire to win made him do something that friends definitely didn't do to each other, especially best friends. He couldn't explain why he did what he did, but when he took hold of his pencil and stared at the blank voting slip, he just couldn't help himself. He took a deep breath and wrote the name 'Arthur' on it. Mr Lee counted the votes whilst the children waited and watched. Arthur felt the blood rushing around inside his head and could feel himself going redder and redder. He couldn't even look at his best friend.

'The result is,' Mr Lee said loudly. 'Samir – fourteen votes, Arthur eighteen votes. Arthur is our School Council representative. Well done to you both.' He clapped and the children joined him, Samir smiled his broad smile, stood up and offered his hand to Arthur to shake, which he did automatically. But Samir's mature attitude in the face of defeat made Arthur feel even worse. He had won by four votes and would have won even if he hadn't voted for himself but he knew that he had broken the rules and he simply couldn't enjoy the moment. Instead of feeling proud that his classmates had voted for him Arthur felt that he had betrayed his best friend. He couldn't stand it any longer and raised his hand in the air. When Mr Lee gave him permission to speak Arthur said, 'I voted for myself. I broke the rules and I don't deserve to be the class councillor.'

There was a gasp from the class. Arthur continued, 'I don't know why I did it but I did and I'm sorry.' He looked at Samir who looked hurt by what Arthur had done, but still managed to smile back at his friend.

Samir then put up his hand to speak. Mr Lee nodded to him and Samir said, 'I almost did the same. I was really tempted and I can understand why Arthur did it. And he would have won anyway.'

Again, he looked at Arthur and smiled. Arthur was already aware of how good a friend Samir was, but the way he had acted in the last few minutes made him realise how true friends should behave towards each other.

Mr Lee certainly had never experienced a situation like this before and asked the class what they thought should be done next. He said that although Arthur had let down himself and Samir, he had also been brave to admit his mistake, particularly in front of the whole class. It was also true, as Samir had pointed out, that Arthur would have won the election if he hadn't voted for himself.

Everyone agreed that the last vote should not count and that a third vote should now take place. For the third time that morning, Mr Lee handed out the voting slips and for the third time that morning, he reminded the children to vote carefully. After what had just happened he decided that he didn't need to remind Arthur and Samir that they were not allowed to vote for themselves. When the Ballot Box had been filled for a third time, Mr Lee emptied it and counted the votes once again. The tension was unbearable as the children watched their teacher dividing the slips of paper into two piles, one for Arthur and the other for Samir. The two boys watched and waited. After counting the votes Mr Lee shook his head, wrote something down in his notebook and began counting again.

'I don't believe this!' he said, exasperated. 'Sixteen votes each!'

This time everyone laughed; it was as if the tension of the situation had suddenly been broken.

'There's only one thing for it,' Mr Lee said. 'This year, for the first time ever, 5L will have two School Councillors!'

Arthur stood up, mightily relieved, walked over to Samir and shook him firmly by the hand. In one morning, they had given the class a lesson in true friendship.

©Adrian Martin and Brilliant Publications

Bill Night's Hundredth Birthday Party

It was Wednesday afternoon and Wednesday afternoon was history and, although Jake didn't ever say it out loud, it was his least favourite afternoon of the week. He just couldn't see the point of learning about things that happened ages ago. He was more of a technology person – he liked finding out how to make things work. He was particularly interested in making something to stop his younger sister biting him. 'Now that would be worth learning about,' he thought, but it was Wednesday afternoon and there was nothing he could do about that and, being a caring sort of person who didn't like upsetting people, he would sit and listen to what Mr Lee had to say and then do whatever task he was given, as well as he could. But then the classroom door opened and as it did, Jake's view of history changed, forever. A stooped, thin and very old man walked slowly into the classroom and shook Mr Lee's hand. Mr Lee immediately helped the man to the leather armchair in the corner of the room. The old man was dressed very smartly; on his feet he wore the shiniest black leather shoes that Jake had ever seen. He wore black trousers with creases which were so straight they looked like they'd been ironed with a ruler and over his white shirt and navy blue tie, the man wore a black blazer with shiny silver buttons down the front and on the cuffs. On the left hand side of the blazer, in a perfectly horizontal line, were six sparkling medals standing to attention. On the side of the man's head was a mop of thick white hair which was accompanied by a pair of white bushy eyebrows and an impressive thick white moustache which curled up at each end, pointing towards his twinkling blue eyes.

'This is our very special guest everyone,' Mr Lee announced. 'Please give a warm welcome to our very own World War II soldier, Mr Bill Night.'

This term the children in Year 5 were learning about World War II and until today Jake had shown little interest in it, but as soon as Bill had walked through the door and began to talk to the children about his war time experiences Jake was hooked. Bill was 25 when he was called up to fight in the war, but a lot of his comrades were just 18 years old. He had taken part in the D-Day landings in France which Jake had never heard of but he was fascinated by Bill's description of what had happened. The armoured boats had stopped in the sea about 50 metres from the shore. Bill described how he and his friends stood on the boat waiting for the steel ramp to be lowered at the front of the boat so that they could wade ashore. His voice trembled a little as he described what happened next. German soldiers were waiting on the beach and bullets rained down on the boat, rebounding off its metal walls and whistling past Bill's ears. He described how many of his friends were killed even before the ramp had been completely lowered. He described how he had somehow managed to avoid being hit and how, as he reached the freezing cold water his best friend Frank got shot in the leg. Bill explained how he had managed

to drag his injured friend to the shore through the freezing water, where they had taken shelter from the bullets behind a rock.

'And this medal here,' Bill said, pointing to the largest and shiniest of his six medals, 'Is the one I received from the Queen for rescuing Frank.'

Jake and the rest of the class were fascinated by Bill's stories. To look at him, now, no one would believe that he was a war hero and that was, without a doubt, exactly what he was. Bill talked for about an hour, at which point Mr Lee asked the class if anyone had any questions to ask. Virtually everyone put up their hand.

'Well, I'm sure Bill's very tired after talking for so long,' Mr Lee explained. 'I'll choose three of you.'

Everyone groaned. Mr Lee knew that history wasn't Jake's favourite subject (it was difficult to hide things like that from teachers), so when Jake's hand had shot up in the air to ask Bill a question, Mr Lee just had to choose him.

'Jake,' he said. 'What would you like to ask Bill?'

Jake wasn't sure whether his question was appropriate or not, but he hadn't ever met anyone with such an amazing past before and he was desperate to know just how old Bill actually was.

'Er, I hope you don't mind me asking, Bill,' Jake stumbled.

'Ask anything you like young man,' Bill replied.

'I'd like to know how old you are please,' Jake asked.

'Well it's funny you should ask me that young man,' said Bill. 'Next week will be my birthday and I hope to be getting something else from the Queen that day.'

Jake had heard his mum talking about how the Queen sends a card to people on their 100th birthday and how she'll be getting fed up writing them now that people are living longer.

'So you'll be 100!' exclaimed Jake.

'Spot on!' smiled Bill, impressed that Jake knew what he had meant. 'What a bright young man you are.'

Jake wondered what Bill would be doing on his birthday, but he didn't have to wonder for long because Millie had already asked him and Bill's answer gave Jake an idea. Bill had no plans. No plans for his 100th birthday! He lived in an elderly peoples' home – he had out-lived most of his friends and any family he had left lived many miles away. Jake felt really sad that such a wonderful man should not have a party on his one 100th birthday. When the children had given Bill a big round of applause Mr Lee asked Jake to show him to the staffroom for a well earned cup of tea.

'This way Bill,' Jake said, pointing down the corridor.

'Bill walked so slowly that Jake had to make a real effort not to walk ahead. When they reached the staffroom door Bill took Jake's hand and shook it firmly.

'Thank you young man,' he said. 'I really enjoyed myself today.'

Jake wasn't sure what to say. It was he who should be thanking Bill and he was about to do just that when Mrs Roberts, the school secretary opened the door and Bill disappeared inside. As Jake walked back to the classroom he made up his mind to thank Bill properly.

Exactly one week later he and the rest of the class were waiting silently outside the lounge door at the elderly people's home where Bill lived. Mr Lee nodded to Jake, the door opened and in they walked. Inside, the chairs had been arranged into a semi-circle leaving a space for Jake to lead his classmates into. After Jake had shared his idea with the class they had spent much of the week learning the words to three wartime songs. They had also done some research on evacuation and had gone to the home dressed as evacuees. When they walked into the lounge Bill's face lit up. He had no idea that they were coming to help him celebrate his special birthday and he was, to say the least, thrilled that they had gone to so much effort for him. The children sang with great spirit and were astonished when Bill and his friends not only joined in with the songs but could remember all of the words. Zoe, who had a talent for baking, had made an amazing

cake and on it was written, 'Happy Birthday Bill Night, War Hero' (Jake's idea). After the singing one of the helpers at the home brought the cake in and placed it on the table in front of Bill, next to his card from the Queen. Everyone sang 'Happy Birthday' and 'For He's A Jolly Good Fellow!' followed by three rousing cheers. The room fell silent and Bill got to his feet. 'I don't know what to say,' he said. 'It's nice to know young people today still care about the past. This has been my best birthday ever!'

And Jake realised that he did like history after all. In fact, he liked it very much indeed.

Caring
Erin Goes Carol Singing

• •

Erin woke up and immediately felt a tingle of excitement. It was her third most exciting day of the year; Christmas Eve. She jumped out of bed, pulled back the curtains, and looked towards the upstairs windows of the house opposite. Lauren lived five minutes walk from Mill Lane Junior School, directly opposite Erin's house, whilst Holly, her other best friend, lived two houses further up the road. The twins, Sam and Joseph, lived next door to Erin. She could hear them through the wall, play fighting. There was a thud as one of them was thrown into the other side of Jess's bedroom wall, followed by a loud shout from their dad; 'Father Christmas won't come if you two carry on like that!' Erin looked over to Lauren's bedroom window – there she was, looking back at Erin. Lauren waved to Erin, mouthed the words, 'See you later,' and then disappeared back behind her curtains. Erin looked up into the sky. It was a beautiful day. The sky was a watery blue colour and cloudless. But even in the warmth of her bedroom, she could sense how cold it was out there. 'It might snow,' she thought. She peered up into the sky and thought about Santa up there, whizzing round in his sleigh with his reindeers. 'Maybe I'll see him tonight,' Erin thought. But there was a lot to do before then. She'd promised Dad that she'd cut out some fish shapes from last week's Sunday paper, so that they could play 'Flap the Fish' tomorrow after Christmas dinner. Dad liked his Christmas games and Flap the Fish was his favourite.

Dad would shout 'Go!' and each person would try to get their fish to the other end of the room by flapping it. 'Any touching means instant disqualification,' he would say, in his best sergeant major voice. Last year, Nana Betty won, but Dad said it was only because her fish was the only one made of kitchen roll so it flapped better. 'And she nudged me,' he said, 'Into the fireplace, with her BIG bottom.' He sulked for a full hour

after that, until Mum gave him a chocolate liqueur and a big sloppy kiss. 'Honestly,' Erin thought, 'Adults can be so childish at times.' Still, at least it was fun, and everyone was there, and they had lots of presents from Santa. They were lucky, very lucky. Erin thought back to Mrs Davies's assembly a couple of days ago on the last day of term, when she had asked everyone to imagine waking up on Christmas Day and having no presents. Not one. Nothing at all. She said that some children in Africa and India and even in our country receive no presents at Christmas. Erin remembered feeling really sad, and at the end she had asked Mrs Davies if she could organise something to raise money for these children so that they could have some presents. Mrs Davies had said what a kind thought that was but as it was the last day of term there wasn't really time to do anything in school. It was then that Erin had thought of the carol singing idea and had asked Mr Lee if he could ask the children in 5L who lived in her road if they would like to join her on Christmas Eve. Mr Lee thought it was a great idea and said that he would ring Erin's mum to ask if she could go along with the children as it wasn't safe for young children to knock on people's doors, even on Christmas Eve. Erin's mum had agreed, even though she was really busy on Christmas Eve, and that was that. At 3 o'clock, seven children and Mrs Brooks, Erin's mum, would meet to sing carols for two hours, to raise money for the children in India and Africa who had no presents. There would be Sam and Joseph from next door, Lauren and Holly, and of course, Tom and Barney, who lived at the other end of the road. Barney plays the trumpet and had been learning Christmas carols in his lessons, so he was bringing that along. Tom didn't play anything, but had asked if he could bring Eric, the gnome he had bought Mrs Knight for her garden. 'I've asked Mrs Knight,' he said, enthusiastically, 'She said Eric would love to go –

• •

©Adrian Martin and Brilliant Publications

Fifty Fantastic Assembly Stories

it would be good for him to get out for a change – see a bit of the world and all that.' The others had looked at Tom with disbelief, as usual, but had reluctantly agreed that Eric could come along.

By ten to three, Erin had finished cutting out the last of the paper fish and Dad had chosen his. 'It's definitely got the look of a winner,' he said, as he tucked the fish into his little paper bed for the night. 'Come on Phil,' he said, 'You need to get a good night's sleep for the big race tomorrow.' Erin's giggles were interrupted by the door bell. She flung open the door, to be greeted by two boys, dressed identically, with matching red and white striped scarves and bobble hats and grinning in a slightly scary way. 'Where's Wally?' she asked. 'Ha ha. Very funny,' Sam and Joseph replied, at exactly the same time. They were followed shortly after by Lauren and Holly, and eventually, at ten past three, by Barney and Tom. 'You're ten minutes late, and I thought you were bringing Eric,' said Erin.

'Wait there.' Tom ran back down the path to the two brick gate posts either side of Erin's front gate. He whistled, as if he was calling a dog, and then walked back towards the house, pulling a long rope behind him. All the children's eyes, as well as Erin's mum's, were fixed on the other end of the rope. After what seemed like ages, the rope stopped. Tom pulled, but it was stuck. 'Ohww!' he muttered, in frustration. He gave it one final tug, and released the rope. And then came the laughter. He'd never heard laughter like it. Everyone simply doubled over laughing.

Tears were dripping down Sam's face. Tom had converted his Go-Kart into Santa's sleigh and there was Eric, sat in the driver's seat, wearing a little Santa suit and hat, and his sack full of miniature presents, in the back seat. 'Hey stop laughing you lot! Mrs Knight spent ages knitting him that suit!' shouted Tom. But it didn't take long before he was laughing as well.

Two hours later, they returned, exhausted, from their carol singing adventure. Barney's trumpet had gone down really well. 'It's nice to see young people making a real effort,' people had said. But the main attraction was … well, it's fairly obvious really. 'Isn't he lovely,' Mrs Peterson had said, when she saw Eric sitting proudly in his sleigh.

'Here's an extra pound for making such an effort with Santa's suit,' said Mr Johnson from number 15. 'He does look a bit like Mrs Knight's new gnome though… Eric. Don't you think?'

The children agreed, and waved goodbye, thanking him for his kind contribution.

Back in Erin's house, Mrs Bentley handed out hot mince pies and juice, while the children counted their money. '£93.17p' exclaimed Erin, excitedly. 'Here's another ten, to take you past 100,' said Dad. 'You deserve it. Well done.'

'Brilliant!' cried Lauren. 'Thanks Mr Bentley. And good luck in the Flap the Fish race tomorrow!'

The money was only sent after Christmas but Mrs Davies made sure it went to the right place, and made a real fuss of the children in the first assembly of the new year.

'This money will make some children who are not as lucky as you, very happy,' she said to the seven children. 'You've been extremely thoughtful.'

Caring
Sid Gets a Hero's Welcome

Sid Troutman loved his job. He'd been Mill Lane's Lollipop Man (or to use his correct title, Crossing Patrol Officer), for 25 years, long before any of the children he helped had even been born. He knew all the children who crossed at his crossing point and all their parents, most of whom he had helped to cross the road when they were children; he even knew most of the grandmas and granddads and of course, everyone who lived near the school knew Sid. He lived with his wife Edna, in a house on Mill Lane just a couple of minutes' walk from the school. Edna worked at the library in the nearby village and, like Sid, she had got to know most of the people who lived in the area. In the evening when they finally sat down to watch a bit of telly, Sid would tell Edna how lucky he was to work with such nice, friendly children

'Hello Sid!' 'Morning Sid!' 'Thanks Sid!' 'See you later Sid!' the children would say as he stood in the middle of the road, allowing them to cross safely. Their cheery, enthusiastic voices made Sid's day and he really couldn't imagine what life would be like without them. He also loved the power of his job; Sid loved the fact that he could actually stop traffic with his lollipop. Over the years he had carefully and safely stepped out onto Mill Lane and stopped thousands and thousands of cars,

vans, motorbikes, buses and even huge, trundling lorries. He would raise his luminous lollipop and wait for the drivers to stop. With lorries, he always had to give them more time as they needed longer stopping distances, he loved the sound of their air-brakes as they hissed to a standstill and waited for Sid's permission to drive on.

When he was a young boy Sid absolutely loved Superheroes, Batman being his favourite; he loved the idea of good winning over evil and longed to be one himself. Being a Lollipop Man was the next best thing to being a Superhero in Sid's mind and he would often imagine himself as the Superhero 'Lollipop Man' whose magic power was to sort out all the traffic problems in the world with his magic lollipop stick. If he saw a driver going too quickly or using a mobile phone whilst driving, he imagined pointing his magic lollipop towards the car, which would stop instantly, the doors locking magically, imprisoning the driver inside until the police arrived.

'If only you could really do that,' Sid would say to his luminous lollipop.

Sid may not have been a Superhero but to the children at Mill Lane Junior School he was a real-life hero. They loved him. He was always friendly, no matter what the weather and, most remarkably of all, he knew all of their names.

If it was sunny he would say, 'Beach weather today!' with a big smile on his face. On a rainy, miserable grey day one of Sid's favourite greetings was, 'Lovely weather for ducks!' and when it was so windy that Sid could hardly raise his lollipop in the air the children would be greeted with, 'Great kite flying weather today!'

Sid was never miserable and everyone loved him because of that, but he saved his best efforts for

©Adrian Martin and Brilliant Publications

Fifty Fantastic Assembly Stories

special times of the year. Last Halloween he made a huge cardboard pumpkin with a smiley face and stuck it to the top of his lollipop. Even though the pumpkin covered the word 'STOP', his lollipop had never been so effective – drivers stopped even more quickly than usual and instead of looking annoyed that their journey had been so rudely interrupted, they laughed and shook their heads in disbelief. At Christmas Sid transformed his lollipop into an enormous Christmas pudding and at Easter it was a huge bunny, complete with floppy ears which had been connected to an electric circuit so that they popped up every time a car stopped. Sid's creations not only stopped the traffic more effectively, but had the added bonus of making the children get out of bed quicker, making him popular with the parents as well!

It wasn't just because he made them laugh that the children loved Sid so much; he was kind too. As he crossed the road on a cold January morning Jake slipped on some black ice and broke his ankle, right in front of Sid. That night, Sid popped a card through Jake's door and every day after that, as Jake's little sister Bella crossed the road, he would ask her how Jake was getting on. When Jake finally had his plaster removed and was able to walk to school again, Sid stuck a 'Welcome Back' sign on the back of his lollipop. He was thoughtful like that.

So when Jake and his friends arrived opposite school one wet morning and the Lollipop Man wasn't Sid but instead was a Lollipop Lady called Betty, they were more than a little worried.

'But where's Sid?' they asked.

'Sid's not very well,' Betty replied. 'Won't be here for a while. I'm Betty and I'll be helping you cross safely 'till he's well enough to return to work.'

Betty was nice and the children liked her, but she didn't seem the type of person to turn her lollipop into a pumpkin, or a giant bunny with pop-up ears

and the children wanted Sid back. Jake told Mr Lee, his teacher, about Sid and wondered if there was any way he could find out just how unwell Sid was and, most importantly, when he would be back. Mr Lee managed to speak to Edna, Sid's wife, on the phone that evening. Sid had had 'a bit of a funny turn' as Edna put it and the doctor had told him to rest for a couple of weeks. Jake suggested that the children have a collection for Sid, so that they could buy him a card and some chocolates; so that he knew they were all missing him. Mrs Davies told the children about the idea in assembly and mentioned that if anyone would like to make a small donation towards a gift for Sid, that would be fine. As it was Jake's idea, the children were told to take any donations to him at break time. Jake held a small, green plastic box as he stood in the corridor next to the playground door at playtime. In it, were three pound coins from his money box. But then the school bell rang, signalling time for break and children began streaming out of their classrooms. As they passed Jake, each one of them dropped some money into his box. After a few minutes a queue had formed and the box was full to the brim with money. Mr Lee arrived and realised immediately that another box was needed.

'Goodness me,' he said, 'Sid obviously means a great deal to you all.'

It took Jake over an hour to count the money. '£115.61p!' he announced to the children in assembly. It was a fine effort and after a short chat about the sort of things Sid enjoyed, Mr Lee came up with a great idea for a present.

Just over two weeks later Sid opened the front door of his house to make the short journey to the crossing point for his first day back at work following his illness. He was quite excited to be back and so was a few minutes early, but as he approached the school he stopped to check his watch.

'Am I late?' he thought. 'What on earth are all these children doing here so early?'

About 60 children, with their parents, lined the pavement at the crossing point. Behind them, attached to the school fence, was the giant banner they had had made. As Sid arrived, Jake walked towards him with a large card signed by them all.

'Welcome back Sid! We've made you this!' he said and as he did so, the line of children stood aside to reveal the banner. Sid couldn't believe his eyes.

It read, 'Always Stop For Our Superhero Sid'.

On either side of the lettering was a picture of Sid in a luminous yellow superhero cape holding his lollipop aloft.

I don't know what to say!' Sid stammered.

Everyone clapped and cheered.

'It'll be there forever,' Jake told him. 'And we hope you will too.'

Sid had no idea how much the children cared about him. Until today that is; a day he would never forget.

For Our
ro Sid!

©Adrian Martin and Brilliant Publications
Fifty Fantastic Assembly Stories

Zoe Does Nanny Finch Proud

It was exactly three months since Zoe's grandma, Nanny Finch, had died. She was only 68 and had been very ill for many months with leukaemia. Zoe had never heard of leukaemia before but had learned that it was when your blood got cancer. Zoe loved Nanny Finch – she had lived with her for two years when she was four, as her mum and dad were going through 'a bad time' as mum had put it and it was decided that the best thing for Zoe was that Nanny Finch looked after her for a while.

When her mum had said, 'for a while' Zoe had thought she meant a couple of days rather than the two years that it turned out to be. But Zoe loved those two years because Nanny Finch was so kind and lovely, she played games with Zoe and took her to the local market every Saturday where everyone seemed to know her. Best of all, and Zoe's happiest memory of her grandma, was that she made the most amazing, huge, creamy cream cakes that anyone could ever imagine. Zoe remembered standing on a stool in the kitchen watching as Nanny Finch mixed the flour, sugar and eggs and then whisked the cream. She would always hand Zoe the whisk to lick the cream. This was Zoe's second favourite part of the cake making process. Her favourite part was an hour after the cake had been removed from the oven and Nanny Finch added the jam and cream, cut a large slice, put it on a plate and yelled, 'Zoe! It's ready. Come and get it!'

Zoe would rush from the swing in the garden or thunder downstairs from her bedroom, take the plate from Nanny Finch's soft, podgy hand and sink her teeth into the succulent, light, creamy, jammy slab of cake.

But now Nanny Finch was gone and Zoe was very, very sad. Her teacher, Mr Lee, had noticed the change in Zoe. She was usually a happy girl, keen to join in but lately she had become sad and withdrawn. He knew why of course; Zoe's mum had told him at the school gate the day after it had happened and he'd done his best to help her through the last few months, but there was only so much he could do to make her feel better. Until today, that was, when Mr Lee had an idea; a very good idea in fact. He'd had the idea in the car on the way to school that morning. The radio was on, and as usual, like most if not all teachers on their way to work, he wasn't listening to it. Instead he was thinking about the lessons he was going to teach that day, what he was going to say to make Simon Ryland stop talking and actually write something in his literacy book, and how he was going to get all his marking done before his favourite comedy programme began at 10 o'clock. But then the car in front braked suddenly, snapping Mr Lee out of his trance-like state and, slamming his right foot on the brake pedal, changing gear and accelerating slowly away again, his attention was drawn to a voice on the radio. It was talking about leukaemia and how more money is needed desperately for research. Mr Lee heard himself saying, 'Leukaemia – that's what Zoe's nan died of isn't it?' And that was when he had the idea. And at break time, he would see what Zoe thought of it.

His plan was to organise a charity event to raise money for leukaemia research and, as he shared his idea with Zoe, her eyes widened and for the first time in several months Mr Lee thought he saw the hint of a smile on her face. After checking his idea with Mrs Davies, the Headteacher, Mr Lee announced it to the class and a discussion followed about what they could do to raise money.

'We could have a sponsored run!' Barney said.

'Good idea,' replied Mr Lee.

'Or a sponsored silence,' suggested Holly.

Fifty Fantastic Assembly Stories

'Now that I do like the sound of,' enthused Mr Lee.

'And we could make games to play with the younger ones,' Jake added.

'But how would we make money for Leukaemia by doing that?' Lauren asked.

'Fair point,' said Mr Lee.

'Well,' continued Jake, 'We could charge them to play the games, ten pence or something and then if they win, they get a prize.' He even surprised himself with his answer.

And as the children became more and more enthusiastic about the idea a strange feeling came over Zoe; she was beginning to feel excited; this was something she actually wanted to do and since Nanny Finch had died, she really hadn't wanted to do anything. She couldn't wait to get home and tell mum and dad and for the first time in as long as she could remember she actually ran home after school that day. Her mum and dad were delighted by idea; like Mr Lee, they had been worried about Zoe but had no idea what to do to help her. This was exactly what she needed.

'Well, you'll have to make cakes,' mum said. 'It's what Nanny Finch would have done. And she did pass her cake-making skills on to you. You're a fantastic cake maker.'

Mum was right. Nanny Finch had not only made gorgeous cakes for Zoe but she had also taught her how to make them herself and Zoe was a natural cook. She just hadn't made any lately but now, at last, she had the perfect reason to do so. And mum was right again; Nanny Finch would have made loads of cakes to raise money for charity and that was exactly what Zoe was going to do. A week later, on a bright Spring day in April, Mr Lee's class raised money for leukaemia research. They began with Mr Lee's favourite part

– the sponsored silence, for two whole hours. Mr Lee himself had sponsored every child in the class fifty pence to do it; that was already sixteen pounds raised. In the afternoon the children from the other classes filed into the hall where Mr Lee's class had set up their games. They had made a terrific effort, not only inventing some great games

but also using their own pocket money to buy prizes.

But the highlight of the day was Zoe's cake stall which she set up at the school gate where the parents meet their children at home time. Mum came along to help and Zoe picked three friends to help her set up and take the money. She had spent

©Adrian Martin and Brilliant Publications

the whole weekend and the last two evenings making cakes and her stall looked amazing. Cakes of all different sizes and types; coffee and walnut, chocolate and of course cakes oozing with jam and cream. Zoe was a little worried at first that no one would buy them, but she needn't have been. Within ten minutes all that was left on the stall were a few crumbs and three tubs full of money.

It took Zoe and her friends an hour to count it all; a staggering £97.20! The girls rushed to tell Mr Lee who said, 'Well we can't have that, here's another £2.80 – now you've made one hundred pounds!'

The girls cheered and by the end of the week all the sponsor money had been collected and the money from the games had been counted by Mrs Roberts, the school secretary.

Mr Lee arranged for Mr Potts from the Charity for Leukaemia to come into school to receive a cheque in assembly. The children sat listening as Mr Lee explained what his class had done and then the moment came for him to reveal the total amount raised. He was clearly very excited as he read the figures from the piece of paper he was holding.

'The sponsored silence raised £85.90,' he said. 'The games raised £162.21,' he continued, 'and Zoe's cake stall took exactly £100! So a grand total of £348.11!'

As he read out the final total everyone in the hall clapped loudly. When the applause stopped Mr Lee told everyone that he would like Zoe to come out to present the cheque to the visitor. As she handed the cheque to Mr Potts and the children clapped again, a wave of happiness came over Zoe; she was almost back to her old self.

'Thanks Mr Lee,' she said, as the children headed home at the end of the day.

'No problem,' he replied, adding, 'But next time you make one of your gorgeous cakes, save some for me!'

Zoe laughed – something she'd not done for a long time. She had certainly done Nanny Finch proud.

Appreciation

Harrison's Breakfast-in-bed Treat to Mum and Dad

● ●

It was a normal Thursday morning in the Whitley household; Harrison and his younger sister Lydia were sat at the kitchen table, slurping away at their cornflakes. Nigel, their cocker spaniel, was sitting in between the two children, his nose pointing upwards, waiting for any scraps that might come his way. Dad had gone to work early today so it was mum's turn to get the children to school. She had heaved herself out of bed at six o'clock to iron the children's school uniforms, make their packed lunches and get the breakfast ready. There was no time for idle chatter – things had to be done quickly if they were to get where they all had to be at the correct times. She was tired and beginning to feel the pressure of being a working mum.

'Toast!' she announced, placing a plate of buttered toast on the table in front of the two children. 'It's a quarter to eight – eat fast. We've got to leave in half an hour.'

Harrison's mum was a manager at a nearby car factory and started work at nine o'clock. The children had to be dropped off at eight thirty at the very latest if she was to get there on time and the traffic at that time in the morning could be horrendous.

'Eat faster you two please,' she instructed, looking up at the clock on the kitchen wall. Of all the days in the week Thursday was the one she least looked forward to – there was always far too much to do and far too little time to do it. Quarter past nine on Thursdays at the car factory was when the weekly management meeting took place and she was the one leading the meeting. Every week she would burst through the door of the meeting room looking flustered – she was always the last one to arrive and as the door opened the other managers would stop chatting and smile at her sympathetically.

Harrison and Lydia munched as quickly as they could. They weren't too keen on Thursday mornings either, knowing full well that mum was in a rush and that there was no time for dawdling. Nigel was the only member of the family who enjoyed Thursdays as he seemed to get more tasty scraps than on any other day of the week. Today was no exception, as Harrison slipped his hand under the kitchen table and pushed a half eaten slice of toast into the dog's mouth. Nigel snaffled the toast in one gulp and wiped his wet muzzle across Harrison's hand in appreciation.

'Right, upstairs, clean teeth, wash faces,' mum barked.

Harrison noticed that when his mum was in a rush she missed words out of her sentences. Her instructions did the trick though as the two children marched up the stairs to the bathroom.

After a few minutes of hurriedly brushing their teeth and splashing cold water onto their faces, another sharp instruction echoed through the house:

'Coats, bags, car. Now!' mum shouted.

Again, the two harassed children obeyed and the final stage of the Thursday morning procedure was complete.

'But it's Walk to School Week' explained Lydia, as she was pushed into the back of the car and strapped into her booster seat.

'No time to walk, sorry,' mum replied.

And within minutes they were at the school gates, car doors were opening, seat belts were being unbuckled and two rather bewildered children

● ●

©Adrian Martin and Brilliant Publications

Fifty Fantastic Assembly Stories

were receiving hugs and kisses from their mum. This bit was, without doubt, Harrison's least favourite part of Thursday morning; any other time and place he liked nothing more than a hug from his mum, but now, here, right in front of all his friends who were pointing and giggling at him? No thank you.

'Mum!' he complained.

But she was back in the car, issuing another shortened message to them both through the open passenger window.

'Half past three. Here. Enjoy. Love you.'

Before she drove away, she watched her two children through the rear view mirror, as they sauntered slowly into the playground towards their friends. Somehow they were washed, fed and even looked smart. She reached over to her handbag on the passenger seat and pulled out a rather soggy piece of toast. This was her breakfast which she chewed on, as she made her way through the endless traffic, the clock on the dashboard telling her that she was going to be late for work, again.

'Right,' she said out loud to herself as she drove, 'Time to plan my management meeting.'

Back at school Harrison walked into his classroom and looked at the whiteboard. Mr Lee had written the words, 'Hand In Homework' in large letters. Harrison quickly scanned his memory bank. He distinctly remembered doing it; in fact he had actually enjoyed doing it. Year 5 were studying the Ancient Greeks and Mr Lee had asked the class to find out as much as they could about the Olympic Games which the Greeks had invented. Harrison had sat at the kitchen table writing down information from the screen of his new tablet whilst Nigel snored rhythmically beneath him, fast asleep on his school bag. But where

was it? He couldn't remember what he did with his homework book when he had finished it. He turned round and walked nervously back to the cloakroom. Once there, he unzipped the main compartment on his bag which fell open to reveal … his homework book.

'Thanks mum,' he whispered to himself and marched happily back to class to hand it in.

At break time, Lydia walked along the corridor to the cloakroom with her friends. They were allowed to bring in a healthy snack and Lydia was hungry, but she couldn't remember putting anything in her bag. She unzipped the side compartment on her school bag, which fell open to reveal … a fruit and nut cluster bar – her favourite healthy snack.

'Thanks mum,' she whispered.

At lunchtime both Harrison and Lydia opened their lunch boxes. They had no idea what was in them but both were delighted by what they saw – their favourite sandwiches, ham and cucumber, accompanied by four baby tomatoes, a shiny red apple and a packet of raisins.

'Thanks mum,' they thought.

Later that afternoon in assembly Mrs Davies was telling everyone how some children grow up without parents and how we should all be grateful to the people who look after us. Her words made Harrison and Lydia think about their parents. Mum had seemed a bit stressed this morning and Dad was in a similar state yesterday, when he had been in charge of getting them to school on time. As they waited at the school gate for their mum to pick them up, Harrison and Lydia hatched a plan to show their appreciation to the people who looked after them. Tomorrow was Friday and on Fridays they went to their nan's after school whilst mum and dad did the weekly shop. Normally they would sit and watch television whilst nan cooked their tea, but this Friday Harrison was going to ask her if she could take them to Doris's shop on the way home to pick up a few breakfast items. They were going to treat mum and dad to breakfast in bed on Saturday morning.

Although this was a lovely idea, Harrison and Lydia had never actually cooked anything before and they were soon to discover that cooking bacon, eggs, beans and tomatoes wasn't anywhere near as easy as mum and dad made it look. The alarm clock had woken Harrison and Lydia at seven o'clock. Mum and dad always had a lie-in until nine on Saturdays and it was now eight thirty. For the last hour and a half the two children had managed to transform the tidy, clean kitchen into something resembling a bomb site in the war. They had used most of the pans in the entire house,

which were now stacked up in a tall, wobbly tower, hissing loudly in the sink. The grill had blackened pieces of bacon stuck to it and the tiles around the cooker were splattered with beans, egg yolk and pieces of tomato skin. Lydia looked at the two plates that her brother was holding. If someone had asked her to describe what she could see at that exact moment she would have only been able to come up with one word – BLACK. She wasn't even sure it actually was food any longer. It didn't resemble any food she had ever eaten and it certainly didn't look even

remotely like bacon, egg, beans and tomato. Even Nigel had gone back to his bed to sleep.

Harrison looked at his sister. 'It's the thought that counts Lydia,' he said. His face was extremely red and he looked as flustered as his mum had done on Thursday morning.

They tiptoed quietly up the stairs, Lydia gently pushed open the bedroom door and into their parents' bedroom they walked. The two adults had been fast asleep until Lydia had opened the curtains to let in the light, at which point Harrison thrust the tray of burnt food onto their bed.

'What on earth… ? spluttered dad, staring wide eyed at the smoking plate of blackness that had somehow made its way onto the bed. Mum sat up, speechless with her mouth open like a goldfish gulping air.

'It's just to say thanks,' Harrison explained.

'Yes, to show our appreciation,' added Lydia, remembering what Mrs Davies had said in assembly.

The two very tired adults looked at the plates, then at each other, and then burst out laughing.

It took the rest of the day to get the kitchen back to normal and some of the pans ended up in the dustbin but for once the parents didn't mind cleaning up the mess because even though they were tired after a very long week, their two children had shown them their appreciation.

'I think we'll eat out tonight,' mum said with a smile.

©Adrian Martin and Brilliant Publications

Fifty Fantastic Assembly Stories

Joseph Becomes More Like his Brother

• •

Sam and Joseph Mohammed were identical twins. They were nine years old and went to Mill Lane Junior School. To see how cool they looked, Sam just looked at Joseph and to see how cool Joseph looked, he simply looked at his brother Sam. They were identical you see. Same height, same weight, same hair colour, same shoe size, same eye colour, same finger length, same toe width, same freckle just behind their left ear, same oddly shaped birth mark on their right elbow – exactly the same sized birth mark, same colour, everything – amazing – everything exactly the same. They even liked the same things and disliked the same things. They both supported Liverpool Football Club, they both loved Burger King burgers but hated McDonald's (although they both liked the McFlurry ice creams). They preferred XBox to Playstation, neither liked fizzy drinks and both were allergic to sprouts (or at least that's what they told their mum). They both loved bananas but hated pears and both loved marshmallows and Jaffa cakes. They both had the same bad habits – occasionally, when watching their favourite TV programme in the same room on the same sofa, they would each take their left sock off, without really thinking about it and without looking, and slowly, oh so very slowly, they would reach down and pick the dry bit of skin on their middle toe. And then, at exactly the same moment again, whilst staring at the television, not even aware of what they were doing, they would get the bit of dry skin that they had picked from their middle toe (now slightly thinner than before), and FLICK that little piece of dried skin over their shoulders, behind the sofa. There was quite a pile of dried skin there now – mum didn't vacuum behind the sofa until the week before Christmas when they moved the furniture around to fit the Christmas tree in and it was only the middle of May – five months of dried skin behind the sofa – not a pretty sight (or smell, for that matter). When eating jaffa cakes they would lick the chocolate until it had all gone, then carefully remove the orange bit and suck it until mum said, 'Stop being so disgusting!'

With marshmallows they'd do something similar, carefully biting the chocolate off and then sucking the fluffy white marshmallow into their mouths in one go. The marshmallow was big – it wasn't designed to be eaten like this. It was supposed to be nibbled carefully by little grey haired grandmas sipping tea from china cups and gossiping with other little grey haired grandmas. So when Sam and Joseph had the whole thing in their mouths, it would make their cheeks puff out as if they were about to burst. And sometimes that's exactly what would happen. Because being twins, they would eat at the same time, and being twins, they would finish biting the chocolate off at the same time, and of course, being twins, they would each suck the fluffy white marshmallow into their mouths – at the same time. And of course, being twins, they would sit opposite each other, noses almost touching, staring at each other, not blinking, having a staring competition, with their cheeks puffing out, not daring to bite into the gooey, marshmallow, filling their cheeks, because whoever bit into the marshmallow first would lose. And losing that was serious. Very serious. So they'd keep staring

• •

Fifty Fantastic Assembly Stories

Becomes More Like his Brother

at each other, and gradually, the marshmallow would become gooier and gooier, filling their mouths with goo, and saliva, filling the gaps in their teeth, tickling the backs of their throats. And they would get redder and redder. And eventually, at the same time, they would burst out laughing, and bits of gooey marshmallow would shoot out, splattering the other's face with the gooey mess. And then mum would come rushing in from the kitchen wondering what all the noise was about and the twins would wipe the sticky mess from their faces, with the same sleeve of their school jumpers. And mum would just look at them both, staring in disbelief, and then walk back to the kitchen, shaking her head and muttering things like 'Why me?'

So you've got the idea – Sam and Joseph were identical twins. But the strange thing was that even though they looked exactly the same and were the same in so many ways, nobody ever had any trouble identifying one from the other. This was because they were different in one very obvious way. Sam appreciated everything that everyone did for him. He knew how fortunate he was to have the friends he had, to go to a great school and to have such kind parents who looked after him. He knew that not all children were as lucky as he was and because he knew that, he made sure that he showed his appreciation whenever he got the chance. When anyone gave him anything – anything at all – something as valuable as the computer he got for his birthday, or something as simple as the pencil Mr Lee gave him when he had forgotten his own, he would smile and say, 'Thank you'. Whenever anyone did something for him – anything at all – something amazing like taking him on holiday to France or something simple like picking up his reading book when it had fallen on the floor, Sam would smile and say, 'Thank you.'

Sam would show his appreciation in other ways too. Whenever anyone needed any help he was always ready to give it. At home, when mum or dad were getting the tea ready, Sam would set the table without being asked. It wasn't difficult and it didn't take him long, but it made his mum and dad's life a little bit easier and they were always grateful that he did it. After they had eaten, he would take the dirty plates and put them in the dishwasher, without anyone asking him to. He kept his bedroom tidy because he knew how much it annoyed his parents when toys, books and clothes were left on the floor and he thought it was the least he could do. After all, it wasn't difficult to pick things up and put them in their correct place. At school, he was always there to help anyone who needed it. When they were doing art he would ask Mr Lee if he needed any help at lunchtime to get things ready. At the end of the lesson he would walk round the class picking things up off the floor and collecting things in, without being asked. At lunchtime he would always say 'Thank you' to the cooks for making his lunch and he would always tell them how tasty it was when he'd finished. If any of the younger children ever knocked their drink over on the table, he would get straight up, go to the kitchen and ask Mrs Parry, the cook, for a cloth to wipe it up. If anyone fell over on the playground he would go straight over to see if they were all right. At Mr Barnes's lunchtime football practice, Sam would always be the one collecting in the cones at the end and making sure all the equipment was taken back to the PE store. The word Sam used the most was definitely 'Thank you,' but there were plenty of other phrases he used every day of his life – phrases such as, 'I'll help', 'Let me do that', 'Do you want a hand with that?', 'Can I help you give those out?', 'I'll pick those up for you.' There was no doubt in anyone's mind that Sam appreciated everything he had and everything anyone did for him. It was no surprise then, that Sam was extremely popular. He received lots of awards at school and was the first to be picked whenever Mr Lee asked the children to work in groups. At Parents' Evenings his mum and dad would always come

©Adrian Martin and Brilliant Publications
Fifty Fantastic Assembly Stories

Joseph Becomes More Like his Brother

out of the classroom after their meeting and beam a big smile at him.

Unfortunately, their beaming smiles would immediately turn into scowls when they looked at Joseph. Joseph was one of those children who seemed to think that his parents, teachers and other children were there to help him and to make his life as easy as possible. He simply didn't seem to appreciate anything he had. 'Thank you' was probably the word he used least. Instead, when people gave him something – anything at all – something as valuable as a computer for his birthday, or something as simple as the pencil Mr Lee gave him when he couldn't find his own (even though it was on the floor under his chair), he would say … nothing. Nothing at all. People would wait for him to say something and often they would remind him to say it, but he either forgot, or just didn't really care that much. When mum and dad were getting tea ready at home, Joseph would be in his room, his very untidy room, with toys, books and clothes all over the floor, playing on his computer or lying on his bed staring up at the ceiling. He knew that Sam would set the table so he couldn't see the point in offering. When he had finished eating he would wander off to watch the television or go back up to his room. He knew Sam would help to stack the dishwasher so there really was no point in him offering. Whenever anyone needed help at school, Joseph tended to slide down on his chair, until there was just a little head sticking up above the desk and then he'd suddenly become very interested in the book that he was supposed to be reading before anyone asked for help. At lunchtime he never thanked the cooks for his meal. He couldn't work out why he should as it was their job after all. At the end of Mr Barnes's lunchtime football practice he would run off the pitch and go straight in to school to get changed so that he could spend the last few minutes of lunchtime playing. It never occurred to him that Mr Barnes may have needed any help.

And just as it was no surprise that Sam was extremely popular, neither was it surprising that Joseph was unpopular. Whenever Mr Lee asked the children to work in groups, Joseph was always the one left on his own. And he could never really understand why. Sam knew of course, but he wasn't the kind of person to be unkind to his brother and he thought that eventually, Joseph would change. And one day, just after another of their 'marshmallow sucking' competitions, Joseph looked Sam in the eye and said, 'How come everyone seems to like you more than me?'

Sam said nothing to begin with – he was still wiping the marshmallow goo from his face. But eventually he realised Joseph was serious and it was time to be honest with him. He looked his twin brother in the eye, and said, very slowly, 'You …never … say … "Thank you".'

And from that moment Joseph began to change. That night he set the table for tea. To his surprise, it took hardly any time at all and when his mum said, 'Thanks Joseph,' he felt better than he had done for some time.

Appreciation
Terry Makes Joseph Realise How Lucky He Is

● ●

This story is best read after 'Joseph Becomes More Like His Brother' (pages 101–103) as it includes the same characters.

There was one particular occasion that changed the way Joseph behaved, forever. Sometimes people have those moments – they go through life happily doing the same things, day after day, behaving in the same way, day after day, wondering why nothing good ever seems to happen to them. And then, suddenly something happens to make them change and as if some magic dust has been sprinkled over their cute little heads, good things start to happen to them.

Something like this happened to Joseph.

You may remember that Sam, Joseph's twin brother, was the one who always offered to help people when they needed help. He was the one who always said 'Thank you' to show his appreciation when someone did something for him – anything at all:

•   The time when his mum handed Sam his new tablet for his birthday; 'Ah thanks Mum – you're the BEST! This is the best present I've ever had.' Joseph, on the other-hand, just ripped the wrapping paper off, threw it over the back of the sofa with the dried skin from his foot and started playing, completely ignoring his Mum, who just shrugged.

•   The time when Barney, one of Sam's friends, picked up his jumper from the playground bench after Sam had forgotten to pick it up; 'Thanks Barn – what would I do without friends like you?' However, people had stopped bothering to pick Joseph's jumper up for him. Why? Because he never said 'Thank you.' That's why.

•   Every Friday evening when dad made the boys' favourite meal – sweet and sour pork in a light crispy batter with fluffy white rice; every Friday Sam would say, 'Dad, this is amazing – I LOVE this meal so much – you are an unbelievable cook, better than Jamie Oliver!' Joseph, meanwhile, was unable to say 'Thank you' because he had stuffed so much crispy pork and fluffy rice into his mouth that his cheeks were bulging outwards horizontally like a particularly hungry and greedy squirrel.

There are hundreds, maybe thousands of examples of times when Sam and Joseph were given things or people did things for them and hundreds, maybe even thousands of times when Sam said 'Thank you' and Joseph said, or did, nothing.

And you may remember that Joseph could never understand why noone ever wanted to be his partner when Mr Lee told the children to work in pairs, whereas everyone liked Sam, his twin brother, who looked exactly like him.

Well, one day, one day in late September, one Monday in late September, one fairly normal Monday in late September in fact, something happened to change the way Joseph behaved for the rest of his life.

It was the end of the day, the end of Monday. The children in 5L had just returned to class from assembly and were getting their things ready to go home. Sam had noticed that Mr Lee, who seemed a little more stressed than usual, had knocked a pile of letters off his desk. Sam being Sam, had immediately nipped across the classroom to help him pick them up. Joseph

● ●

©Adrian Martin and Brilliant Publications

Fifty Fantastic Assembly Stories

was standing on one of the letters, completely unaware that Sam was kneeling on the floor beneath him waiting for him to lift his shoe.

'Oh thanks Sam – you're ever so helpful,' said Mr Lee, when Sam had finally forced his brother's shoe off the floor and returned the letter to his teacher.

'Now everyone there is an important letter to go home tonight – don't forget to take one from the table as you leave.'

Sam knew Joseph wasn't listening and knew that he would have to take a letter for his brother. Joseph, of course, wasn't listening. He was facing the wrong way, staring out of the window, with his left index finger lodged firmly in his ear. He appeared to be trying to find something in there. His desk was a mess; a mixture of clothes, pens, rubbers and unfinished work.

'How can he be my brother?' Sam thought. 'He's so embarrassing.'

But as if someone had pointed a remote control at him, Joseph's ears suddenly pricked up. Mr Lee had said something that he found interesting. In fact Mr Lee had said something that Joseph found very interesting. He had said the word 'chocolate.'

Teachers and other adults, said many words and most of them didn't register in Joseph's brain, but there were a few that got his attention. 'Football' was one. He liked football. 'Marshmallow' was another. He really liked marshmallows. 'Jelly', that was another one – he loved jelly, especially with runny cream. And finally 'chocolate'. Yes. Chocolate. And on the few occasions that adults said any one of these words, Joseph would listen. And this was one of those occasions. And suddenly Joseph was all ears. He even removed his finger from one of them so that if Mr Lee mentioned the word 'chocolate' again, he would be ready. And thankfully, Mr Lee did exactly that:

'So everyone, as you know,' Mr Lee announced. 'It's Tom's birthday today. He's reached the grand old age of ten and to celebrate this momentous occasion he's brought in some chocolate bars to share with you all!'

There it was again. 'Chocolate'. And this time it had been followed by the word 'bars.' Bars, with the letter 's' at the end, which meant that there was more than one. Mr Lee was speaking again and the children were lining up to go home.

'There's enough for everyone so you don't need to push. Make sure you say 'Thank you' and wish Tom a Happy Birthday as you leave.'

Joseph had been so busy daydreaming in his own little world that he had ended up at the very back of the line behind Terry Johnson. Terry had only been at the school for a week but already Joseph had noticed he seemed to have more friends than him. Joseph hadn't bothered to speak to him yet, but as he stood behind him he noticed that Terry's shirt collar was grubby and his jumper was ripped at the cuffs. There was also a hole on the shoulder where the material had frayed. Joseph's eyes scanned down to Terry's trousers which he noticed were too short for him – they didn't even cover his socks which appeared to be slightly different colours. His shoes were scuffed and looked uncomfortably tight, the backs of his ankles almost bursting out of them. Joseph thought back to the moment Mr Lee had introduced Terry to the class. Even on his first day he had looked like this. Joseph remembered overhearing his brother Sam talking to Terry. Terry had told Sam that his dad had moved away and that his mum didn't have a job. It began to dawn on Joseph that Terry's family did not have much money. That's why Terry's clothes were old and didn't fit him properly. But despite his scruffy clothes, Terry still had more friends than Joseph.

Slowly but surely the line of children moved forwards, each child thanking Tom and wishing him a happy birthday as they took a chocolate bar from the bag. Joseph and Terry were near the door now. Most of the children had got their chocolate bar and were on their way up the corridor and out of school, chatting and munching away. Lauren Booth was in front of Terry:

'Thanks Tom and Happy Birthday!' she said enthusiastically and skipped out of the classroom to join her friends.

Now it was Terry's turn. But something was wrong. He was standing still, looking at Tom with an awkward expression on his face.

'There's only one left Tom,' he said.

'I don't believe it,' said Tom. 'Mum said there would be enough for one each. 28 chocolate bars. 28 children in the class.'

'But there are 29 children Tom, now that Terry has joined us,' Mr Lee explained. 'Your mum must have used last year's class numbers. Don't worry I'm sure we can sort it out.'

But before he could say anymore, Terry turned to face Joseph and placed the chocolate bar calmly in his hand. 'It's yours Joseph. I've got one in my bag anyway. It's fine. Honestly.'

Joseph looked at Terry in disbelief. He knew Terry didn't have a chocolate bar in his bag because he never had anything to eat at break times or on the way home. He could not believe that Terry was prepared to give up the chocolate bar. It was one of the most generous acts Joseph had ever

witnessed. And it was a generous act which had an amazing effect on Joseph; without thinking he said a word that he hardly ever said. He just couldn't help himself. He even looked surprised when he heard it come out of his mouth. And he was surprised about how it made him feel.

'Thanks Terry,' Joseph said.

He felt good. But it wasn't anything to do with having the chocolate bar. This was a different kind of good. And before he could do anything more he'd said something else which made him feel even better.

'Tell you what Terry, let's have half each,' he said and broke the bar into two equal pieces.

Terry smiled, took his half of the bar and said, 'Thanks Joseph' in return. The two boys then walked home together, chatting away, sharing the chocolate bar. And it was the best half a chocolate bar Joseph had ever had; in fact it was much better than any whole chocolate bar he had ever had.

And that was the moment that changed Joseph's life forever. Terry had changed his life. Terry, who had very little, was prepared to give up something he was given and that made Joseph realise how lucky he was. From then on, he showed his appreciation, by saying two words more than any other:

THANK YOU.

Colin Thinks Life's So Unfair

● ●

Colin had developed a bit of a reputation at his school for being one of those children who didn't really try very hard at anything he did. He wasn't naughty and never got himself into any real trouble, it was just that he never did anything really well. He was one of those children who got up in the morning, did what he needed to do during the day and then went to bed at night and that was about it. Everyone knew it – his friends knew it, his teachers knew it, and his parents knew it. The only person who didn't seem to know it was … Colin.

He was ten years old and had been at his Junior School for over two years now and if he was asked what he thought about school he'd probably say, 'It's okay.' At Mill Lane Juniors the teachers believed in rewarding children for their effort and they would find themselves frustrated by Colin because he never seemed to show any determination to do his best. Each week on Friday all the children and staff would gather in assembly and Mrs Davies would give out lots of awards to children who had tried really hard on something that week; children were rewarded for a range of things; last week for example Barney received a certificate for working particularly hard on his drawing of Queen Victoria whereas Alicia Wright in Year 3 had been rewarded for being determined to improve her forward rolls in PE. For over two years Colin had sat in Friday's assembly, listening to Mrs Davies reading out the awards from her special book. For over two years he had sat and watched children next to him, in front of him and behind him getting to their feet and making their way to the front of the hall, where they would stand proudly holding their certificate, waiting for the rest of the children to give them a deserved round of applause. But not once had Colin's name been read out. Not once had he stood up and made his way to the front of the hall, not once had he been given a certificate and

not once had he received a round of applause from the rest of the children. Although his teachers and his friends and his parents all knew why, Colin just didn't understand it. In fact, there were many things that happened at school that Colin simply didn't understand:

His best friend Ian Dobson, or Dobbo, as he was known, always seemed to get certificates – for his hard work, for always completing his homework on time, for his lovely manners, for his neat handwriting, for his kindness to others, for his determination to improve at maths, his weakest subject, and for many other things that Colin thought he should have been rewarded for. In Colin's mind, Dobbo was lucky, and Colin was unlucky. Life, in Colin's mind, just wasn't fair.

It will come as no surprise then, that Dobbo loved Friday's celebration assembly whereas Colin hated it.

Colin couldn't understand why he was never given any responsibility by his teachers. Dobbo, on the other hand, was always being asked to take messages to other teachers or to hand the books out or to take things to the office. No one ever asked Colin to do things like this.

Neither could Colin understand why he was never picked to represent the school in any of the teams. Dobbo was in the football team, the basketball team, the choir, the drama group, the cricket team, the art club and was one of the school's head gardeners.

At playtime, when children were picking teams for a game, Colin was never picked first, or even second or third for that matter and, again, he simply couldn't understand why. When a game needed a captain it was always Dobbo who was picked and never Colin. When a game needed

● ●

Fifty Fantastic Assembly Stories

someone to go 'on', Dobbo always volunteered whereas Colin didn't like the sound of that.

And when Mr Lee asked the children to get into groups for an activity Colin would often be left on his own and then grabbed at the last minute; Dobbo was always the one everyone would rush over to – everyone wanted to work with him. Colin also noticed how Dobbo's group always seemed to finish their task really well, whereas the children in Colin's group always ended up arguing and never finished what they were supposed to do.

Colin never understood the point of homework.

'I work hard enough at school. Why do I need to do more at home when I could be doing more interesting things like eating crisps, or watching telly, or playing on my computer, or sleeping, or tormenting Booboo (his cat)?' he thought.

Dobbo, on the other hand, quite liked his homework. He knew that he could spend the time he needed on it, without his teachers telling him how much time he had left, and without his friend Colin constantly asking him for a spare pencil, or a rubber to rub out his mistakes. Dobbo enjoyed handing his homework in before anyone else, knowing that for the rest of the week he could spend time watching telly, or playing on his computer, or playing with his pet cat Freddie.

Colin could never understand why he needed to be 'organised' as his teachers and parents were always telling him. What did they know? If he needed a pencil he could just ask his best friend Dobbo – he always had a spare one. If he made a mistake he could always borrow Dobbo's rubber – Dobbo didn't mind.

Dobbo loved being organised. He particularly loved going back to school in January, when he had a brand new pencil case with a set of brand new pencils, sharp and shining, and a set of brand new rubbers, not yet borrowed by Colin. His

desk was always spotless so that he knew where everything was. There were more things under Colin's desk than on it. No wonder he never knew where anything was.

And now it was the first Friday in January at the beginning of the Spring term (even though it was freezing cold outside) and time for the first celebration assembly of the year. Colin was sitting there waiting for his name to be called out, finally, for a certificate. Next to him, sat Dobbo. As Colin sat there he vaguely remembered the assembly earlier on in the week when Mrs Davies had talked about how it was a new year and a new year was always a good time to be determined to change the things you don't do so well and a great time of the year to be determined to try even harder than you have before. And he vaguely remembered thinking, 'What's the point in changing when you do everything well already?'

He remembered glancing over at his best friend Dobbo as Mrs Davies was speaking. He appeared to be listening to every word the headteacher said and seemed to be concentrating really hard because he was nodding as she spoke as if he agreed with her completely.

As he sat there, in the first Friday celebration assembly of the year, Colin thought about the first week of the Spring Term. Dobbo had seemed even more enthusiastic in lessons. He constantly had his hand up when the teacher asked a question and when Colin had asked him for a spare pencil he had looked at him with disgust, as if he had done something terribly wrong. Colin, on the other hand, had had the same sort of week as he always had, carrying on as normal and as usual, people had seemed quite grumpy with him.

And as he sat there, in the first Friday celebration assembly of the year, Mrs Davies began reading out the names of the children who were to receive

©Adrian Martin and Brilliant Publications
Fifty Fantastic Assembly Stories

the first certificates of the year. And to his dismay, to his utter disbelief, when it came to the turn of the children in Year 5, Colin could not believe his ears when yet again his name was not called out. And to his dismay, to his utter disbelief, Colin could not believe his ears when yet again Dobbo's name was called out and all the children and staff clapped as he received his certificate, a beaming smile across his face.

Dobbo sat back down next to Colin, still grinning.

'I never get a certificate,' muttered Colin. 'Why do you always get them? It's not fair.'

Dobbo took a deep breath.

He decided it was time to tell Colin the truth once and for all; 'It is fair Colin. You never change,' he whispered. 'You never try hard enough. If you got a certificate it would be unfair.'

And with that, he stood up again, because his name had been called out again, because he had been chosen to represent the school at a really important event that Colin had already forgotten the name of.

Colin just sat there. And for the first time ever, he realised that maybe, just maybe, it was time for him to be a little bit more determined to do things better.

Determination

Neil Shows Incredible Determination
● ●

Neil Hampson loved to run. He loved running so much that he ran everywhere. Absolutely everywhere. In the mornings when his dad told him it was time to get up he would roll out of bed and run across his bedroom floor to the door at the other side of the room. After putting on his dressing gown he would run out of his room, across the landing and down the stairs, missing out every other step as he went. Once downstairs, he would run across the hallway and into the kitchen, skidding to a stop at the kitchen table, where he would sit down and grab a piece of toast from the plate in the centre. Neil only ever had one thing on his toast, apart from butter and that was honey, but not solid honey, oh no. There was only one kind of honey Neil had on his toast and that was runny honey. He liked runny honey because, well, it was runny. And anything that was runny was good enough for him (apart from his brother's nose that is. That was often very runny and Neil definitely did not like that).

After eating his breakfast, Neil would slide back his chair and run back upstairs to get dressed for school. He always wore his trainers to get to school and changed into his school shoes on the playground.

School was a mile's walk from Neil's house, or in his case, a mile's run. He was in Year 5 now and after a great deal of discussion, mum and dad had said that Neil could go to school on his own. On the Sunday before the new school year began he and his dad had planned a route from home which meant that Neil only had to cross one road and that was right outside school, where Sid the lollipop man would be able to help him across safely.

So every morning since the beginning of September, Neil stood at the front door with his trainers on, his rucksack strapped tightly on his

back and a stopwatch in his right hand, waiting for his dad to tell him he could go. His first attempt, early in September, took him 9 minutes and 52 seconds but he did have to stop a couple of times to make sure he was going the right way. Since then, he had knocked over 2 minutes off this time, his best being 7 minutes and 12 seconds. His dad had done some research on the internet and reckoned that this time put Neil in the top 5 percent of runners for his age, in the entire country. 'And I bet they didn't do it with their school uniform on and a rucksack on their backs with their books and school shoes in,' he told Neil, proudly.

Running was Neil's life and if there was any opportunity to run anywhere, he would.

'You couldn't run to the paper shop and get me a magazine Neil?' his mum would ask on a Saturday afternoon.

A normal nine year old boy would probably need some persuasion to do something like this, but not Neil. Within seconds of hearing the question he had grabbed a five pound note from her purse and was gone, leaving the front door wide open as he sprinted away from the house towards the shop at the end of the road.

'I don't suppose anyone would mind taking one of the litter pickers out at break time to tidy up the playground?' Mr Lee asked 5L after a particularly windy spell at school.

Neil's hand shot up and at break time the children and teachers watched, speechless, as he sped round the playground, litter picker in one hand, bin bag in the other, sprinting from one item of litter to another. Within minutes the playground was litter free and Neil had enjoyed every second.

● ● Neil Shows Incredible Determination ●

©Adrian Martin and Brilliant Publications

There were plenty of activities for the children to do after school – football, netball, drama, basketball, science, orchestra and a whole host of other activities. But to Neil's bitter disappointment, there were no activities which focused entirely on running. At least there weren't until Mr Lee made an announcement to the class, causing Neil to become very excited indeed:

'I've got an exciting announcement to make,' Mr Lee said. 'This morning I received a letter inviting me to enter a team of children into a triathlon event. I can take eight children who must be able to swim, cycle and run. If you're interested stay behind after maths.'

Neil had heard Mr Lee say his favourite word, 'run' and immediately went into a trance. 'At last,' he thought. 'A running event at school. I'm in.'

He wasn't a great swimmer but could get by and his cycling was okay but that didn't matter. There was running involved and everyone knew that Neil was the best runner in the school by a long, long way.

Exactly eight children stayed behind to find out more about the triathlon.

'Great,' said Mr Lee. 'You're my team then. It's next Thursday afternoon. Take a letter each so that your parents know when it is and bring me back your permission slips as soon as possible please.'

Neil's permission slip was signed and in Mr Lee's hand before school had even begun the next day. In the days that followed, all he could think about was his opportunity to test himself against children from other schools in a proper running race. Worryingly though, he had been so wrapped up in the running part of the event that he hadn't really thought about the swimming and cycling. And now he was stood at the side of the pool with the rest of his team, waiting for

the start. He was the weakest swimmer so would be the last to go. The pool had been divided into lanes and Neil's team were in Lane 3. Gradually, as those in front of him began their races, he got closer and closer to the water. He looked to his left; unlike him, the boys in Lanes 4, 5 and 6 were wearing swimming caps and goggles. They were circling their arms around their heads in a way which made them look serious. He looked to his right. The boys in Lanes 1 and 2 were doing the same exercises and were also wearing swimming caps and goggles. Neil began to feel nervous.

Mr Lee was standing behind Neil and sensed his nervousness. 'Don't worry Neil,' he said. 'Just do your best but leave yourself some energy to cycle and run.'

Neil looked over to the seating area at the side of the pool. His mum and dad were sat watching. They seemed nervous too, but gave Neil the 'thumbs up' sign when he looked at them.

'On your marks …' the official said in a loud, clear voice.

The other boys took a step forward so that their toes gripped the edge of the pool. Neil followed.

'Get set …' the official raised his right hand in the air, his finger on the trigger of the starting pistol.

Neil watched as the other boys assumed a crouching position with their arms held straight out in front of them. Again, he did the same but unlike them he wasn't used to standing in this position and began to wobble. He could feel himself losing his balance and just as he was about to fall, the official pulled the trigger and a loud bang started the race. While the other boys dived powerfully into the water, Neil fell in with a splash, making a disastrous start to the race. By the time he had recovered himself and begun to swim, the rest of the competitors were half way

for him. All the other competitors and the rest of his team were well on their way. Neil grabbed the bike, pushed his damp feet into the trainers and forced the helmet onto his head. He could see the others in the distance and was determined not to let them get too far ahead. He knew that if he was close enough at the running stage he would be in with a chance of catching some of them up.

'It's two laps!' shouted Mr Lee, as Neil cycled away pedalling furiously. Each lap was half a mile, so a mi

down the pool. It had been a while since he had done the crawl properly and he had forgotten how tiring it was. It was a two length race and as he reached the wall at the end of his first length he began to worry that he might not be able to complete the second. Some of the boys were beginning to climb out at the other end now and were running from the pool to the cycling area. He pushed off from the wall to begin his second length but instead of breathing in air he took a gulp of water causing him to cough and splutter. In a moment of panic he attempted to put his feet down but was out of his depth and his head disappeared beneath the water. Before he knew what was happening the lifeguard had hooked a long pole under Neil's arm and dragged him to the side. Once there Neil was able to regain his breath and despite the lifeguard encouraging him to get out, he swam back to his lane and made it to the end of the pool. The spectators and his mum and dad in particular, clapped and cheered enthusiastically. Mr Lee greeted Neil as he clambered from the pool.

'Well done Neil – that took real courage,' he said.

'Where do I go now?' Neil asked, determined to get to the run.

Mr Lee directed him to the field where a bike, a pair of trainers and a cycle helmet were waiting

Neil couldn't be certain but it seemed like he was closing the gap on the other riders. With half a lap to go Neil could see some of them getting off their bikes and beginning the mile long run. The fastest he had run a mile so far was 7 minutes and 12 seconds but that was with his uniform and bag. As he approached the end of his second lap and the crowd of parents cheered him on, he wondered how much energy he had left after his difficult swim and a mile of cycling at full speed.

As he jumped from his bike his legs felt weak, causing him to wobble for the second time that day.

'Stand still for a moment and take your helmet off Neil,' Mr Lee said, calmly. 'You've made up lots of ground on them all – you may even catch some on the run,' he continued.

©Adrian Martin and Brilliant Publications

Fifty Fantastic Assembly Stories

After a few gulps of air Neil's legs felt stronger. The crowd of parents were just a few metres away. 'Ready Neil?'

It was his dad and he was holding the stopwatch in his hand.

'Go!' he shouted, and Neil was off.

The crowd watched, astonished, as the boy who had struggled so much in the pool sprinted towards the rest of the runners. Within a minute he had caught up with the slower runners and was now making his way towards the rest. By the end of the first lap he was in fourth position and was closing fast on the three boys ahead of him.

'3 minutes 40 seconds!' Neil's dad shouted.

His muscles were hurting now but he kicked on and increased his speed even more. He was on his last lap now and was determined to give it his all. The boy in third place was definitely slowing

down and before long Neil had caught him. Only two to go but time was running out. The boys in first and second place were still 20 metres ahead of him and only had about 200 metres left to run.

The boy in second place stumbled a little and with one final push Neil accelerated towards him. With just 100 metres left Neil secured second position and focused his attention on the tall, dark haired boy who was breathing heavily and nervously looking over his shoulder.

With the finish line just metres away the two boys were level but the dark haired boy lunged forward, bursting through the finishing tape. They fell to the ground exhausted. Neil had finished second but had provided everyone who was watching with a spectacular display of determination.

Neil lay on his back looking up at the sky, taking in deep breaths of air. The two smiling faces of Mr Lee and his dad blocked his view.

'Unbelievable,' his dad panted. '7 minutes and 11 seconds – your best yet!'

'Not bad,' said Mr Lee. 'Not bad at all. But you definitely need to work on your swimming!'

And with that, Neil got to his feet to cheer the rest of his team to the finish line.

Determination
Robert Finally Speaks Out

●●●

It was the first day back after Christmas and Mr Lee, 5L's teacher, was speaking to his class for the first time in the new year.

'Good morning and a Happy New Year to you all.'

'Happy New Year,' the class mumbled back.

'Goodness me,' replied Mr Lee. 'Is that the best you can do? It sounds like you've all been eating too many chocolates and playing on those computers for too long over Christmas. Let's try that again shall we? Good morning and a Happy New Year to you all.'

The class responded, louder, and more enthusiastically than before. They loved their teacher and didn't like seeing him upset.

'Well that's a lot better,' he said. 'Now let's wake up our brains with our first discussion of the new year.'

It was true – they had eaten too much chocolate, and they had spent too long in front of their computer screens. Sam and Joseph, the twins, had each got tablets for Christmas and from Christmas Day morning until the last day of the holiday, they had played, in silence, on their games. Mrs Mohammed, their mum, said they were the best presents she had ever had as well and couldn't thank Santa enough – she had had two whole weeks of peace and quiet. But, although the games kept the two boys quiet, they hadn't had a conversation for a fortnight, and they were a bit shocked when Mr Lee asked them a question. He was right – their brains certainly did need waking up.

Lauren Booth simply loved chocolate – she couldn't get enough of it. The first time she was given dinner money by her mum when she was six she spent it on two Galaxy bars, a Crunchy and a Twix at the shop on the way to school and had eaten them all before the bell went at nine o'clock. Father Christmas knew that she loved chocolate too – every present she got she could eat – Selection boxes, boxes of chocolates, huge chocolate bars, chocolate cookies, chocolate cakes, bags of chocolates, chocolate coins, and her favourite present of all, a mobile phone made out of … chocolate. It took her three minutes to eat it, and that included two minutes pretending to phone her dad at the other side of the room. From Christmas Day morning until the last day of the holiday, she had eaten chocolate. And now she was beginning to feel like she'd had just a little too much. Mr Lee was right – her brain did need waking up.

Lauren looked round the class at the faces of the other children – Sam and Joseph looked confused, as if they didn't know where they were. She wondered what they had been doing for the two weeks. 'Probably playing on their tablets,' she thought. Erin and Emily, her best friends, looked tired – they had been watching television and eating too much, just like her.

Despite the fun they had had over Christmas, the children in 5L were actually glad to be back at school with their friends, and getting their brains going again.

'So,' continued Mr Lee; 'Let's go round the class and find out what our New Year's resolutions are. I'll begin; I'm going to try to do more exercise. All that chocolate this Christmas has done nothing for my figure!'

The class laughed. Lauren nodded in agreement. And around the class they went, finding out what everyone's New Year's resolutions were. Sam and Joseph were both determined 'to spend a bit less time in front of the telly,' Erin and Emily were aiming 'to do a bit more exercise.' Lauren, of course, was determined 'to eat less chocolate,' and Barney

●●●

©Adrian Martin and Brilliant Publications

Fifty Fantastic Assembly Stories

Smith was, 'determined to get into the school football team.' Mr Lee continued around the class, who all listened to each other's resolutions, some funny, some serious until eventually it was Robert Jackson's turn. Robert hated speaking in front of the class. He was fine with his best friend Neil and some of his other close friends, but whenever he was asked a question in class, he froze. It was almost as if someone had super-glued his lips together. His tongue always felt really heavy, like it was made of lead! He could sense the eyes of his classmates staring at him, his ears would tingle and go red, and the longer his teacher would wait for his answer, the redder his ears would get. There was nothing he could do to stop them getting redder and redder. The class would fall silent and Robert would hear the ticking of the clock on the wall, ticking, agonisingly slowly. In his head the clock ticked louder and louder and he would completely forget the question he was asked, and that was that. This first happened at the Infant School – he would never forget what happened. As his ears got redder and redder, he told the teacher, Miss Patel, that he had forgotten the question, and everyone laughed, even Miss Patel, and ever since then, he hated answering questions in class. He never put his hand up and he never answered questions. When the class had a discussion, he sat listening. He hadn't answered a question in front of a class of children for five years.

Mr Lee was very aware of this but it didn't stop him asking Robert questions. He knew that one day Robert would answer and so he would give him five seconds and then move on to someone else. The other children no longer stared at Robert. They understood that speaking out just wasn't for him.

Robert knew a question was coming. He had sat listening to all the other children telling the class what they were going to do less of, or more of, and so he had plenty of time to prepare.

'Now Robert – what will your new year's resolution be?' asked Mr Lee.

Robert knew exactly what he wanted to say. He had been preparing the words in his head for the last half hour. But as soon as Mr Lee said his name and looked him in the eye, his lips stuck together, his tongue went heavy, his ears began to tingle and go red and the ticking of the clock grew louder and louder.

'It can be anything Robert – anything at all,' Mr Lee said, encouragingly. 'But it must be something that you have to be really determined to do.'

And from somewhere deep within himself, Robert somehow managed to shut out the sound of the clock and to unglue his lips. And from his mouth shot an answer which amazed everyone, including himself.

'I'm determined to answer more questions in class Mr Lee!' he yelled.

The class were so amazed to hear him say this that they clapped.

'Well that's one question you've answered already Robert. Well done, and good luck with your resolution,' beamed Mr Lee.

Later on that day, in assembly, Mrs Davies was talking about New Year's resolutions.

'I wonder if anyone would like to share their new year's resolution with us all?' she asked. Most of the younger children at the front put their hands up, but Mrs Davies looked towards the back of the hall, where the older ones sat. Before he knew what he was doing, Robert's hand had shot up into the air – he hadn't asked it to, it just, well, did. He looked at it, as if it didn't belong to him. Neil, and the rest of 5L, including Mr Lee, looked at him too. But worst of all, Mrs Davies was looking at him. She also knew about Robert's reluctance to speak in front of other people. She had heard the teachers talk about it in the staffroom and she had certainly never seen

Robert put up his hand in assembly before. There were nearly 300 children sitting there after all. She wasn't sure what to do. If she asked him and he couldn't answer it would be terrible. He may never speak again!

'Oh no,' thought Neil. 'She's going to ask him. I just know she is. And he won't be able to answer, and his ears will go red, and it'll be awful – he'll never answer another question again.'

Mrs Davies looked at Mr Lee and he gave her a nod. He just had a feeling that this could be a big moment for Robert.

'Yes Robert?' said Mrs Davies, 'Tell us what you are determined to do this year.'

And before his lips could glue themselves together, before his tongue could turn to rubber, before his ears could begin to tingle and go red and before the giant clock on the hall wall began to tick in his ears, he said it.

'I'm determined to answer more questions in class,'

Robert said.

Neil gasped – the whole of 5L, including Mr Lee, gasped.

'Well you've made a terrific start Robert. Well done,' replied Mrs Davies. 'That was very brave of you.'

Robert felt fantastic. Rather than his ears tingling, he had a funny tingle down his spine. He had conquered his fear at last – he'd not only spoken in front of his class, but in front of the whole school.

And do you know what happened next? One week later, Robert's name was called out again in assembly. This time it was to receive the weekly award for achieving something really special. Mrs Davies read out the award:

'This week's achievement award goes to Robert Jackson, for being determined to answer more questions in class. Congratulations Robert – you're well on your way to achieving your new year's resolution.'

©Adrian Martin and Brilliant Publications

Fifty Fantastic Assembly Stories

George Walsh Learns to Ride a Bike

George Walsh sat, wobbling, on the living room carpet of Number 42, Bolton Avenue. He was eleven months old and, to the amusement and slight concern of his parents, was still unable to crawl forwards.

'He's just a slow developer,' the doctor had told Barbara, George's mum. 'You just need to be patient.'

At this moment Barbara was losing her patience as her son sat there unsteadily, giggling to himself.

'Sam next door was crawling forwards when he was five months old. He's nearly walking now,' she thought.

'George!' she called, snapping her fingers at him to get his attention. 'Georgie! Come to mummy!'

George knew what he had to do. He rolled onto his tummy and, looking determinedly at his mother, began to crawl. Unfortunately for George and for Barbara, instead of crawling towards his mum he went backwards, moving further and further away from her with every push of his arms until eventually, he could go no further, as he'd hit the living room radiator. At this point, now much further away from his mum than he was before, he did what most babies would do; he cried!

'Oh Georgie Porgie!' Barbara said, scooping him up in her arms. 'You just have to be patient my darling.'

But her patience was quickly running out.

'Why can't he be like Sam next door? Who ever heard of a baby who could only crawl backwards? she asked her husband Andrew.

'The doctor said 'be patient', remember?' Andrew replied, reassuringly. 'He's just a slow developer.'

The doctor was, of course, correct and a few weeks later George Walsh did crawl forwards, much to his and everyone else's amazement. But he was a slow developer and it wasn't just crawling that George seemed to be slower at than other children.

Even at the age of nine as he now was, he was extremely slow at getting dressed. At home his younger brother Harry would be dressed and eating his breakfast whilst George sat, perched on the edge of his bed, fiddling with his shirt buttons. Even when his favourite smell in the whole world drifted through the house on Saturday mornings as his mum sizzled bacon in the pan, Harry was onto his second slice when George finally arrived in the kitchen, puffing and panting, his T-shirt on back to front and odd socks on his feet. At school Mr Lee had to send George in from PE five minutes early to start getting dressed so that he could start the next lesson at the same time as everyone else.

But it was being unable to ride a bike that troubled George most. All of his friends could, his younger brother Harry could, but he just couldn't balance

and despite his dad spending endless weekends helping him, running behind him holding the seat, as soon as the stabilisers were removed, George would crash to the ground. After three years of trying, at the age of seven George had understandably lost patience and given up.

'It's not the end of the world George,' his dad would say. 'And we can always give it another go when you're older.'

But George had had enough of trying to balance on two wheels and whenever his friends asked him why he didn't have a bike he simply told them it wasn't his thing, which was, in fact, very true. It didn't bother George that much; his friends seemed to understand and as he'd never actually ridden a bike he had no idea how much fun it was so he didn't know what he was missing. But lately, cycling to school was being encouraged more and more to try to reduce the number of cars on the road outside school. A man, introduced in assembly as 'Bob the Bike Man', had told the children how much fun cycling was and how much healthier it was than travelling in a car. Bob also told everyone that he had some exciting events lined up for the year ahead, the first of which was in a few weeks. He called it a 'Biking Bacon Breakfast' – everyone would meet on their bikes a mile from school with their parents, cycle to school together and then – and this was the part that George really liked the sound of – bacon sandwiches served on the playground. George loved bacon. But he couldn't ride a bike. It was time to get his patience back. Apart from the bacon sandwiches, Bob the Bike Man had announced something else that had caught George's attention.

'I can teach anyone to ride a bike in an hour,' he told the children.

Mr Lee looked a little surprised by this bold statement but had reminded his class of it when they got back from assembly. 'I'm sure you can all ride,' he said. 'But remember what Bob said, 'If you can't, he can teach you, so there's no excuse

to miss the Biking Bacon Breakfast.'

But George did have an excuse. He was nine years old and still couldn't ride a bike and even if he could, he didn't actually own a bike. There was always Harry's of course – he had three bikes and didn't even like cycling. Somehow he was going to have to learn and Bob The Bike Man just might be the man to help. George was embarrassed about his inability to ride but trusted his teacher Mr Lee, so decided to share his secret with him. Mr Lee was great; he arranged for George to spend an hour after school with Bob the very next day. Bob was one of the most enthusiastic people George had ever met; he brought along a special bike with pedals that could be easily removed. He began by lowering the seat and told George to sit on and to use his feet to push himself forward. George did exactly what Bob instructed, but amazed both himself and Bob by going backwards into the wall – it was just like crawling all over again! Bob had never seen anyone do this before and an hour later, after George had fallen off a lot, he was still unable to ride a bike. He was now able to push himself forwards for a couple of seconds, but he certainly wasn't ready to have the pedals put on yet.

'I'm going to need more time with him,' Bob told Mr Lee. 'I've never known a wobblier child.'

But Bob remained calm and never once got annoyed with George. 'Be patient George. You'll do it,' he said, over and over again. Half way through their third session together George hadn't fallen off and was able to scoot along on the bike for the length of the playground, his legs sticking out on each side.

'Pedals!' Bob shouted. 'Time for pedals!'

George sat nervously on the seat looking straight ahead. Bob had attached the pedals and they were ready to go.

©Adrian Martin and Brilliant Publications

His mum and dad were delighted when George burst through the door to tell them although they already knew because Mr Lee had been keeping them updated on his progress.

'That's fantastic news George,' his dad said. 'You'll be able to go on the Biking Bacon Breakfast with Harry now.'

'What?' George asked. 'Harry's going? But I thought he didn't want to.'

'Changed his mind. All his friends are doing it,' replied dad.

'But that means I can't use his bike and his other two are tiny,' George complained.

'Not a problem,' dad said, opening the door to the lounge. 'This is your new bike.'

George looked at the gleaming, red mountain bike with thick, black wheels and sparkling silver spokes.

'We've been waiting a long time to buy you your first bike,' smiled mum.

'Just do as you have been doing,' Bob said encouragingly. 'Look straight ahead and instead of pushing the floor with your feet push the pedals instead. I'll be right behind you, holding the seat.' George pushed down on the pedal with his right foot and the bike immediately lurched to the right. He shut his eyes waiting to hit the ground but Bob steadied him and pushed him forward. George automatically pushed down on the other pedal with his left foot, then his right again. 'You're doing it!' Bob panted, running with George, holding the seat. 'You're riding!'

'Don't let go Bob!' George shouted.

'Don't worry, I won't!' Bob replied.

But he already had, and for the first time ever, George was riding a bike on his own. He got to the end of the playground grinning. 'I'm riding!' he shouted. 'On my own!'

'Wow! And I've been waiting a long time to ride it!' added George, climbing onto the seat.

The Biking Bacon Breakfast was fantastic. George stayed at the back for most of the ride and was a little wobbly but managed to stay on the whole way. After leading the long line of bikes to school Bob served the bacon sandwiches to the children.

'And remember everyone!' he shouted. 'If you know anyone who can't ride a bike, tell them to come and see me. I can teach them in … .' He paused as he caught sight of George waiting in the queue. '… . In three hours!' he said, laughing.

Patience

Hattie Fisher's Prize-winning Garden

The children of Mill Lane Junior School were sitting in the school hall. Mrs Davies, the Headteacher, was about to announce the winner of the competition to design a garden for the Southport Flower Show. Everyone had entered and so, it seemed, had most of the children in the north west of England. The Southport Flower Show was a big event in the area – the television cameras were always there – and a few days ago, Mrs Davies had told the school that she had received a letter informing her that one of the pupils from Mill Lane Juniors had won the competition. The winner's design would actually be created at the show and the winner would have his, or her photograph taken standing in the garden. They may even be interviewed on the local news! Mrs Davies had received the letter on Wednesday and told everyone that the winner would be revealed on Friday. Like most Headteachers, Mrs Davies enjoyed knowing things that other people didn't know; she liked creating a feeling of excitement. And now it was Friday and it would be fair to say that there was a high level of excitement amongst the children and staff.

'All right,' announced Mrs Davies, with a smile. 'It gives me great pleasure to reveal that the winner of the Southport Flower Show's Garden Design Competition is … '

The staff edged forwards on their chairs. The children leaned forwards, desperate to hear the news that had been kept from them for two full days.

Hattie Fisher was particularly keen to hear who the winner was – she had thought of little else for two days. Hattie was not good at sport, she was terrible at art and was just about all right at writing and maths. But she was a talented gardener. Since the Gardening Club had begun at school three years ago Hattie had been every week and

was now even allowed to come at the weekends with her grandad (to whom Mrs Davies had given a key), so that they could water the plants and vegetables and do a bit of weeding. When visitors came to look around the school, Mrs Davies would often take them to see the garden – she was proud of it and of course she knew that most of the garden's success was down to the hard work of Hattie and her grandad, George.

Whilst she sat there on the school hall floor waiting for Mrs Davies to announce the winner, she thought back to the moment she had first become interested in gardening. Even though it was five years ago when she was four, Hattie could remember the moment like it was yesterday. She was on a very busy bus in Greece with her family during the summer holidays. It was a really hot day and her grandad, George, was holding her hand tightly, as they were standing up in the aisle and the bus was lurching from side to side to avoid the pot holes in the road. As she stood there, swaying from left to right, holding her granddad's hand for balance, Hattie became fascinated by a Greek man sitting in the seat to granddad's left. The man, who had a large nose at the centre of a deeply suntanned, wrinkly face, was wearing a straw hat which he kept touching nervously. He had huge, podgy fingers and Hattie couldn't help noticing that his finger nails were full of soil. The gentle way he continually touched his hat made Hattie wonder if there was something underneath it that the man didn't want the other passengers to see. She was desperate to find out what it was and moments later, his secret was revealed in a very unusual way.

As the bus bobbed and jolted along the road, a Greek cat, asleep on the pavement in the distance, decided it was a perfect time to stretch, stand up and saunter across the road to the café on the other side. The bus driver, happily chatting

©Adrian Martin and Brilliant Publications

Fifty Fantastic Assembly Stories

away to one of the passengers standing next to him, only saw the cat at the very last moment and slammed his foot down onto his brake pedal just in time. However, all the standing passengers lurched forwards and George's free arm shot up into the air in search of the grab rail to prevent him and Hattie from falling over. But before George's hand reached the rail, it flicked the rim of the man's hat, sending it flying through the air. The eyes of every passenger on the bus were fixed on the hat, wondering where it was going to land. But Hattie's eyes went straight to the man's head, and his secret was revealed.

Sitting there, on the top of his head was the biggest, reddest, shiniest tomato she had ever seen. Just sitting there. The second his hat flew off, he raised his hands to his head with the speed of a magician performing a trick, grabbed the tomato and buried it deep into a shopping bag between his knees. Meanwhile his hat was being passed back from where it had landed and returned to its relieved owner. After placing the straw hat back firmly onto his head, he looked

around to see if anyone had seen the tomato. No one seemed to have noticed, except an English girl who was standing nearby, looking at him with a very confused expression on her face. The man leaned over to Hattie and whispered in broken English, 'Prize winning tomato. Very special.'

From that moment on Hattie was fascinated with growing her own vegetables, tomatoes to start with, but she would happily try her hand at anything. She had her own vegetable plot at the bottom of the garden at home and currently had fine crops of leeks, onions (both red and white), chillies, sweetcorn and of course, tomatoes.

When she heard about the competition she began work on her design the minute she arrived home from school. It was to be done for homework and the children had two weeks to complete it. Unlike most of the children in 5L, Hattie spent at least two hours each night and five at the weekend on her design. It was a vegetable garden, predictably, but as Southport was a seaside town, she had drawn an open topped bus travelling beside the sea and instead of passengers, she had drawn a tomato on each seat, each wearing a straw hat. There was a beach area, with sesame seeds for sand and mushrooms on sticks for the parasols. At the centre of the design was a fountain with water shooting out of a huge red tomato. Every part of the design was labelled neatly and coloured in meticulously. Hattie had never worked as hard on anything before.

'It gives me great pleasure', Mrs Davies said.

Hattie wouldn't have to wait any longer.

'To reveal that the winner of the Southport Flower Show's Garden Design Competition is Hattie Fisher!'

There was a gasp from the children around her. Hattie couldn't believe her ears but everyone was looking at her and clapping their hands and Mrs

Davies was beckoning her to the front of the hall.

To her astonishment her mum and dad appeared from a door just outside the hall, followed by Grandad George. That's why Mrs Davies had not told everyone for two days – she had wanted Hattie's parents and granddad to be there when the winner was announced. They had known since Wednesday and had kept it a secret from her.

Hattie didn't normally achieve things like this but everyone agreed that she thoroughly deserved to win the competition. For years she had shown the patience and determination to develop her gardening skills and her patience had finally paid off.

Six weeks later, Hattie, her mum and dad and, of course, her grandad, George, walked through the crowds of visitors, towards the Garden Design Area at the Flower Show. When she first saw the garden she was completely speechless;

the design that she had spent hours and hours drawing and colouring at home on a piece of paper was now a real, life sized garden. There was a model bus with model seats, each with a real tomato 'sitting' there with their straw hats on, looking through the window to the beach. Even the driver was a tomato! It reminded her again of her bus journey in Greece.

But she had little time to enjoy her garden because the photographers had gathered, determined to get a photograph of the young garden designer. As she was instructed, Hattie stood in front of her prize winning garden at the show. Over her shoulder, water shot upwards into the air from an enormous red tomato. After having her photograph taken by all the local newspaper photographers, one reporter asked, 'So Hattie, what gave you the idea for such an amazing garden?'

She looked at Grandad George. He smiled. 'That's our secret I'm afraid,' she said, with a grin.

©Adrian Martin and Brilliant Publications

Michael's Patience Finally Pays Off

●●

If ever there was a child who lived up to his name it was Michael Smiley. He was, quite simply, the happiest, smiliest, most enthusiastic boy anyone could wish to meet. He always did the best he could in everything he did even though, to be perfectly honest, he wasn't particularly good at anything (apart from smiling of course).

Over the years he had played a range of animal parts in the school plays, including the donkey in the Christmas Nativity in Year 1, a penguin in the Easter story in Year 4 (even though he was never completely sure what a penguin was doing in the Easter story) and, his favourite so far, a dancing bear in the Year 5 pantomime, Snow White. Never before had an audience seen such an enthusiastic and happy bear – the school hall always became very warm when it was full of people, as it was on the evenings of the pantomime. The added heat inside the bear costume would have dampened the spirits of most actors, but not Michael. He jumped around the stage as no bear had ever done before and when he exited the stage, following his unique performance, the audience applauded thunderously.

He loved playing football but wasn't very good at it and spent most of his time standing in the middle of the pitch watching the ball as it flew over his head or rolled between his legs. He would stand and watch in amazement as the ball seemed to be glued to the feet of some of the other children, their control was so good. Whenever anyone passed the ball to him he would try to control it but it just seemed to take on super bouncy qualities when he touched it with his foot and off it went. But he loved being part of the game and whether his team were winning or losing he would always have a big smile on his face. He wasn't the fastest runner, in fact 'fast' was a speed that he rarely managed to achieve, unless he was running down a very steep hill. He was hopeless at catching a ball, although he often remembered fondly the occasion in a school rounders match when Kevin Gallagher, the school's best hitter, smashed the ball high up into the air only for Michael, running in the wrong direction, to catch it completely by accident in the hood of his tracksuit top! His 'catch' meant that his team won the match so for once Michael was the hero of the hour that day – and even Kevin Gallagher saw the funny side of it!

But Michael wasn't at all bothered about not being very good at sport. There was nothing he could do about that and as his mum said, 'There's no point in worrying about something you can't help,' so he didn't worry. But there was one part of school life that did worry him; a very important part of school life in fact. He was constantly frustrated with his reading. He was in Year 5 now and week after week of his school life so far he had heard his teachers say how important it was to read as often as possible. He knew how important it was – his bedroom shelves were lined with wonderful looking books but when he actually sat down and opened one to read, he couldn't do it. Most of his friends loved reading and when they weren't playing on their tablets or running around with a ball outside, their heads were firmly focused on the latest adventure series. Even that was like a competition for them; when they arrived on the school playground each morning they would discuss where they were up to in the story and discuss what they thought was going to happen next. Michael wasn't able to read the books his friends had and so he just had to listen to the strange characters and the amazing adventures they described; this made it all the more frustrating for him. He just didn't get it – he was still a 'Home Reader' and unlike his friends who could choose any book they liked from the school library, he had to make his choice from a small number of books

●●●

Fifty Fantastic Assembly Stories

in the 'Red Band'. If Michael was asked what he really thought of these books, he'd probably say that they were too young for him, even though he still struggled to read them. When he looked at the page, the letters in each word seemed to dance around making it very difficult for Michael to read what they said. In Year 4 his parents had been told that he had something called Dyslexia and ever since then he had been given extra support by Mrs Brady, who he loved as she was very kind and helped him so much to make sense of the dancing letters.

'Just be patient Michael,' Mrs Brady would say. 'We'll get there in the end. Just be patient.'

And Michael believed her and so here he was in Year 5, continuing to try his best and continuing to be patient, waiting for the day when reading would become as easy for him as it seemed to be for everyone else.

It was only when Michael's dad found him upset, sitting in his bedroom trying to read a book that one of his friends had given him, that Mr and Mrs Smiley decided to see what else could be done.

'I think my patience is running out Dad,' Michael said, tearfully.

Mr and Mrs Smiley knew that the school had done all they could, but they had some savings put aside and had been told a while ago by a specialist that Michael may benefit from wearing some special coloured glasses. There was no doubt in anyone's mind that Michael deserved all the support he could get and so his mum and dad agreed that it was worth a try and the special coloured glasses were ordered. They were expensive and took two weeks to arrive but Michael was used to being patient and it was well worth the wait. Michael arrived home from school one spring afternoon to find a deep red leather glasses case sitting on the dining room table. Like most ten year olds, Michael was not

the most organised of children, so his mum and dad had decided to pay a little extra to have his name printed on the case. Michael looked at the gold lettering and despite each of the letters jumping and twitching, he could easily recognise the overall shape of the words, spelling out his name. Each letter had been pressed into the lid of the case and gold ink filled each one so that the words stood out from the surface. Michael ran his fingers across the case from left to right, feeling the smoothness of each letter against the leather. He opened the box and as the lid sprung back solidly, his eyes widened as he looked inside. The glasses were cool. They had red frames and blue lenses and lay neatly on a gold cleaning cloth. He put them on and closed the case again. It made a satisfying clunk as its jaws snapped shut. And then Michael saw something that he had never, ever seen before; his name, in gold, completely and utterly still – the letters weren't dancing or twitching, or moving in even the slightest way and because of this he could read them instantly, quickly. He read them over and over again and as he did so he said his name. And as he said his name, his voice got louder and louder:

'Michael Smiley … Michael Smiley … Michael Smiley… Michael SMILEY!' Until he was saying his name so loudly that his mum ran into the room wondering what on earth was going on. Michael looked at his mum.

'They're not moving,' he said.

'What aren't moving love?' Mum replied, beginning to worry about her son.

'The letters – they're not moving. They're completely still. AND I CAN READ THEM!' he shouted.

And beneath his very cool red rimmed glasses with the blue lenses, was the biggest, broadest, smiliest grin Michael Smiley had ever smiled. His patience had finally paid off.

©Adrian Martin and Brilliant Publications

Adam Solves a Mystery

• •

Recently Shelley Watson always seemed to be in the wrong place at the wrong time. Whenever there was something not quite right, Shelley was there, or had been there moments before. A few months ago Shelley's mum had had a baby daughter, Alice, and although Shelley loved her new sister very much, she had felt strange ever since the little bundle had arrived home from the hospital. It was as though Shelley's world had been completely taken over by this tiny baby. Mum and dad suddenly seemed unable to utter a sentence without the name 'Alice' in it. They looked at her constantly, fed her, cradled her, bathed her, sang to her and spent most of the night trying to get her to sleep. Shelley struggled to remember the last time either of them had asked her how her day at school had been and although she understood that Alice had to be looked after, she was beginning to feel very left out. It was at this time that things began to get a little troublesome at school.

On two occasions last week, when something had gone missing, Shelley had found it in a place where no one else would have looked. First of all Stephen Heywood lost his glasses case. He was quite often losing his glasses, but had never before lost his glasses case. After searching the cloakrooms, everyone's desks and bags, Mr Lee was beginning to become a little irritated, when Shelley found them, right at the very back of the art cupboard.

'How did they get there?' asked Stephen, 'I've not been anywhere near the art cupboard.'

'You obviously left them there when you were tidying up the paints for Mr Lee,' replied Shelley.

'But I haven't been tidying the paints up,' said Stephen, mystified. 'Thanks though Shelley.'

'No problem,' she said, and walked back to her place, with a smirk on her face.

A day later, after PE, Adam McMahon's watch went missing from the hall. Mr Lee always made the children take off their watches and put them on the piano in the corner of the hall before PE, to avoid anyone getting scratched. Adam had forgotten to get his at the end of the lesson and only remembered when he was changed. After asking Mr Lee if he could go back and get it, he scampered off to the hall, but stopped dead in his tracks when he reached the piano. His watch wasn't there. The lesson had only finished five minutes ago and no one else had been in the hall since. He simply couldn't understand where it could have gone. As he made his way back to class he replayed the beginning of the lesson in his mind. He had walked into the hall and when Mr Lee had reminded everyone to put their watches on the piano he had done exactly that. He had walked over to the piano and waited for the children in front of him to take their watches off – Robert Jackson and Erin Bentley and then he had done the same. Behind him was Shelley Watson who was waiting to take off her watch and then the lesson had started. So what had happened to his watch? No one else's had gone missing. When he got back to class he told Mr Lee that his watch wasn't on the piano and after a series of questions, the teacher decided that the only thing for it was to organise a search. The watch was a birthday present from Adam's grandma and he was getting worried. Mr Lee asked the whole class to go back to the cloakrooms and to look in their bags. He asked Adam three times if he was sure he had left it on the piano. Each time Adam replied that he was certain he had done. No one found the watch. They had to carry on with lessons but Mr Lee told Adam that they would have another look when everyone else had gone home. Adam couldn't

• •

Fifty Fantastic Assembly Stories

concentrate for the rest of the afternoon. What would mum say when he told her? She was bound to blame him. With about ten minutes to go before the end of the afternoon Shelley Watson asked Mr Lee if she could go to the toilet. When she returned back to the room she was holding Adam's watch.

'Where did you find that?' asked Mr Lee.

'It was underneath the book shelf outside the toilets Mr Lee,' Shelley replied. 'It must have been accidentally kicked under there.'

'Right,' said Mr Lee, suspiciously. He didn't seem convinced by Shelley's explanation. 'Well thank you Shelley. You really are becoming an excellent detective aren't you? Adam, look what Shelley's found.'

Adam was delighted, but couldn't help wondering how his watch had managed to make the journey from the piano in the school hall to underneath the book shelf outside the toilets at the other end of the school corridor. He also couldn't help noticing how Shelley had looked at him when she made her way back to her desk. He couldn't quite put his finger on it, but something wasn't quite right.

And then something really odd happened. It was Monday morning and the children were coming in from the playground after their break. Adam sat down at his desk and noticed Shelley wiping her eyes with a tissue. She looked upset. Mr Lee was looking very serious and asked everyone to listen very carefully to what he had to say.

'You may have noticed that Shelley is very upset today,' he began.

Everyone looked at Shelley, who wiped another tear from her eye.

'The reason Shelley is upset,' Mr Lee continued, 'Is

because someone has written a note to her and put it into her bag. The note was not very nice. In fact, it said some unkind things in it about Shelley.'

Everyone in the class looked at each other. No one said a word.

Mr Lee continued, 'I don't suppose anyone will admit to writing the note, but I am warning you all right now – whoever it was make sure it never happens again.'

Everyone remained silent. Many questions were going through the children's minds – 'Who would write a nasty letter to Shelley?'; 'What did it say?'; 'Why would someone write a letter to her?'

The children worked silently for the rest of the lesson and at lunchtime, some of them comforted Shelley whilst everyone else chatted about who could have written the letter and what it might have said.

But when the children came back into class after lunch, things had got worse. Mrs Davies, the headteacher was standing next to Mr Lee. She was looking very serious.

'5L,' she said, 'You are aware of the letter to Shelley Watson found in her bag this morning?'

The class nodded. No one dared speak.

'Mr Lee warned you that it must never happen again?'

Again, the children in 5L nodded.

She held up a piece of cream coloured paper.

'This,' she said, 'Was found in her tray at lunchtime.'

There were gasps around the room.

©Adrian Martin and Brilliant Publications

'Someone has written another letter and pushed it into her tray. Another unkind letter. She found it when she came back into class at lunchtime to get her dinner money.'

There wasn't a sound. Adam looked around the room. His eye caught Stephen's. After Shelley had found Stephen's glasses case and Adam's watch the two boys had chatted to each other. Both were suspicious of Shelley and were sure that they had not been responsible for the disappearance of their things.

Mrs Davies repeated the warning Mr Lee had given the class. She said that whoever had written the letter was a coward and a bully. She left the class by shutting the door with a bang. She was not happy, and 5L knew it. No one was happy when Mrs Davies wasn't happy.

After school Adam and Stephen walked home together.

'What d'you think of all that then?' Adam asked Stephen.

'It's not me if that's what you're thinking,' replied Stephen.

'I wasn't thinking that. It's not me either. But who could it be?'

The next day – Tuesday, things got worse. Shelley's parents had come into school to see Mrs Davies. They had arrived that morning with another letter. This one had been posted through their front door last night. All three letters were written on the same cream paper, in the same red ink, and all were written in block capital letters.

Mrs Davies was back in 5L.

'If this doesn't stop I'm going to start keeping you in at break time,' she said. I've had enough of

this!' And for the second time in as many days, the classroom door was shut with a bang.

When Mrs Davies had left the room the children were told to get their trays and put them on their desks. Mr Lee asked each child to check their partner's tray.

'You're looking for paper like this,' he said, holding up the backs of one of the letters.

No one found anything. Everyone's tray had been searched.

'Everyone's, except Shelley's that is,' thought Adam.

Shelley was still with her mum and dad in Mrs Davies's room.

After break she came back into class and the children in 5L carried on as well as they could.

At lunchtime the children were in the dining room eating their lunch. Adam noticed Shelley asking one of the mid-day assistants something. She then walked out of the dining room on her own. He put his hand up and asked if he could go to the toilet. It was a white lie, but he had to follow Shelley.

Adam walked out of the dining room as quickly as he could without being called back for running. As he left the dining room and rounded the corner into the main corridor, he just caught sight of Shelley disappearing into 5L's classroom. He quickly walked up the corridor and reached his classroom door. In the top half of the door there was a window and Adam peered through it into the classroom. At first he couldn't see anyone but after a few moments he spotted her. Shelley was crouching in the far corner of the room and he could see that she appeared to be writing something. As she stood up he quickly moved his head away from the window so that she wouldn't see him, but when he looked back he saw her pushing something into her reading book on her desk. It was a piece of paper. More importantly it was a piece of cream coloured paper. He knew it. She was writing the letters, the unkind letters, to herself! Unbelievable! He rushed back to the dining room, his mind racing. What should he do? Should he tell Stephen? Should he confront Shelley? She had taken his watch – he was sure about that now. And Stephen's glasses case. He knew something wasn't quite right about that look she gave him.

A couple of minutes after Adam had returned to the dining room to finish his lunch, Shelley arrived back to finish hers. He gobbled his food down and made his way out of the dining room.

'Where are you going so fast?' Stephen asked. 'Things to do,' replied Adam, and was gone.

He went straight to the staffroom and knocked on the door.

'How do you know there's another letter Adam?' Mr Lee asked.

'Because I know who's writing them and I saw the letter being written,' he replied.

He led Mr Lee into 5L's classroom and showed him the letter in Shelley's reading book. The ink was still wet and as Mr Lee removed the letter from the book some of the writing smudged.

'Did you do this Adam?' Mr Lee asked.

'No Mr Lee. Look in Shelley's tray.' Adam's teacher did what he asked and pulled

the tray out from its shelf.

'Well?' he asked.

'It's in there somewhere I know it is,' Adam stuttered, beginning to doubt his own eyes.

Mr Lee took out Shelley's books one by one. Nothing.

'I think you've got some explaining to do,' he said, holding Shelley's scrap book and pointing it in Adam's direction.

But before Adam could reply something caught his eye as his teacher jabbed the book in the air. A piece of paper, cream coloured, had made its way out of the scrap book and was now floating down to the floor. Mr Lee stared at it. Adam stared at it.

'I … don't … believe … it,' stammered the teacher.

He opened Shelley's pencil case and emptied it out onto the desk. The last thing to fall out was a red pen.

Shelley immediately admitted what she had done and when Mr Lee spoke to her mum and dad the reason for her behaviour became obvious to them; ever since baby Alice had arrived Shelley had had no attention and her deceitful behaviour was her way of getting it. Unfortunately for Shelley, her actions had got her the wrong kind of attention and it would be a while until her classmates would be able to trust her again.

©Adrian Martin and Brilliant Publications

Charlie Harper's Lies Go One Step Too Far

Charlie Harper was not a person anyone could trust. He often promised to do things but then never actually did anything.

At the beginning of their topic on Egyptians, Charlie had told everyone that he had been to Egypt and he had some really important Egyptian artefacts at home. Mr Lee, Charlie's teacher, said, 'Well it would be great if you could bring them in to show us Charlie, with your parents' permission, of course.'

'No problem Mr Lee. My dad's already told me I can bring them in to show the class. I'll bring them tomorrow.'

But he never brought them in and whenever anyone asked him he'd say, 'My older brother's taken them into his school. I'll bring them in as soon as he brings them back.'

Charlie always had an answer.

In the playground Charlie was always boasting about going to the Old Mill down Smithy Lane, about half a mile from school. The Old Mill used to make cotton in Victorian times and was about 160 years old. It had been closed for a long time now and although it still looked the same on the outside, the inside was falling to pieces. There was a large sign on the front door which read, 'Danger! Do not enter under any circumstances. Floors are extremely unsafe and could collapse at any time.'

The council wanted to knock the building down, but local people had protested, saying that it was a valuable historical building, so it had just been left to rot slowly away.

Monday mornings on the playground were when Charlie was at his worst. He would tell anyone who would listen that his brother had taken him to the Old Mill at the weekend and that they'd had a great time

exploring inside. He hadn't, of course, but he wanted people to think he was brave and interesting. In actual fact he'd spent the whole of Saturday watching television as many 9 year old boys did.

After a while the other children became a little fed up with Charlie's stories and he often ended up standing on the playground on his own with no one to talk to. But one particular Monday morning he noticed a child he'd never seen before walking around the playground looking a little confused. The boy was Reuben Peters and today was his first day at the school. Charlie decided to talk to Reuben and couldn't believe his luck when he found out that Reuben was going to be in Mr Lee's class. Reuben seemed genuinely happy to talk to Charlie and before long, they were talking about the Old Mill.

'I think that's near where I live,' Reuben said. 'Can you take me sometime?'

'Sure,' replied Charlie, and before he could think, went on to say, 'How about this Saturday?'

Unfortunately, Reuben didn't know that the Old Mill was dangerous. Nor did he know that his new friend Charlie was not someone to be trusted.

'Sounds good,' he said. 'Ten o'clock?'

'I'll be there,' smiled Charlie (although inside, he wasn't so sure. After all, he'd never actually been to the mill).

As the week went on Charlie began to dread Saturday, but he couldn't admit to his new friend Reuben that he'd never actually been to the mill. What would he think of him? He'd have to go through with it, but little did he know, that what was about to happen at the Old Mill, would change both their lives forever.
'How do you get in?' Reuben asked Charlie, as

they stood looking at the huge wooden door.

Charlie didn't have the faintest idea, but a blackbird, which he saw fly into the mill through a side window, came to his rescue.

'The window,' he said, pointing to the right of the door.

Reuben said nothing, but skilfully jumped over some of the old bricks and timber lying on the ground, to the side window.

There was no glass in the window, but it was a lot higher than it looked and neither boy could reach the sill, even on tiptoe. Charlie looked around amongst the rubble on the ground and spotted a box. He and Reuben dragged it to the wall just under the window. Quick as a flash, Reuben had climbed up on the box and had heaved himself up onto the window sill. From there he jumped down onto the floor of the mill.

'Are you coming or not?' he shouted, from inside. Impressed by Reuben's brave approach, Charlie climbed up onto the box, and followed into the derelict building.

Once inside, Charlie looked around. The room they were in was completely empty, apart from a wooden ladder in the far corner, which disappeared through a square hole in the ceiling above.

'Well, what do you do in here that's so exciting? Reuben asked.

'Climb,' replied Charlie, pointing to the ladder. 'Is it safe?' questioned Reuben.

'Perfectly,' lied Charlie.

'But what about the sign on the door?' asked Reuben.

'It's just there to keep people out, 'Charlie lied

again. 'It'll be fine. I've done it hundreds of times. Trust me.'

To Charlie's amazement, Reuben did seem to trust him. He nodded to Charlie and walked across the floor towards the ladder.

The mill had four floors in total; the ground floor, which was solid, and three others, each made of wood, and each with a wooden ladder in the corner. The original stairs had collapsed a long time ago and so the only way of getting to the top floor was by climbing the ladders. If this wasn't dangerous enough, the ladders on each floor were in opposite corners of the room, so to get to the level above meant walking across the whole of the wooden floor to the next ladder.

Unlike Charlie, Reuben was not afraid of heights and he was beginning to enjoy himself.

He reached the top of the first ladder and stepped from it onto the wooden floor of the second room. The floor on this level was not as solid as the one on the ground floor and when he put his weight onto it there was a loud creak. Reuben decided that the best thing to do was to walk quickly, but with every step he took the floor boards beneath him seemed to sag and weaken. He made it to the bottom of the next ladder and quickly grabbed onto it. The ladders were attached to the wall and he knew that once he was on the ladder he was safe, or at least safer. But he'd got this far and was determined to keep going. There were only two more ladders to climb and if he made it to the top Charlie would be really impressed with him. What Reuben didn't know, was that the floor he had just walked across had not been walked across for many years and the wood that the floor was made of was rotten. And that if he were to walk across it again, as he would have to on his way back down, it would collapse in a very large cloud of dust taking him with it.

But Reuben didn't know that and the shouts from

©Adrian Martin and Brilliant Publications

Charlie on the bottom floor asking him how he was getting on were growing fainter the higher he climbed. The wood on the third floor creaked even more than the second and Reuben was very relieved to reach the safety of the ladder in the far corner. As he did so, he thought he heard a cracking sound, but he decided it must have been his imagination.

Charlie had got fed up with shouting up to Reuben and getting no reply and had decided to climb back through the window to see if there was anything more interesting on the outside of the mill.

As Reuben reached the top of the third and final ladder, a beam of light hit him full in the face. At the far end of the top floor was a huge window and the sunlight was streaming in through it.

'I bet the view's great from the top,' he thought, and decided that before heading back down he'd make his way over to the window. Although his first few steps weren't too bad he was in no doubt that this floor was definitely the worst. As Reuben got just past half way, there was a definite creak and the floorboard he was standing on began to give way. The creak became a worryingly loud crack which was followed by the sound of several more even louder cracks, making Reuben quickly realise that going back was not an option. He made a run for the window ledge as the floor began to give way beneath him. With every step the floor behind him was collapsing. Large splinters of wood were being thrown into the air. He focused on the window ledge and made a desperate leap for it. His fingers grasped at the bricks and he used all his strength to heave himself up onto the safety of the ledge which was deep enough to sit on. The noise was louder than anything he'd ever heard before. He pressed his hands over his ears and slammed his eyes shut. A few minutes later he opened his eyes and dared to look back over his shoulder. When the cloud of dust eventually cleared he could see that the floor he had just run across had gone completely. Worse still there were no floors left below that. They had

all collapsed, leaving a huge pile of rubble on the ground floor, where he and Charlie had stood only half an hour ago. A sickly feeling swept over him as he remembered Charlie. Reuben didn't know that Charlie had got bored and climbed back out of the mill.

Meanwhile, on the outside of the mill, a similarly sickly feeling had swept over Charlie. The noise of the collapsing floors had made him jump back in fright and he was sure Reuben must have fallen with the rubble.

'Reuben?! Are you all right?' Charlie shouted, desperately.

Reuben looked out through the window, over the edge of the mill, down to Charlie, way down below.

'Up here!' he shouted.

It took Charlie a few moments to work out where Reuben's voice was coming from. As soon as he saw Reuben he shouted, 'Don't move!' and ran up the lane away from the mill. Within half an hour a fire engine was parked outside the mill and a metal, extending ladder was making its way towards Reuben. For the first time in his life, Charlie had acted in a trustworthy and responsible way. After getting his new friend into terrible trouble, he had done the right thing and got him out of it.

The next step Reuben took was onto the safety of the rescue ladder. As it lowered him down slowly to the ground he remembered Charlie's words to him before he climbed the first ladder. 'It'll be fine. I've done it hundreds of times. Trust me.'

He decided there and then that in future, he'd only trust people who he knew were telling the truth.

As for Charlie, he'd learned a very important lesson; if he continued to tell lies, no one would ever trust him.

Trust

Jack Simpson Finally Wins Mr Lee's Trust

● ●

Jack Simpson was one of those boys who always seemed to be in the wrong place at the wrong time. His heart was in the right place, but whenever anything went wrong, he was always close by. In fact, sometimes, he was what went wrong. Jack had been in Year 5 now for just over a term, and his teacher, Mr Lee, had begun to find himself repeating the same things to Jack, over and over again – 'Don't you think it's about time you became a little bit more trustworthy, Jack?', 'I'm sorry, but I'm not entirely sure I can trust you with that job, Jack.'

Jack was aware of the reputation he was getting – he would be ten years old soon and he had spent the last nine years trying to prove to people that he was someone to trust, only for things to go badly wrong.

When he was three years old, he was left alone with his baby sister Hannah in the kitchen for no more than two minutes, whilst his mum 'nipped' upstairs for something.

'I'm just nipping upstairs for something. Keep an eye on your sister for me Jack. She's in her high chair. I'll be back down in five minutes,' she said.

Five minutes later, mum walked into the kitchen and was horrified by what she saw. Hannah was no longer sitting in her high chair but instead, was sat, wobbling on top of the kitchen work surface. She was eight months old and could not walk, but somehow she had managed to get out of her high chair, and onto the kitchen work surface, which was twice her height. Her cute, pink face was no longer cute, nor pink. Someone, using a permanent marker pen, had drawn a pair of glasses, a beard and a moustache onto Hannah's face. She now looked like a very small hairy man. Her jet black, spiky hair, which mum had spent fifteen minutes brushing that morning, was no longer black,

and no longer spiky, and worse still, some of it, was missing. Her hair was now yellow because someone had covered her head in thick yellow custard. Except the bit that was missing. This bit was still black, but was not attached to her head. This bit was lying on the kitchen table, nowhere near Hannah's head, next to a pair of scissors.

Jack's mum looked at Jack. Jack shrugged. 'Wasn't me,' he said. Hannah chuckled, as a delicious droplet of custard dripped from her nose onto her lips.

No one knows to this day how the whole thing happened. No one, that is, except Jack (and maybe Hannah), but this was the first of many occasions which led to the reputation Jack now had, of someone who was difficult to trust.

But on the first day of the new year, like so many other children, he made a decision; from that moment on, he was going to be more trustworthy. He had to change. Mr Lee was right. He had plenty of friends, but he was beginning to think that they were his friends for the wrong reasons – they loved it when he did silly things, when he got himself into trouble. They liked him because he made them laugh, but by making them laugh, he was getting himself into trouble.

On the first day back in the new year the rest of the class looked at him doubtfully when he told them he was determined to change, but this didn't bother him. He knew it wouldn't be easy. Every time Mr Lee asked for a volunteer for something, Jack put up his hand.

'I need someone to take a message to Mrs Newall's class please,' Mr Lee said, at the end of maths. Jack's hand shot up. His was easily the first to go up. But Mr Lee waited for other hands before he made his decision. 'Thanks Liam – I

● ●

©Adrian Martin and Brilliant Publications

Fifty Fantastic Assembly Stories

know I can trust you,' he said. Jack tried not to show his disappointment.

'The caretaker would like five volunteers to help with some litter picking at breaktime – can anyone help?' Mr Lee asked.

This was another chance for Jack to show he could be trusted. Again, his hand was up straight away. Surely he stood a chance with this one – Mr Lee would struggle to get five other children to give up their breaktime to pick up litter in January. Jack looked around the room. 'Casey', Liam, Adam and Lauren all had their hands up, but that was only four. Mr Lee had to choose him this time.

'Is that it 5L? Come on. You can do better than that.'

All around the room, hands slowly went up.

'Thank you. I should think so too.' And once again, Jack was overlooked.

He was beginning to realise that the reputation he had developed was not going to be easy to shrug off.

Over the next few weeks Jack stuck at it, staying out of any trouble and putting his hand up whenever anyone asked for help. It was February now, and after four weeks, he still had not been trusted with any responsibility by his teacher. He was beginning to wonder whether Mr Lee would ever trust him to do anything, when, at the end of the art lesson, one Tuesday afternoon, it finally happened. 5L had been sketching objects arranged in the middle of each table. One of the objects on Jack's table was a vase which Mr Lee had constantly told them not to touch, as it was extremely valuable and belonged to Mrs Newall, the Year 3 teacher.

'Right everyone, before we tidy away, I need someone I can trust to take the vase back to Mrs Newall.'

Jack really didn't know whether to even bother putting his hand up. There was no way Mr Lee would choose him to do it. He didn't even trust him to pick litter up. But he put up his hand anyway, and to his amazement, he was the only one who did. No one else was prepared to risk taking the vase all the way to the other end of the school. Mr Lee looked at Jack thoughtfully. 'He does seem to have changed recently,' he thought. 'Maybe it's worth a try.'

'Okay Jack,' he said. 'Off you go to Mrs Newall's classroom. But remember, it's very valuable. Be really careful. Don't let me down.'

'It will be safe in my hands Mr Lee,' replied Jack confidently.

He picked the vase up carefully, and began the walk to Mrs Newall's room – down the corridor, through the main entrance hall, and then down a second corridor to the end. 3N was at the other end of the school to Jack's classroom. He was determined to do it. Mr Lee had finally put his trust in Jack and he wasn't going to let him down. He walked slowly and carefully down the corridor, with one hand underneath the vase, the other holding it firmly around the middle and before long, he was standing outside the door to Mrs Newall's classroom. He was about to peer through the glass to attract someone's attention when he heard a noise coming from the cloakroom opposite. He looked in, and saw a small boy struggling with something. It was Peter Knight. 'What's the matter?' Jack asked.

'I'm stuck,' replied Peter. 'I've got my tie caught.'

'Hold on,' said Jack. There was a table outside Mrs Newall's room. He carefully placed the vase on it, and then went to help the boy. Somehow Peter's tie had got caught on one of the coat hooks, and after several minutes, Jack had unravelled it, releasing Peter who, after a quick 'thanks', disappeared back into class.

Jack Simpson Finally Wins Mr Lee's Trust

'Leave the door open!' Jack called after him. But it was too late. Peter was too keen to get back into class and had closed the door behind him ….. with some force. Enough force, as it turned out, to cause the table with the vase on to shudder. And when the table shuddered, the vase wobbled. Jack was a few metres away, at the entrance to the cloakroom. He watched as the vase rocked from side to side, fell sideways onto the table and rolled slowly over the edge. Jack took one step forward and dived towards it. He caught the vase in both hands, centimetres before it hit the floor. Unfortunately, as he dived, he skidded forwards and his knuckles rapped against the wall. The pain caused him to jerk his hands away, and in doing so, one side of the vase knocked against the wall. Jack stared at the part of the vase that had been knocked. A crack had appeared, and as he stood up, a triangular piece fell into his hand. He couldn't believe his luck.

'That's that,' he said to himself. 'No one will ever trust me again. I've done it again. I can't believe it. I've even messed this up.'

He placed the piece back in the vase, where it had fallen from. And to his surprise, it fitted perfectly. It had been a clean break. 'Maybe,' he thought, 'If I just click the piece back in, no one will know it was me.'

And before he could think it through any more, someone had opened the door for him and Mrs Newall, who was reading a story to the class on the carpet, was pointing to her desk. 'Leave it on my desk please Jack,' she said. He had no choice. It would be rude to interrupt the story. Hannah, his sister, who was now in Year 3, smiled at him as he left the room. He didn't smile back, but simply walked quickly out of the room, leaving his sister looking puzzled.

At home that evening, Jack had a bad feeling in his stomach. The next day when the bell went at nine o'clock he marched purposefully to Mrs Newall's room. If he was going to be trusted, he needed to tell the truth. The classroom was empty. The vase was on Mrs Newall's desk. He walked over to it and picked it up, expecting the piece to fall out. It didn't. He gave the vase a shake. Nothing. He held the vase where it had broken between his fingers and pulled. Nothing. The piece had been glued in place. Someone tapped him on his shoulder. He put the vase down and turned round. It was Hannah, smiling a big, broad grin.

'Did you …?' but he never completed the sentence. Mrs Newall arrived with her class. 'Hello Jack. Have you come to take the vase back to Mr Lee?'

'Er … no Mrs Newal … I just thought I'd check to see if it was still in one piece. Got to go. See you later Hannah.'

Minutes later, he was back in his own classroom, where Mr Lee called him to his desk.

'That vase Jack,' began Mr Lee. 'Did you get it to Mrs Newall in one piece?'

Jack knew that this was an important moment. This was his chance to tell the truth and to show that he could be trustworthy.

'Well, actually Mr Lee,' he began.

And when he had told his teacher the entire story Mr Lee smiled at Jack and said, 'Jack, I'm proud of you. You obviously broke the vase by accident and we would never have known about it if you hadn't told us. Well done. And guess what?' he continued. 'It wasn't really valuable you know. Oh no. Mrs Newall got it at a car boot sale at the weekend. She knew I needed some objects for art. Ten pence I think she paid. I just wanted to see who would be trustworthy enough to take it back to her. Well done Jack. It seems that you've finally become someone I can trust.'

©Adrian Martin and Brilliant Publications

Fifty Fantastic Assembly Stories

It's What You're Like on the Inside That Matters

● ●

It was the last day of term and the holidays were about to begin but as Mark woke up and realised what day it was a feeling of dread came over him.

He was looking forward to the holidays but before they began he had the last day of term to contend with. You might be wondering what was so bad about the last day of term? Well for most children it was fine, great fun even, but not for Mark; he hated it. He hated it because on the last day of each term Mrs Davies allowed the children to come in their 'normal' clothes rather than their uniform and for Mark, wearing normal clothes at school was the last thing he wanted to do.

Mark's dad had disappeared when he was seven years old; Mark never really understood where he'd gone. Mum just said, 'He wasn't very nice and we're all better off without him.'

And mum was left to bring up Mark and his younger brother Tim who was six. Although mum was the manager at the local supermarket, which sounded impressive, Mark was beginning to realise that she didn't get much money for doing it. He was also beginning to realise how hard it must be for his mum to look after him and Tim. They were both growing fast and always seemed to be going shopping for new stuff – for them, not her. Recently he'd noticed how tired she was beginning to look. 'It can't be easy working full time and bringing up two boys,' he thought and he did what he could to help her. They all got on well together; Mark even quite liked his little brother, although he'd never admit it of course and Tim secretly looked up to Mark.

Whenever he could, Mark would help mum out around the house. He would always give her a hand with the washing up, try to keep his room tidy and help to get Tim ready for school. This was his favourite job as it usually involved trying to drag

his brother out of bed by his feet. But Mark was frustrated at not being able to help his mum when she needed to buy things for them. Sometimes he wished he could just fast forward his life to when he could get a job so that she wouldn't have to do everything for him and his brother.

There was a boy at school who was the same age as Mark, but who could not have been more different; Andy Smith, or Smithy, as he told everyone to call him.

Unlike Mark's dad, Andy Smith's dad hadn't left when he was seven years old. Oh no. Andy Smith's dad was, as Andy himself told everyone, 'loaded'. No one was quite sure what he did (even Andy didn't know), but whatever it was, he seemed to get lots of money for it. He would drop Andy off at school every morning in his huge, silver Mercedes with blacked out windows so that no one could see inside. He'd also be there at the end of the day to pick Andy up. He would park his huge car (usually on the yellow zig-zags where people are not allowed to park) and stand at the gate waiting for his son. He had dark curly hair and always wore sunglasses even when it wasn't remotely sunny. He wore his shirt with the buttons undone revealing a hairy chest and several gold medallions which hung on thick gold chains around his neck. On his feet he wore long, pointy shoes. He obviously thought he looked fantastic. Mark wasn't so sure.

It wasn't any real surprise then, that Andy was one of those boys who seemed to have everything. Unfortunately every opportunity he got to show off the things he had, he took and the last day of term, when the children could wear their own clothes, was one of the best opportunities Andy got to do just that.

Mark and his friends had been standing chatting on the playground for some time before Andy

● ●

©Adrian Martin and Brilliant Publications

arrived. They heard a screech of brakes and looked towards the road to see the silver Mercedes come to a stop on the zig-zags.

'Andy's here then,' said Warren.

'Mmm. I wonder what he'll be wearing this time?' Robert asked.

'Something new, no doubt,' said Tom, with a knowing look on his face.

The other boys rolled their eyes. They knew exactly what Andy was like, but it wasn't them who Andy would say sarcastic things about, it was Mark. They didn't like it, but Mark didn't ever seem that bothered, so they decided not to say anything. Of course it did bother Mark. It bothered him a great deal but the last thing he wanted to do was to let Andy know how much his remarks hurt him inside. Mark's friends had absolutely no idea how their friend really felt.

As Andy approached them it quickly became clear that he was wearing a brand new tracksuit which was shiny and bright blue with yellow stripes down the arms and legs. On his feet he wore a brand new pair of bright yellow trainers with stripes to match his tracksuit.

'All right boys,' he said as he arrived. 'What do you think?' And he actually did a full 360 degree turn so that they could all admire his new outfit.

They nodded and made the sorts of comments they thought he expected them to make.

He then unzipped his brand new tracksuit top to reveal the latest Everton Football Club shirt. As he performed yet another turn, he pulled down his tracksuit top to reveal the name 'Smithy' on the back of his shirt.

'Didn't you get a new Everton kit last weekend?' asked Rob.

'Yeah but this is the away kit,' replied Andy. 'I'm a true fan you see! Not a part-timer like you lot.'

As he said this Mark noticed that Andy was also wearing a small medallion around his neck. 'I don't believe it. He's turning into his dad,' Mark thought, and even though he knew what was about to happen, he had to do his very best not to laugh out loud.

Mark had made sure he was standing behind his friends. His clothes were not new. In fact, they were the same clothes that he had worn at the last non-uniform day, a few months ago; jeans, t-shirt and trainers – unlike Andy, who seemed to know the brands of all his clothes, Mark didn't have a clue what make his were. His mum had ordered them from the catalogue. He knew they weren't what Andy would call 'trendy'.

Mark looked up at the playground clock. Five minutes to go before the whistle was blown. Five minutes before he could go into school to safety. Unfortunately, as it turned out, five minutes too many. Andy had finished showing off his new clothes and was now focusing on what his friends were wearing. This was the moment Mark was dreading. It was always the same. 'Ignore him,' he told himself.

'Ignore him,' Warren, his best friend, always said.

'Now then, let's have a look at Mark,' Andy said sneeringly. 'It's catalogue boy! Hiya catalogue boy. Don't you know the way to the sports shop huh? Didn't you have those on last term? Hey everyone, have you seen Mark's trainers? Ha! How uncool are they? Catalogue Boy! That's gotta be his new nickname. CB. Catalogue Boy!'

Mark looked up. His friends were looking back at him awkwardly. Andy was laughing but none of them joined in. Mr Lee appeared on the playground and blew his whistle. They trundled towards the door. Andy pushed past them all,

©Adrian Martin and Brilliant Publications

eager to show his new outfit off to Miss Morris, who was an Everton fan.

'You okay?' Warren asked Mark as they walked from the playground into the corridor. 'He's unbelievable isn't he?'

Mark hated this day. He hated being different because different meant that he was made fun of, even though it was by someone for whom he had no respect. And even though he hated it and it made him feel horrible inside, he knew one thing; he would never be like Andy; he would always respect other people, no matter how different they looked.

A few months later, the last day of term arrived again and with it, the next non-uniform day. But this one was completely different. Mark still wore the same clothes. Nothing had changed in that way. But he had noticed a change in Andy over the last few weeks. He didn't seem as confident for some reason. Mark had also noticed that Andy had been walking to school lately and walking home on his own. Warren had mentioned something about Andy's dad losing his job. Maybe that was it.

And on the morning of the last day, Andy was earlier than normal. Perhaps most surprisingly of all, he was wearing the same blue tracksuit with the same yellow trainers as he had worn for last term's non-uniform day. But they were no longer very shiny and beginning to look a little tatty and worn.

Instead of showing off to everyone and making nasty comments about Mark's clothes like he

normally did, he was really quiet. Mark walked over to him.

Andy looked up at Mark.

'I suppose you've come over to get your own back have you?' he asked.

'No, what do you mean?' replied Mark.

'You know. I've got the same stuff on as last time. Dad's lost his job and he can't afford to buy me any new stuff,' Andy said, flatly.

Mark looked at Andy and took a deep breath. This was his chance for revenge: his chance to get even with Andy for all those unhappy days he'd caused him; his chance to gain revenge for all those horrible comments about his clothes; for making him dread coming to school. For making him feel different, not as good as anyone else. Should he go for it? Should he tell him how he felt? Should he tell Andy how untrendy he looks now in his old tatty tracksuit and how his trainers are out of date?

'You live on the same estate as me,' Mark said. 'Do you fancy walking home together after school?'

Andy could not have looked more surprised. A broad smile spread across his face. It was the first time he'd felt really happy for a very long time. By not taking revenge, Mark had taught him a very important lesson. It's not how you look that matters, but what you're like on the inside.

William Accepts Kofi for What He Is

It was a very special day for Kofi Ecuban. For today was his first day at his new school. But Mill Lane Junior School wasn't just his new school; it was the first school he had ever attended in England. Kofi's family had recently moved to England from Ghana. He had only ever known his school in Africa and for Kofi, this was the start of a completely new life.

'This is Kofi, everyone,' announced Mr Lee, 5L's teacher.

Kofi was standing nervously by Mr Lee's side. He could almost feel the thirty pairs of eyes staring at him, multiplying his nerves further. But as the teacher continued, explaining to the class how difficult it must be for Kofi, starting a new school in a new country and how everyone needed to be especially kind to him, Nathan Gibson had stopped listening and so, it seemed, had the rest of the children. There were no other African children at Mill Lane Juniors and despite trying really hard not to, Nathan just couldn't stop himself from staring. Kofi's skin was a deep brown colour, his hair a mass of tight black curls.

Mr Lee was coming to the end of his speech:

'So, Nathan,' he said.

The mention of his name shook Nathan from his hypnotic state.

'Yes Mr Lee?' he stammered.

'Nathan, I'd like you to look after Kofi today. Make sure he knows where everything is, make him feel welcome.'

'Yes, of course Mr Lee,' Nathan replied, putting on his most responsible voice.

His friends looked on enviously. Mr Lee told Kofi to sit at Nathan's table and for the whole of the first lesson, Nathan enjoyed the responsibility of helping his new, interesting friend to settle in. A highlight for Nathan was watching Kofi's eyes widen in amazement when Mr Lee activated the interactive whiteboard with his remote control pad. It was becoming clear to Nathan just how different Mill Lane Juniors must be to Kofi's school in Ghana.

Mr Lee had shown great trust in Nathan, choosing him, from everyone else in the class, to look after Kofi and he was determined not let him down. However, he wasn't quite prepared for what was about to happen and more importantly, neither was Kofi. It was about to become very clear that Nathan wasn't the only one to be fascinated by Kofi's appearance. The bell for playtime rang loudly and Mr Lee dismissed the class, reminding Nathan to take good care of his new pupil. Nathan quickly led Kofi out of the classroom and down the corridor before all the other children filed out of their classrooms. It was a dry day and the door to the playground was wide open. Nathan stepped outside, closely followed by Kofi. The second they set foot onto the playground, the majority of the children in 5L surrounded them. They only wanted to say 'Hello' and to introduce themselves to their new classmate but Kofi wasn't used to this level of attention; his school in Ghana had only 34 pupils in total. There were only six in Kofi's class. As the children got closer and closer, smiling and telling Kofi their names, he began to panic and try as he might, Nathan could do little to calm him down. Things became even worse when the children began touching Kofi's hair. 'It's so springy!' Nathan could hear them saying.

Tears began to well up in Kofi's eyes and thankfully, when they realised he was becoming upset, the children immediately backed away, leaving Nathan standing beside him, his arm on

©Adrian Martin and Brilliant Publications

Fifty Fantastic Assembly Stories

Kofi's shoulder. They hadn't meant any harm, but Mr Lee gave a firm and clear message to them all when they returned to the classroom.

'I know you were only being friendly,' he said. 'But it would be a very good idea if you gave Kofi some 'space' for the rest of the day (and stop touching his lovely hair).'

As the weeks passed Kofi became more accustomed to his new school and to his new classmates and got on especially well with Nathan. But it was no longer Kofi who Nathan was worried about. Ever since Kofi's arrival at Mill Lane, Nathan had noticed a change in one of his closest friends, Will. Will loved football but ever since Kofi had arrived, he hadn't played once. At lunchtime, Will always sat with Nathan to have his lunch but since Kofi had arrived, he had chosen to sit somewhere else to eat. Nathan thought back to Kofi's first day – Will was one of the few children in 5L not to surround Kofi to say 'hello'. In fact, the more he thought about it, Nathan could not remember one occasion when Will had even talked to Kofi and he had been at the school

nearly half a term now.

It was playtime and the Year 5 football game was in full swing. Kofi, who was brilliant at football, had just scored from the half way line and was being swamped by the rest of his team. Once again Will wasn't playing and Nathan scanned the playground for his friend. There were groups of children everywhere; some were skipping, some were running, chasing each other, laughing. But there was one child sat on a bench on his own, playing with nobody and very clearly not enjoying himself; Will. Nathan went over to him.

'All right?' he asked.

'Fine,' Will replied, coldly.

'Wanna play footy?' Nathan ventured.

'Nah. Gone off it,' Will lied.

'What?' gasped Nathan. 'You love football. You're football crazy! I've never known anyone more obsessed with football.'

'It's just …' Will's voice trailed off.

But Nathan wasn't stupid. He had worked out exactly why Will had taken a sudden dislike to the sport he loved so much six weeks ago and he wasn't going to let him avoid the issue any longer.

'It's Kofi isn't it?' he said. 'Ever since he arrived you've been like this. Why don't you like him?'

Will didn't speak to begin with. He'd never actually said the words out loud before.

'He's … ' he began.

'What?' asked Nathan. 'He's what?'

'Different. Not like us. He's from … ' Will tailed off again.

'Africa?' Nathan completed Will's sentence. 'So what? What difference does that make? He's exactly the same as us.'

Nathan couldn't believe what Will was saying. They had been friends even before they had started school and had never disagreed on anything before but Will's attitude had really made Nathan angry. He just couldn't understand why he was behaving like this.

'And he's never spoken to me,' Will continued.

'That's because you've never made the effort to speak to him!' Nathan said, astonished by Will's attitude. 'You didn't even say 'hello' to him on his first day.'

But Nathan had had enough and decided it was time to take charge of the situation. He called Kofi's name and beckoned him over.

'What are you doing?' asked Will.

'I'm going to introduce you,' Nathan said.

But before Will could answer Kofi was standing in front of them both, slightly out of breath as he'd just been swamped by his team mates again after scoring another great goal.

'What's up?' he asked.

Will didn't know what to say. He didn't want to admit it to Nathan but unlike everyone else in the class, he hadn't been excited by Kofi's arrival at the school. From the moment Kofi had arrived Will had got it into his head that he was different – he was from Africa and he looked different and because of this Nathan liked him more than Will. This, of course, was not true at all but it was what Will thought and the only way he could cope with the situation was to be on his own. And now of course he realised he was wrong but he didn't know what to do to sort it all out.

Fortunately Kofi had absolutely no idea what all the fuss was about and rescued Will from his dilemma. He pulled Will's sleeve. 'C'mon,' he said. 'There's only five minutes of playtime left and we're losing.'

Will followed Kofi to the football pitch and Nathan followed, smiling to himself.

Five minutes later Mr Lee blew the whistle for the end of playtime. Will had just scored the goal that won the game for his and Kofi's team, but for once, Nathan didn't mind losing one bit. He watched his two friends laughing as they walked into the line together.

'Mission accomplished,' he thought to himself.

©Adrian Martin and Brilliant Publications
Fifty Fantastic Assembly Stories

Nathan's Mum Learns an Important Lesson

May was Nathan's favourite month of the year. Each year during the May half-term holiday, his mum and dad would take him and Sam his brother, to Cornwall, where they rented a cottage in St Ives, a few metres from the sea. They would spend the week swimming, body boarding, fishing for crabs and generally having a fantastic time. But just before this holiday each year, on May 23rd, was Nathan's favourite event of the year: his birthday. Today was May 9th, exactly two weeks to go and Nathan's mum had decided it was time to tell him what was organised for his party.

'Your dad and I have booked you a trip to the safari park – you've got your own private tour with a ranger and you're allowed to take five of your friends,' she said. 'Then you can all come back here for some food and party games.'

'Oh fantastic!' Nathan yelled. He loved animals and had wanted to go to the safari park for ages but had always been told that it was too expensive.

'And I can take five of my friends?' he asked, just to make sure he had heard mum correctly.

'The maximum number for the tour is six,' she explained. 'So yes, you and five others. Who should I write the invitations for?'

'Easy,' Nathan said. 'Michael, Robert, Terry, Adam and Kofi.'

'Kofi Jones?' Mum asked.

'No, Kofi Ecuban,' Nathan replied.

There were many times so far in Nathan's nine years, eleven months and two weeks on Earth, that his mum had had to ask him to repeat what

he had said – mainly because he mumbled a lot, but occasionally it was because she simply couldn't believe what he had said. Like the time he was telling her what Adam had been given for his birthday;

'A tablet, a stunt scooter, a bike and a telly?' she had asked, flabbergasted, for the second time, after Nathan had repeated the list to her.

'Well don't you expect so much for your birthday. That's ridiculous. We're not made of money you know.'

Nathan knew full well that his mum and dad were not 'made of money'. He also knew that Adam was spoilt but it wasn't his fault and at least it meant Nathan got to play with all his presents.

Nathan's mum was often asking him to repeat what he had said, but never in his memory had he ever had to ask her to repeat something. Until now. Because he simply could not believe what she said when he told her who he wanted to come to the safari park with him.

'Well, we can't have Kofi Ecuban here. I mean, he's from Africa. He's not like us. He just wouldn't fit in.'

After hearing her say it a second time, Nathan had left the room, upset because he couldn't invite Kofi to his party, but also confused by his mum's attitude. What did she mean, 'He just wouldn't fit in' and what was he going to say to Kofi when he gave out all the invitations? He just couldn't understand her. Kofi had become one of Nathan's best friends since arriving at the school from Africa in September. He was brilliant at art, worked harder than anyone else in class and was a fantastic footballer. Even more importantly, he always laughed at Nathan's jokes, even when they weren't that funny.

Nathan's Mum Learns an Important Lesson

The next day at school Nathan walked into the playground clutching five red envelopes, each containing an invitation to his birthday party. He quickly scanned the groups of children standing on the tarmac surface. The Year 5 boys were standing in their usual place by the wall with the school logo painted on it. Kofi was normally standing with them but obviously hadn't arrived yet. Nathan seized his opportunity and made his way over to his friends to give out the invitations. He had chosen Will Clarke instead of Kofi and Will was delighted to have been chosen by Nathan.

'Great, thanks Nathan. I love the safari park!' Will said, as Nathan pushed the envelope awkwardly into his hand. He felt bad for Kofi and also guilty that Will had not been on his original list of five.

'Don't mention it,' Nathan replied.

But apart from meaning, 'It's no problem' Nathan also wanted to say, 'No really, DON'T mention it. Don't say anything about this to Kofi.'

The party was a fortnight away and those two weeks were the longest in Nathan's life. Every time he saw Kofi he felt odd, awkward. Thankfully, Kofi acted no differently but Nathan just didn't know what to say to him. Although nothing had been mentioned about the party Kofi must have known about it but he just didn't seem to mind. But the worst moment was still to come – a moment which would change the way Mrs Gibson, Nathan's mum, judged people in the future.

It was the day of the party and the boys had just returned from the safari park. They had had a fantastic time. The ranger, Brad, was really cool and had allowed Nathan and his friends to feed the ring tailed lemurs which was amazing fun – the lemurs lived on 'Lemur Island' in the middle of the safari park's river and the boys had gone across to it on a small motor boat. As they got close to the shore one of the lemurs called Kevin actually jumped onto the boat and straight onto

Nathan's shoulder.

'That's Kevin,' said Brad. 'He's the cheekiest one of the lot – he's worked out it's your birthday because of your badge and he knows the drill – the birthday boy is always the one who gives the most food out!'

It was true – Kevin didn't leave Nathan's side (or shoulder) until he had given all of the food out from his bucket. After leaving Lemur Island and saying 'goodbye' to cool Brad, the boys persuaded Nathan's dad to take them through the monkey enclosure in his car. He wasn't keen as he had heard lots of stories from the other dads about the monkeys causing damage to their cars. The sign just beyond the entrance did even less for dad's confidence; it read, 'The safari park accepts no responsibility for any damage the monkeys may cause to your car', but it was too late then – they were already in and they couldn't turn round as it was a one-way system. The monkeys immediately surrounded the car. One jumped onto the roof and began swinging on the aerial whilst two others sat on the edge of the bonnet and tore the wing mirror clean off. At that point dad put his foot down on the accelerator pedal, despite the signs telling him to drive with caution, and zoomed out of the park. The boys found the whole thing hilarious and even

©Adrian Martin and Brilliant Publications

though he would have to get himself a new aerial and wing mirror, dad chuckled to himself several times on the journey home.

When they arrived home Nathan's mum had prepared a feast of pizza, spicy chicken wings, scrummy sandwiches and cake. The boys sat in the lounge munching away as Nathan opened his presents. Unexpectedly, there was a knock at the door.

Mum went to answer it and soon returned to the lounge, her face a deep shade of red, redder than Nathan had seen it before. She looked embarrassed for some reason.

'You okay mum?' Nathan asked.

'You've got a visitor,' she replied awkwardly, moving aside to reveal Kofi, who was grinning from ear to ear and holding a box wrapped in birthday paper with a bow on top.

'Happy Birthday Nathan!' he said, stepping into the lounge and thrusting the gift towards his friend.

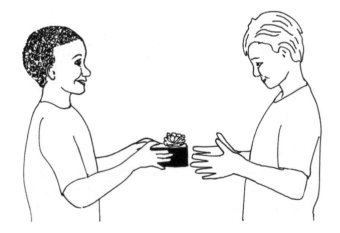

The boys stood up and surrounded Kofi, slapping him on the back and high-fiving him to make him feel welcome.

'I'll go and start the washing up,' mum said, gathering the empty plates and making her way

to the kitchen. She was too embarrassed to stay in the lounge.

'I hope you're going to stay for the afternoon, Kofi isn't it?' said Nathan's dad. 'I've got some great games lined up!'

Kofi nodded enthusiastically and stayed for the rest of the afternoon, enjoying the silly games, 'Pass the Parcel', 'Charades' and his favourite, but most confusing of all, 'Pin the Tail on the Donkey'. After a while, Nathan went into the kitchen and pulled his mum into the lounge by the arm, saying nothing. She plonked herself down on the sofa next to Nathan's dad and watched the boys having a great time together. One thing stuck in her mind more than anything else about Kofi – when he won a game he just smiled and if he lost he immediately congratulated the winner. 'How incredibly polite he is,' she thought to herself.

Later that evening, when everyone had gone and Nathan lay in bed reading, his mum popped her head round the bedroom door.

'Great day Mum, thanks again,' he said.

'Wasn't it just?' she replied. 'Dad and I are shattered though!'

And before Nathan could say another word, she added, 'Kofi's a nice boy isn't he? Very kind … and thoughtful … and so polite. How about inviting him round for tea next week?'

'Really? That would be brilliant,' Nathan replied.

And with that, he turned the bedroom light off and closed his eyes, delighted that on his tenth birthday, his mum had learned a very important lesson – never judge anyone until you know what they are really like.

Accepting others

Sean Patterson Gets What He Deserves

It was Monday morning, the morning Warren hated the most. He hated all school days, but Monday was the worst. He hated school, he hated everything about it. He didn't even like himself very much. He could hear his mum downstairs. It was difficult not to. Cupboard doors banged, dishes rattled on the kitchen work surface, cups clanged together. He was sure she did it on purpose, to make him get out of bed. But it wasn't going to work. Not this time. He was NOT going to school today.

'Warren!' screamed his mum.

'What is it about mums?' Warren thought. 'They seem to be able to scream louder than any other living creature.'

He was sure that if his mum had been around when dinosaurs roamed the earth, she would have killed them all in one go with just one of her piercing screams. He decided to pretend not to have heard. He pulled the pillow over his head and snuggled back down under the covers. It was warm and safe under the covers. No one could get him there. He'd stay there for the whole day – warm and safe. He'd go to school tomorrow. Tuesdays weren't so bad. It was ICT club on Tuesdays, so he didn't have to go outside at lunchtime.

'WARREN!!!'

Even from deep under the covers his ears rang. He could actually feel his eardrum vibrating. 'How did she do that?' he thought. 'How could she produce such a sound? Was it something all mums could do?'

He pulled the pillow more tightly over his head. But not tightly enough. There was one thing scarier than his mum's scream; her footsteps. And when her footsteps were loud, and fast and getting louder and faster, it could only mean one thing. She was on her way up the stairs. Warren's mum hated Mondays too. She had to go to work which meant getting up early, making Warren's breakfast as well as her own, driving ten miles and then sitting in an office taking orders from her boss. And when Warren was pretending to be sick, as he seemed to be doing a lot lately, it made her Monday morning even worse.

From deep under the covers, Warren heard the whoosh of his bedroom door being flung open. Two loud footsteps entered the room. He lay, perfectly still, holding his breath. Maybe she couldn't see him.

'If you honestly think I can't see you in there Warren, you're dafter than I thought. OUT! NOW!'

'Not well,' he groaned, in his best, croaky, groany voice.

It didn't work. He felt a blast of cold air as the covers were ripped off the bed, revealing him huddled in a ball, in his Spiderman pyjamas.

'Porridge is going cold. We've got to be out in ten minutes.' With that, his mum left the room.

In what seemed like no time at all, Warren was dressed, washed, fed and standing reluctantly by the door, with his school bag over his shoulder as his mum rushed around him in a blur.

A few moments later, the car screeched to a halt where Mill Lane and Elm Street met, and Warren was being pulled from it, hugged, kissed, and pushed in the direction of Mill Lane Junior School. She beeped the horn and waved as she drove off, the tyres of the car screeching on the tarmac. But now he was on his own. And another terrible

©Adrian Martin and Brilliant Publications

Fifty Fantastic Assembly Stories

day at school lay ahead. He had only been here for two weeks, and they had been the worst two weeks of his life. He was smaller than the other children of his age and he had glasses, and coming to this new school seemed to make his differences even more different.

He ran round the corner of Elm Street and into Mill Lane. Two large, black shoes blocked his path. He looked up. It was Sean Patterson.

'Dinner money, titch,' he said.

'I've got none. Mum forgot to give me any,' Warren replied, his voice trembling.

Sean ripped Warren's school bag from his back, causing the straps to dig into his shoulders. He undid the buckles with ease. This was not the first time he had undone them.

'Two quid? Is that it? Suppose it'll have to do shorty. See you later.'

And with that, the older boy thrust the bag into Warren's stomach, knocking him to his knees.

Warren picked himself up, threw his bag back over his shoulder and ran, head down, as fast as he could, until he arrived, breathless, at the school gates. His new friend, Johnny Price, was just getting out of his mum's car right outside school. 'Why can't my mum drop me off here?' Warren thought.

'All right Warren?' Johnny asked. 'You been running again? Always runnin' you are. Training for the Olympics I reckon.'

'I'm fine Johnny. Come on, the bell's about to go.'

Warren glanced over his shoulder. Sean Patterson was turning the two pound coins over in his hand, smiling at him. But it wasn't a friendly smile, and Warren knew that Sean had more meetings

planned for the two of them that day.

Just before break, Mr Lee, Warren's teacher, asked for volunteers to help him with a job at break time. This was a lifeline to Warren, and he took it. He took his time helping Mr Lee, making sure he didn't have to go outside. It worked. But he had no such luck at lunchtime.

He had only been at Mill Lane Juniors for two weeks, and for the last eight days, Sean Patterson had taken his dinner money. His excuses for not having any money when he arrived at the lunch till were running out.

'You've not forgotten it again have you Warren?' the lady at the till asked.

'Sorry,' Warren replied. 'Mum was in a rush this morning.'

Little did Warren know that his mum now owed £16.00 for the lunches he hadn't paid for. Even more serious, there was a letter in the post that day telling his mum exactly that. Warren ate his lunch with Johnny, who had looked after him since he arrived. As they left the dining room, Johnny asked Warren if he'd like to play football with him.

'Thanks Johnny,' said Warren. 'But I've got a bit of a stomach ache.'

Johnny was beginning to worry about his new friend. Every time he asked him to play, Warren gave the excuse of not feeling very well. He never complained to Mr Lee and he always looked all right in the afternoon. He decided to give Warren a few minutes to himself and then to see if he was all right. But a few minutes later, Johnny was shocked by what he saw. Warren was standing by the bins, just away from the main playground. But he wasn't alone. Sean Patterson from Year 6, was talking to him. At first, Johnny thought Sean was just being friendly, but when he saw the older boy take Warren's glasses off, stamp on them, and then run away laughing, he realised something much more serious was going on.

It became very clear to Johnny exactly what was happening. His friend Warren, who never had any dinner money, who never wanted to play football (despite being really good in games lessons), and who always arrived at school late, and out of breath, was being bullied. And Johnny knew exactly what to do.

That evening when Warren arrived home, his mum was sitting at the kitchen table, reading a letter. She had her serious face on.

'What's this?' she asked.

'What's what?' he asked back.

'Don't get smart with me young man. This, is a bill, for £16.00, for the dinner money I owe the school.'

Warren gulped. The colour drained from his face.

'Have you been spending the money I give you at the shop Warren?' she asked.

This was his chance. This was the opportunity Warren had been waiting for, to tell his mum what he had been going through ever since he arrived at his new school. To tell her that he pretends to be sick every morning because minutes after waving him goodbye and beeping the horn, he has his dinner money taken by an older boy. To tell her that at breaks and lunchtime he is called names and threatened by this older boy. To tell her that today he ripped his glasses from his face, jumped on them and ran off laughing. To tell her everything.

She asked him again:

'I said, 'Have you been spending the money I give you at the shop?''

He took a deep breath.

'Yes. I have. I don't like the dinners at my new school,' he said.

He couldn't tell her. He just couldn't do it. He knew that if he did she'd be up to school to make things worse. And Sean Patterson would know he'd said something and then he'd be in real trouble.

'Well you'll just have to get used to them. Do you think I'm made of money? I can't afford for you to spend your money on junk from the shop. And where are your glasses? I've told you – if you don't wear them, your eyes will get worse.'

She went on and on and on. Warren just couldn't bring himself to tell her the truth. He thought it was his fault. He hated being small. He hated having glasses. He hated being different. Why couldn't he be like Johnny?

He didn't bother pretending to be ill the next day. He knew there was no point. He would just have to put up with Sean Patterson. Perhaps after a while he'd get fed up, and bother someone else instead. And at least it was ICT club today.

To his amazement, Sean wasn't waiting for him at the corner before school. 'Maybe he's found someone else to bully,' Warren thought.

He managed to get another job to do at morning break, and was just beginning to think this was his best day so far at his new school, when, after having his lunch (and actually paying for it), he arrived at the ICT room to find….a notice on the door from Mr Croft:

'Sorry everyone. ICT Club cancelled today. I've had to go to a meeting. See you next week.'

For the first time since he'd been at Mill Lane Juniors, Warren actually felt sick. He was relying on ICT club to keep him away from Sean Patterson. 'Back to the bins then,' he thought, and scurried off to hide.

It wasn't long before Sean found him.

'Missed you this morning,' the older boy said. 'More important things to do. But I'm here now. Give us it then.'

'I've spent it,' said Warren.

'Oh yeah. We'll see about that.'

Sean grabbed Warren by his legs and lifted him upside down.

'Let's see if titch is telling the truth shall we?' he laughed, as he began to shake Warren. The only things that fell from his pocket were his broken glasses.

'Stop that NOW!'

It was Mrs Davies, the Headteacher. She had been waiting out of sight behind the bins.

Sean immediately put Warren down. 'Just playing Mrs Davies. Titch…er.. Warren loves it, don't you mate?'

'Does he love having his dinner money taken every day? Does he love having his glasses broken? Does he love being called names? Does he love … being bullied?' asked Mrs Davies.

For once, Sean's face went pale and Warren wasn't sure, but he thought he actually saw Sean's bottom lip wobble.

'Come with me. Warren – I'll talk to you later. Everything will be alright from now on. I promise,' Mrs Davies said, with a reassuring smile.

Warren made his way back to the main playground. Johnny was waiting for him, smiling. Neither boy said anything. There was no need. Warren knew that he'd found himself a true friend.

Someone who didn't care how different he was and someone who was prepared to do the right thing when he knew something was wrong.

That night, Warren was watching television with his mum – she had calmed down a little now – when the doorbell rang.

'It'll be the milkman,' she said. 'You get it love, I'll get my purse.'

Warren opened the door. As surprises go, this was up there with the best.

It was Sean Patterson, with his dad. Sean had very red, blotchy eyes, and his dad….well he was just red. He was obviously very angry with his son.

'Well go on then,' Mr Patterson said.

'I'm really sorry,' blubbed Sean. 'I won't do anything nasty to you again. And here's the money I owe you. 'Fourteen pounds.'

'Sixteen actually,' Warren's mum chipped in from behind Warren.

After Sean and his dad had apologised several more times, and promised to pay for a new pair of glasses, they went, leaving Warren and his mum to discuss what had happened.

'Promise me Warren. That if anything like this happens again, you'll tell me.'

'Promise,' he said.

'Now get on that phone and invite Johnny for a sleep-over at the weekend.'

And for the first time since moving to his new school, Warren felt good – really good.

Andy Learns what Teamwork Is

● ●

Andy Smith LOVED football. He was 10, and for the last 10 years he had loved football, and he was going to love football for the rest of his life. He was BRILLIANT at it. He knew it, and everyone else knew it. He told everyone else, that's why.

Kevin Gallagher HATED football. He was 10, and for the last 10 years he had hated football, and he was going to hate football for the rest of his life. He was RUBBISH at it. He knew it, and everyone else knew it. Everyone else told him, especially Andy Smith. At break, he would be the last one on the football pitch. The bit he hated the most was when the teams were picked. He would stand there while all the other boys and girls were picked before him. The most humiliating time ever was when Andy Smith and Ian Dobson (the second best player in the school) were picking the teams. Kevin stood there … and stood there … and stood there. After a few minutes everyone had been picked except him and a girl called Fiona Pembleton. She was 7 and in Year 3. Kevin was 10 and in Year 5. It was Andy Smith's turn to pick. He looked at the two children standing there. He looked at Kevin, up and down … at his feet, at his legs….at his face … took a deep breath, pointed at him, and then said, 'Fiona!' and laughed. Everyone laughed. Kevin trudged over to the other team. They stopped laughing – they had realised that Kevin was on their team.

One day in assembly, Mrs Davies finished with a message which made the children extremely excited – all the children except one – Kevin Gallagher.

'As you all know it's the World Cup this year,' said Mrs Davies. 'So the teachers and I have decided to organise our own World Cup Competition here in school.'

Andy Smith actually whooped. Kevin's heart sank.

But it sank even more when he heard what Mrs Davies said next.

'The competition will be for Years 5 and 6 only. Years 3 and 4 will get their turn next year. There will be 20 teams, each with 5 players and you have to pick them. When you've got your team, let me know and I'll give you a name.'

Out of the corner of his eye, Kevin could see Andy Smith pointing at Ian Dobson and nodding. He then pointed at three other boys in Year 6. They also nodded. Andy Smith had his team picked before the end of assembly. Along the rows in Years 5 and 6 boys and girls were pointing at each other and nodding. Mrs Davies had to calm everyone down.

'No one is to pick their team yet,' she said. 'Wait until break time.'

But it was too late. Most of the children had got their teams sorted. Noone pointed at Kevin. And even if they had done, he wouldn't have seen them. He was looking at the floor, wishing a big hole would appear and swallow him up and take him to a place where there was no such thing as football.

The competition was due to take place on Friday afternoon – Years 3 and 4 were being allowed to watch, so they were very excited. On Friday morning all the teams were sorted out. There were only two children in Year 5 and 6 who weren't involved. Jackie Miller, who had broken her arm falling off her scooter on Tuesday, and … Kevin. Mrs Davies had asked him to be a linesman, whatever that meant. He had to bring his kit in and would be given a yellow flag to wave whenever the ball went over the line.

At lunchtime, all the teams were either sitting

©Adrian Martin and Brilliant Publications

Andy Learns What Teamwork Is

discussing tactics, or practising their skills with the various balls scattered around the playground. With minutes to go until the end of lunch time bell, Kevin noticed a commotion in one area of the playground. Children were gathering round, as they do, and Mrs Shelby, one of the lunchtime supervisors, was moving everyone away. When Kevin arrived at the scene he could hear someone crying. Mr Lee had arrived and Kevin saw him bend down at the centre of the crowd of children. Within seconds he was up again, carrying a child in his arms. It was Tom Bassett, and it looked serious.

Mr Lee was shaking his head. 'You'll be okay Tom – nothing's broken, but you've got a nasty bruise on your knee and there's no way you can play in the tournament today I'm afraid.'

Kevin saw Andy Smith smile. Tom was a good player and was in the second best team for the competition – the biggest threat to Andy Smith's chances of winning. The rest of Tom's team looked as if their worlds were about to end.

'What do we do now?' asked Jake. 'We can't play with four.'

Jake, and his team mates looked at each other. Almost at exactly the same time, they realised what Tom's injury meant. They had a choice:

1.   Withdraw from the tournament

2.   Ask Kevin to play on their team

They went into a huddle. Kevin could see some of them shaking their heads. Then they separated. They all turned towards Kevin. Jake walked towards him.

'Will you play on our team Kev?'

Kevin had never been called 'Kev' before. 'All right,' he said.

'Come with us,' replied Jake. 'You need a kit.'

Before Kevin could even begin to worry about letting anyone down, he was wearing Tom Bassett's football kit, including shin pads and boots. He'd never even worn football boots before, or shin pads, and they made him feel strong, as if he was wearing battle armour. For the first time ever in his life, Kevin was looking forward to playing football. And it was all because of Jake. Kevin had never really spoken to Jake before. He was one of the good footballers, and even though they were in the same class, they sat at opposite sides of the classroom. But Kevin decided pretty quickly that he liked Jake. The first thing Jake did was to get the team together to introduce them to Kevin.

'Everyone, this is Kev. Kev, this is Johnno – he's the keeper, Bagsy – our goalscorer, and Freddo – he's our main man in midfield. You and me will be the defense – nothing will get past us. Not even Andy Smith. Okay lads?'

They got themselves in a circle and bent down. Kevin, not knowing what else to do, joined them. Jake put his right hand towards the centre of the circle. The others put theirs onto his. Kevin did the same. Then came a low, groaning noise, started by Jake. The noise got louder and higher in pitch. As it got higher the boys, who were still crouching, started to rise, still with their hands on top of each others. When the noise got to a certain volume and pitch, they all raised their hands towards the sky and shouted, 'Oi!!'

They then patted each other on the back and ran onto the field to join the other teams. He wasn't sure why, but this strange ritual made Kevin feel different, stronger.

Just before the first game, Jake showed Kevin where to stand.

'Right Kev,' said Jake. 'You stay on this side, and I'll

do the other side. If the ball comes anywhere near you, kick it as hard as you can, THAT way.'

And he pointed towards the other team's goal.

Kevin nodded.

A couple of minutes into the game the ball came towards Kevin. Three players from the other team were chasing it. Kevin could hear their studs ripping into the grass as they ran.

'Hoof it!' shouted Jake.

Kevin focused on the ball. He could feel the eyes of the children in Years 3 and 4 watching him. The three opposing players chasing the ball were hoping he would miss it. He drew his foot back just as the ball reached him and, 'BAM!'

The ball went sailing over the three players' heads. There was a gasp from the crowd. The ball not only sailed over the three players' heads, but over the goals at the other end of the pitch.

'Nice one,' said Jake, admiringly.

Kevin couldn't believe it. He'd never actually had the chance to kick the ball a long way before. The game usually just went on around him. He'd found something he could do. With a football. At last.

Shortly afterwards Bagsy scored a great goal after a lovely pass from Freddo and to Kevin's amazement, his team won their first game. And to his absolute amazement, they won their second match and their third and the quarter final and the semi final. Before he knew it, Kevin was in the final of his school's World Cup and his team hadn't let a single goal in.

'What a team. Well done boys,' said Jake. 'Now let's go and win the final.'

Meanwhile, Andy Smith's team had won all their

games and Andy had scored all their goals. Kevin would meet Andy in the final. In fact, it was his job to stop Andy Smith scoring.

Don't worry,' Jake said. 'Andy Smith doesn't know what teamwork is. He's greedy. There's no way he can beat us by himself. Just stick together. We'll be fine.'

Mr Barnes blew his whistle and the two teams walked onto the pitch for the final.

Andy walked past Kevin and as he did so he muttered something under his breath:

'You're rubbish at football Kevin Gallagher. Always have been. I'm going to dribble the ball past you and score the winning goal.'

Kevin gulped when he heard these words. Jake noticed something was the matter and called the team together. They gathered round in their circle and put their hands in the centre.

'One last time,' he said. 'May the best team win.'

And with that, Mr Barnes blew the whistle and the match was underway. Like most finals, there were very few chances. But with a few minutes to go, Kevin's team got a penalty, after Freddo was fouled in the penalty box.

'No way Mr Barnes!' screamed Andy Smith.

Mr Barnes was not happy with him and gave him a severe telling off. Bagsy stood over the ball, ready to take it. Andy Smith stood just behind him and Kevin could hear him muttering something over and over. He got closer and realised that he was saying things to Bagsy.

'You're gonna miss this Bagsy. You're never gonna score. You're gonna miss, and I'm gonna get the ball, run all the way to the other end, and score. And then the whistle will go. And we'll have won.'

©Adrian Martin and Brilliant Publications

Kevin couldn't believe what he was hearing. But before he could do anything about it, the whistle was blown for the penalty to be taken and Bagsy was running towards the ball. As he drew his foot back, the ball moved slightly off its spot. It was too late to do anything about it and he kicked the edge of the ball rather than the centre, sending it wide of the post.

'Ha!' shouted Andy Smith. 'Told you.'

Within seconds, Andy had the ball at his feet. Kevin turned and ran back to his defensive position and waited. The rest of his team were still in shock after the penalty miss. Andy sprinted with the ball towards goal. His control was excellent – the ball was always at his feet and he was running at full speed. Kevin stood his ground and waited. Andy got closer and closer, expecting Kevin to run towards him. But Kevin just stayed where he was, waiting for Andy to make a mistake. And a couple of metres away from Kevin, Andy did make a mistake. For once. Just for a split second, he let the ball get away from his feet. Kevin seized the opportunity. He ran towards the ball, which was now an equal distance between them. He shut his eyes, and kicked. As hard as he could. He definitely kicked something. Two things in fact. The ball, and Andy Smith, who was now lying on the floor, groaning.

'No foul!' shouted Mr Barnes.

But the crowd weren't looking at Andy or Kevin. They had their eyes on the ball, which was way up in the air, but heading towards the goal.

Their goalkeeper was out of position. He'd been watching Andy's run and was waiting to celebrate his goal. The ball was coming down. Fast. The goalkeeper attempted a desperate dive. The ball skimmed the under side of the bar and bounced up into the roof of the net.

The crowd went wild. Kevin opened his eyes. He couldn't quite understand what all the fuss was about. Jake, Johnno, Freddo and Bagsy were running towards him with scary grins on their faces. He didn't know what to do. Should he run away? Too late. They pulled him to the ground and jumped on top of him, rubbing his hair and screaming, 'YYYYYEEEESSSSS!!!'

Mr Barnes blew the final whistle and Kevin was lifted onto his team mate's shoulders.

'What a team,' said Jake, grinning like a Cheshire cat.

Kevin looked over to where Andy Smith had been lying. His team mates were standing around him. He was shouting at them:

'I would have scored if he hadn't fouled me. I'm the best player in this school. I would have been better on my own. I don't need team mates. I'm the best.'

Kevin couldn't believe his ears. He looked at Jake, who smiled and said, 'I, I, I – that's all he ever says. Well we've just proved that there's no 'I' in team!'

Teamwork
Mill Park FC Don't Lose!

● ●

Mill Park Football Club had played 17 games so far this season and had lost every single one. Worse still, they had lost every game by a lot of goals. In fact, they had broken the record for the most number of goals ever scored against a team in one season; 391 goals had been scored against them, an average of 23 per game. And there was still one game left to play. They had also broken the record for the fewest goals ever scored by a team in one season; in 17 games they had not scored one goal. They had hit the post in their second game against Brookdale FC, but that was only because Brookdale's goalkeeper accidentally kicked the ball against the back of Brendan's head and it had rebounded back, hitting the post. It was the closest they had come to scoring and Brendan was quite proud of himself for being the one to nearly do it. They had lost that game 26–0. Mr Jenks, Harry's dad, wasn't quite sure how he had ended up becoming the manager; he only went along to watch Harry. The manager that day had stormed off because one of the other parents had suggested his formation was all wrong. At the end of the match all the other parents had approached Harry's dad and asked him to be the new manager. He couldn't work out why to begin with as he hadn't a clue about football, but after a few weeks he realised why they had asked him. He owned a fruit and vegetable shop and had a van for transporting all his produce in. This meant he could take the whole team to the matches in the van which meant none of the other parents would have to go and watch! On the whole he enjoyed it – the boys were fun to be with and didn't seem to mind losing, which was just as well, and they always thanked him after each game. There were, of course, many problems with the team but the main one, as far as Mr Jenks could see, was Martin Smith. Martin was a nice lad, there was no doubt about that, but he just didn't seem to fit into the team – he was just too good at football. Whenever he got the ball he would try to beat the other team entirely on his own. He never once passed the ball to any of the players on his team.

'You've got to pass the ball Martin,' Mr Jenks told him at half time against Townfield Rovers. They were 9–0 down at the time.

'But we're no good dad,' Harry said. 'You can't blame Martin for not giving the ball to us – we'd only lose it.'

The rest of the team nodded, agreeing with Harry. Harry's dad didn't know what to say.

'Off you go,' he said, eventually. 'And enjoy yourselves!' he added. He had heard one of the Premiership managers on the television say that he always told his players to enjoy the game because if they didn't enjoy playing they'd never win.

Townfield scored 15 goals in the second half, winning 24–0.

'At least we enjoyed it Mr Jenks,' smiled Jake.

'They certainly did,' replied Harry's dad, gesturing to the Townfield team who were whooping and cheering in the distance, celebrating their biggest ever victory. 'But I'm not so sure Martin did,' he added.

Martin was sat on the grass on his own, taking his boots off, muttering and shaking his head.

'I've got to do something to make Martin trust his teammates,' thought Harry's dad. 'And preferably before our last game.'

Later that night, in the middle of the night in fact, he had an idea.

● ●

©Adrian Martin and Brilliant Publications

Fifty Fantastic Assembly Stories

Mill Park FC Don't Lose!

'Got it!' he said, sitting bolt upright in bed.

'What's the matter?' exclaimed Harry's mum who had been rudely awakened by her husband.

But Mr Jenks had gone to find a pen and a piece of paper. He had to write his idea down before he forgot it – his memory was not quite what it once was.

'I can't see the point of this,' groaned Martin as Harry's dad tied the blindfold around his head.

'You will,' he laughed.

It was the day before their final game and Harry's dad had set up a series of obstacles on his lawn. He had invited the whole team over to the house and, working in pairs, one blindfolded, the boys had to make their way around the course. Each pair would begin with ten points and each time the blindfolded boy touched one of the obstacles, the pair would lose a point. Harry's dad moved the obstacles around occasionally and made sure they all swapped partners so all had a turn with each other.

'The idea is that the one who can see has to guide the blindfolded one around the course,' Mr Jenks explained. 'So if you're blindfolded, you've got to communicate really clearly.'

To his surprise, the idea worked perfectly. The activity required two very important ingredients of teamwork; listening carefully and communicating clearly and as the afternoon progressed, something very interesting happened. Most of the boys worked really well together and only hit the obstacles a couple of times. But the obstacles were hit over and over again whenever Martin was involved – he simply seemed unable to listen when he was blindfolded and was utterly hopeless at giving clear instructions, when he was the one who could see. At the end of the afternoon the boys sat on the grass together. It had been fun,

but most of them had realised why Harry's dad had done it and one of the boys understood more than anyone else. It had been quite a lesson for Martin. He had watched his friends working really well together, but knew that he had been unable to do what they could. He walked into the kitchen where Harry's dad was pouring out some orange juice.

'I'll pass the ball tomorrow Mr Jenks,' he said.

'I'll look forward to it,' came the reply.

The final game of the season was at their home ground, against Portland United. They were fourth in the league and had beaten Mill Park FC 26–0 earlier on in the season. All the parents had come to watch, but none of them were expecting to see what they saw. Harry's dad sat the team down before the match.

'Okay boys. Our last game of the season. I don't care what the score is, but you're a team, so I want to see you playing TOGETHER!' he said, ruffling Martin's hair. 'Now off you go and enjoy

Fifty Fantastic Assembly Stories

yourselves!'

Some of the Portland boys were smirking and nudging each other as their opponents made their way onto the pitch. They were obviously expecting an easy game.

Mill Park kicked off. Brendan passed the ball to Martin who ran forward. Normally Martin would have dribbled passed several Portland players before losing the ball, at which point the Portland players would probably have passed it between themselves and scored. But this time Martin dribbled the ball round one Portland player and then listened. Brendan had continued to run forwards towards the Portland goal and Martin could hear him calling his name. He passed the ball to Brendan in the penalty area, Brendan took the ball in his stride and hit a low shot passed the Portland goalkeeper, but against the left post; the second time Brendan had hit the post that season, but at least this time deliberately. Brendan turned away, annoyed with himself for missing a scoring opportunity but a loud cheer went up from the Mill Park supporters at the side of the pitch. Brendan looked over to them, wondering why they were cheering. Harry's dad was jumping up and down like a chimpanzee with a bee in its ear. Martin had continued running and as Brendan's shot had

rebounded off the post, he smashed the ball into the net. Brendan ran over to Martin and the whole team jumped on top of them both, screaming with delight. The Portland players were stunned and when it was still 1–0 at half time the smirks on their faces had been well and truly wiped away.

The second half did not go quite as well as the first. To be fair to Portland, they had hit the post four times in the first half and had lots and lots of shots which had just missed the goal. Harry's dad wasn't quite sure how the score had remained 1–0 for so long but Portland scored two goals in the second half, making it 2–1 to them.

To the delight of their supporters, Mill Park continued to play as a team, passing the ball to each other, led by Martin, who impressed everyone by constantly encouraging his teammates. With a minute of the match to go, Jake kicked the ball up-field, Martin headed it on to Brendan and this time he managed to miss both the posts, hitting a great shot into the back of the net.

At the end of the game Portland's manager came over to the Mill Park team. 'My team could learn a thing or two about teamwork from your boys,' he said to Mr Jenks.

Mr Jenks beamed with pride. He knew that he couldn't teach Martin to be a better footballer, but he had certainly taught him a lesson about teamwork. Martin looked up at Mr Jenks and smiled; he may not have won the game, but he had never felt so good.

Sophie Learns Some Home Truths

'There are two kinds of people in this world,' Mr Lee was saying to the class. He had just been sorting out yet another problem with Sophie Evans and when he got cross he tended to remind everyone of his expectations:

'There are those who can work well with others and those who can't.'

This was one of his favourite phrases and he said it regularly. Terry Johnson agreed with his teacher and although it wasn't really for him to say which of the two types he was, he felt he got on fairly well with people. He had plenty of friends, he never got himself into any trouble and he was very patient with his younger sister, even when she bit him on his arm, which was quite often. And Terry was right. His teachers and friends thought the world of him and Mr Lee often used him as an example of a good team player. His sister Beth adored him and only bit him to get his attention, which it always succeeded in doing.

Sophie Evans, on the other hand, never really understood what Mr Lee meant by his silly phrases.

'There are far more than two types of people in the world,' she thought. 'What a ridiculous thing to say.'

Unlike Terry, Sophie already knew that she was a good team player. She always had brilliant ideas when she worked with other children – it wasn't her fault that they just didn't understand what she meant. Of course, this was Sophie's view; the other children in her class, and all of her teachers for that matter, had a very different opinion of her. Whenever the children had to work in groups, the rest of the class dreaded having to work with Sophie; she always took over the task, speaking loudly and interrupting and she never listened to anyone else's ideas. More often than not there would be an argument in her team and Mr Lee would have to step in to sort things out.

'So, this afternoon I'm going to set you a task which will really test your teamwork skills,' Mr Lee told the class. 'You will work in groups of four. And before you all start choosing each other, I've already decided the groups.'

The class groaned – they knew that when Mr Lee chose the groups they wouldn't be able to work with their friends.

'It does you good to work with people you wouldn't normally work with,' he said. 'After all, that's what happens in the real world.'

Sophie was glad that the groups had been chosen. When Mr Lee allowed the children to choose their own groups, she was always left on her own and she could never really understand why.

The task was to build a tower from newspaper which would support a tennis ball. Each group would have 30 minutes to complete their tower and the tallest one would be the winner. Terry's heart sank when Mr Lee read out the groups. There were 32 children in the class which meant there would be eight groups and with seven groups announced there were just four children remaining; Millie Thompson, Declan Murphy, Terry and Sophie Evans. Declan put his head on his desk, Millie rolled her eyes. It was obvious what they thought about the group they had been put into. Terry remembered another one of Mr Lee's phrases; 'If you have nothing nice to say, say nothing.'

With this in mind, he did not react when Mr Lee

Fifty Fantastic Assembly Stories

announced the names of the children in Group 8. He caught Sophie's eye as their names were read out. She clenched her fist and mouthed the words, 'We'll win' to him. Terry wasn't so confident as he had seen what happened when Sophie worked with others in the past and he could never remember a group with her in winning anything. When the four of them sat down together he became even less convinced that the next 30 minutes would be a success.

'This is going to be so easy,' Sophie announced. 'I know exactly what to do, just listen to me.'

Each group had been given some paper to draw their ideas on. Sophie had already snatched a piece and the group's one pencil and was drawing her idea on it for the others to see. She had drawn a tower that was made of tightly rolled up pieces of newspaper, forming a series of cubes sat on top of each other. At the very top of the tower was a cross piece.

'The cross piece is for the tennis ball to sit on,' she explained. 'Easy!'

Even though she hadn't asked any of the other members of the group and had completely taken over the task, Terry could see that her idea was a good one; not perfect by any means, but not bad. It just needed a few adjustments here and there. Unfortunately Millie wasn't so sure:

'I think that will fall over,' she suggested. 'It needs some cross pieces to join the corners of each cube – that will make the cubes into triangular structures and Mr Lee showed us that triangles make strong structures last week when we were looking at bridges,' she continued. Declan agreed with Millie.

'But we've only got 30 minutes,' Sophie replied. 'There's definitely no time for all of that. It's the tallest tower that will win, not the strongest.'

'But it won't be the tallest if it falls over,' Declan added.

And that was when the discussion turned into more of an argument. Sophie would not be persuaded that there was enough time to make the triangular structures whereas Millie and Declan were convinced that Sophie's design would collapse.

At this point Terry hadn't said a word. He had just sat and listened to the other three members of his group. 'If only Sophie would just listen to someone else's ideas,' he thought. Her design was good, but she wouldn't let anyone change it. The noise level in the room was beginning to rise. He looked over his shoulder to see the other groups beginning to make their towers. In his group there was a stand-off. Ten minutes of the 30 had gone already, leaving only 20 minutes until Mr Lee would be judging each group's tower. Five more minutes passed in which Sophie continued to try to persuade Millie and Declan that her design would work. She didn't say anything different, Terry noticed, she just said the same thing over and over again, but increasingly loudly. This strategy didn't seem to be having the desired effect as Millie and Declan sat there with their arms folded, becoming sulkier and sulkier. Once again Terry looked around the room. Newspaper towers of various shapes and sizes were slowly growing upwards and children were busily rolling, cutting, sticking and building. None of the groups, Terry noticed, were arguing. It was time for him to contribute to the group:

'Look,' he said. 'We've wasted 15 minutes arguing and now we've only got 15 minutes to build the tower. We'll have to go with Sophie's idea.'

'At last,' Sophie said. 'We're going with my idea. I'm in charge.'

Terry couldn't believe her attitude. Reluctantly,

realising they had no choice, Millie and Declan agreed to follow Sophie's instructions. They began frantically rolling and sticking sheets of newspaper, leaving Sophie to build the tower. Although it grew quite quickly and was soon as tall as many of the others in the room, the taller it became the more it wobbled, just as Millie had predicted. But Sophie remained unconcerned, focusing only on making the tower as tall as possible.

'One minute to go!' announced Mr Lee.

'Where's the tennis ball?' Sophie snapped.

Terry handed the ball to her.

'Thanks Terry,' she said.

Sophie had been impressed by Terry. He hadn't argued. He hadn't wasted any time. He had done everything she had asked him to do and he hadn't tried to take over like Millie and Declan. But what Sophie still didn't realise was that her group were about to fail the task because she simply wouldn't listen to the ideas of the others. Neither did she realise that Mr Lee was standing over her shoulder and had been keeping a very close eye on her through the whole task.

'There are two types of people in the world,' he whispered in Sophie's ear.

Sophie had no idea that Mr Lee was there but before she could answer him he had moved away and called, 'Time's up!'

Everyone moved away from their towers.

Terry looked around the room. Sophie's tower was probably the tallest of them all. But it certainly wasn't the most stable. The class watched as Mr Lee approached each tower with the tennis ball. 'Group 8,' he said. 'We'll begin with yours. Impressive height, but it does look a little wobbly.'

He placed the tennis ball onto the cross section at the top of the tower. Sophie held her breath. The tower held firm.

'Right, let's measure it then,' Mr Lee continued.

But there was a creaking sound, followed by a ripping sound. And the tower lurched worryingly to the left. Within a second it had crashed to the floor, the tennis ball coming to rest at Sophie's feet.

'Oh dear,' said Mr Lee. 'Not stable enough I'm afraid.'

Millie and Declan shook their heads and for once, Sophie said nothing.

Group 6 won and as they stood proudly admiring their tower, Terry pushed Sophie's drawing towards her, with Millie's triangular sections added. It was exactly the same as the winning tower. He decided to complete the other part of Mr Lee's favourite phrase.

'There are those who can work well with others and those who can't,' he whispered, so that no one else could hear. 'Argue less, listen more,' he added.

Sophie was grateful that he had whispered it to her and for the first time, she understood what she needed to do to become a better team member.

Lightning Source UK Ltd.
Milton Keynes UK
UKHW05f0433090418
320729UK00003B/6/P